HANDBOOK FOR TEAM–BASED QUALITATIVE RESEARCH

HANDBOOK FOR TEAM-BASED QUALITATIVE RESEARCH

EDITED BY
GREG GUEST AND KATHLEEN M. MACQUEEN

ALTAMIRA PRESS
A Division of Rowman & Littlefield Publishers, Inc.
Lanham • New York • Toronto • Plymouth, UK

ALTAMIRA PRESS
A division of Rowman & Littlefield Publishers, Inc.
A wholly owned subsidary of The Rowman & Littlefield Publishing Group, Inc.
4501 Forbes Boulevard, Suite 200, Lanham, MD 20706
www.altamirapress.com

Estover Road, Plymouth PL6 7PY, United Kingdom

The poem on p. 1 is from *Chiyo-ni: Woman Haiku Master*, translated by Patricia Donegan and Yoshie Ishibashi. Boston: Tuttle Publishing, 1998.

The poem on p. 99 is from Anselm Hollo, *Outlying Districts*. Minneapolis: Coffee House Press, 1990.

British Library Cataloguing in Publication Information Available

Library of Congress Cataloging-in-Publication Data
Handbook for team-based qualitative research / edited by Greg Guest and Kathleen M. MacQueen.
    p. cm.
  Includes bibliographical references and index.
  ISBN-13: 978-0-7591-0910-0 (cloth : alk. paper)
  ISBN-10: 0-7591-0910-9 (cloth : alk. paper)
  ISBN-13: 978-0-7591-0911-7 (pbk. : alk. paper)
  ISBN-10: 0-7591-0911-7 (pbk. : alk. paper)
  1. Public health—Research—Methodology. 2. Anthropology—Research—Methodology.
3. Social sciences—Research—Methodology. 4. Qualitative research. 5. Research teams.
I. Guest, Greg, 1963- II. MacQueen, Kathleen M.

  RA440.85.H36 2008
  362.1072--dc22

                                                            2007002042

Printed in the United States of America

∞™ The paper used in this publication meets the minimum requirements of American National Standard for Information Sciences—Permanence of Paper for Printed Library Materials, ANSI/NISO Z39.48-1992.

CONTENTS

Preface

THIS BOOK IS THE CULMINATION OF YEARS' worth of trial and error. Both of us had worked on and managed multidisciplinary research projects over the past decade and experienced first-hand the issues and problems that are described in the chapters that follow. Working in teams is challenging—politically, operationally, and methodologically. Personalities and individual interests often clash. The cohesive vision that birthed a study can get lost in the multilayered research process. Reliability of data can erode as they pass from one point in the research process to the next. With large, multisite research initiatives, all of these problems are exacerbated, and many new ones arise. Communication becomes more difficult, particularly if the study is multicultural. Data must be handled and coordinated over distances, spawning a whole new set of logistical and ethical issues. Add to this already complicated situation the relatively unstructured nature of qualitative inquiry, and the potential for frustration (at best) or a research fiasco (at worst) is enhanced further.

We found that we needed to develop ways to rein in the entropic nature of team-based qualitative work. Bit by bit, project by project, we and colleagues who found themselves in similar situations catalogued the lessons learned and began to establish methods and procedures to deal with the incipient chaos of designing and implementing large qualitative research studies. These procedures tended to reside within the confines of individual researchers' psyches (aka "experience") or take the form of project-specific working documents. With a few exceptions (e.g., chapter 6), they weren't published or otherwise brought to the attention of an external audience. This all changed during a taxi ride through the Nigerian countryside one hot and dusty afternoon.

The two-hour drive from Lagos to Ibadan is fraught with the not-so-ordinary: military checkpoints, crater-sized potholes, stalled trucks, overfilled and unstable vehicles overtaking at high speeds, and the occasional roadside corpse. It's not a particularly pleasant journey, which may explain why everyone on the road is in such a hurry. It also probably explains why we distracted ourselves that afternoon by discussing qualitative research methods and the pitfalls associated with large, multisite studies. We lamented the dearth of published works that addressed the research challenges we seemed to face on an almost daily basis. At some point in our conversation the revelatory lightbulb flickered and we began working on an outline for a book. By the end of our two-hour trip, we had penned an annotated table of contents, which ultimately formed the foundation for this book.

Many excellent articles and books have been written about qualitative research methods. The same can be said for the concept of teamwork. What was lacking, in our view, was a synthesized treatment of both topics. This book is intended for any researchers who engage in team-based sociobehavioral research. While a few of the chapters are specifically relevant to qualitative inquiry, the majority are applicable to all kinds of team research. We also tried to give the book a more practical, rather than theoretical, perspective to help researchers cope with the day-to-day vagaries of working in research teams. We hope that it minimizes the amount of trial and error that you, the reader, have to endure throughout the research process.

RESEARCH DESIGN
AND IMPLEMENTATION

I

hyakunari ya tsuru hitosuji no kokoro yori

a hundred gourds
from the heart
of one vine

CHIYO-NI

An Introduction to Team-based Qualitative Research

1

KATHLEEN M. MACQUEEN AND GREG GUEST

The great jazz ensemble has talent and a shared vision (even if they don't discuss it), but what really matters is that the musicians know how to play together.

PETER M. SENGE, *THE FIFTH DISCIPLINE* (1990:236)

QUALITATIVE RESEARCH IS FIRMLY ROOTED in a tradition of independent scholarly exploration undertaken in a culturally foreign setting for a prolonged period of time. In this tradition the researcher, perhaps accompanied by a spouse but just as likely to be alone, spends day after day talking with people and observing their everyday lives, followed by night after night writing up field notes and transcribing interviews. This would go on for a year or two or sometimes longer. Then, over the course of perhaps decades, the resulting textual data would be meticulously winnowed, sifted, analyzed, and synthesized into articles and books by the researcher who collected it.

In contrast, team-based qualitative research involves multiple players, large data sets, complex protocols, and compressed timelines. As such, it requires a set of skills and a mindset that is alien to many traditionally trained qualitative researchers, including those who may have experience with peer-based academic collaborations. Designing and implementing a traditional qualitative study as part of a large interdisciplinary project is not the same as fielding a team that divides tasks and yet makes a coherent whole in the end. The former requires an ability to manage one's self in the company of others; the latter also requires an ability to lead and be led.

3

Team-based qualitative research is increasingly common for many reasons. Globalization brings with it a need to integrate multiple perspectives (e.g., cultural, political, scientific), disciplines (e.g., anthropology, economics, public health, ecology), and scales (e.g., temporal, environmental, geographic). Simultaneously, rapid advances in information technology have provided the tools needed to support such integration. Yet too often researchers give lip service to teamwork and integration without considering the work needed to make it happen. "Team" research may be little more than a group of reasonably congenial scientists who collaboratively obtain funding, conduct multidisciplinary research in parallel, and then separately publish their findings with minimal conceptual integration. As Rhoades et al. (1986) observe, team research more often resembles the bumbling choreography of the Three Stooges than the coordinated efforts of the Three Musketeers, and is often fraught with interdisciplinary conflict.

Alternatively, research "teams" may embody a disciplinary hierarchy where the contributions of some are relegated to technical assistance on narrow topics while dismissing the potential for more substantive contributions and leadership (Rhoades 2006). Even when true interdisciplinary research is the stated goal, obstacles exist. Qualitative researchers who collaborate with biomedical researchers and others in the so-called hard sciences often find their contributions minimized or ignored because the major journals in those fields tend toward a narrow disciplinary focus and impose strict page limits that preclude adequate—hence, convincing—presentation of the richness of qualitative research. Or, in a misguided effort to ensure publication of rigorous qualitative research, such journals may impose narrow standards that preclude important and often innovative methodological approaches better suited to integration (see chapter 10). Nevertheless, multidisciplinary collaborations that include qualitative research are evolving toward true interdisciplinary teams, with mutual learning, integrated study designs, analytic strategies enriched by multiple types of data and observations, and results with sufficient breadth and depth to inform decision making in a world subject to both global and local influences (Fernald and Duclos 2005, Garland et al. 2006, Rhoades 2006). It is with this goal in mind that we conceived this book.

If Teamwork Is So Good for Us, Why Is It So Hard?

> *"Fool of a Took!" he growled. "This is a serious journey, not a hobbit walking-party. Throw yourself in [the well] next time, and then you will be no further nuisance. Now be quiet!"*
>
> J. R. R. TOLKIEN, *THE FELLOWSHIP OF THE RING* (1966:327)

There is an extensive literature on the highs and lows of teamwork and management, including theoretical works, empirical studies, fiction, and even cartoons such as *Dilbert*. According to one commonly cited definition, "A team is a small number of people with complementary skills who are committed to a common purpose, performance goals, and approach for which they are mutually accountable" (Katzenbach and Smith 1993:45). The notion of complementary skills is important: team members build on each other's strengths. A person does not have to be skillful in all aspects of the intended research in order to be an excellent team member. Because the work is not about any one person, it is also important that each team member feel a sense of commitment and responsibility to the work of the group and not just his or her own particular focus. This includes the team leader or lead investigator. Each person must be willing to be present and to participate in ways that facilitate the work of others, even at some cost to time and energy that could be directed to one's personal priorities. Team members need to listen to, question, and challenge each other. Respect is key, trust essential.

Teams go through a process of development, and inevitably the going will be rocky at times. Tuckman (1965) famously described this process as having four stages: forming, storming, norming, and performing. In the forming stage, the team members get to know each other and the project in what is often described as the honeymoon period. Of course, the honeymoon ends as the need to actually do the work is impressed on the team. Implicit assumptions and expectations emerge and arguments often ensue with regard to who does what, when, and how. This storming phase is a time of negotiation and conflict resolution that should ultimately evolve into a set of accepted normative expectations. With norming comes a sense of team pride as people learn to work together to accomplish their increasingly shared goals. Now they are performing as a team—and likely as not, the project is also coming to an end. The team development process takes a lot of time, relative to the amount of time spent on a project. Most people woefully underestimate the amount of time and effort involved in the teamwork process, even if they have been through it before (Garland et al. 2006).

The process need not be linear, of course. The team may get stuck in storming or noodling about with norming and never progress to sustained, effective performing. If a project lasts more than two or three years, an effectively performing team may need to go through the cycle again as old members leave and new ones come on board. Human relationships need constant attention.

As described by Arrow et al. (2000), groups (including teams) are composed of members, tasks, and tools that are linked in a dynamic, functional structure the authors call the *coordination network*. The initial group-formation period generally overlaps with a process whereby the coordination network is elaborated. This is a critically important period for future group functioning. Evidence suggests that the interaction and work patterns established in the first meeting of a group persist unquestioned and largely unconsciously for at least half the life of the group (Gersick 1988). Team leaders should never underestimate the importance of getting off on the right foot. From the first meeting, they need to foster a shared understanding of expectations about roles, responsibilities, and relationships among team members and foster the emergence of a maximally functional coordination network (Fernald and Duclos 2005).

The implications of team size also need to be carefully considered. Larger groups require significantly more resources to support and manage—not because there are more people but because there are more relationships. The number of potential dyadic relationships increases geometrically with the addition of each new person to the group, and it is relationships that are at the crux of group functioning (Arrow et al. 2000).

The larger the group, the larger the resulting coordination network will be and the less amenable it will be to informal coordination. This is true even if all the team members work in the same setting and can hold regular face-to-face meetings. For example, spontaneous conversation is difficult to sustain when more than four people are present (Dunbar et al. 1995), which means that people are more likely to feel excluded in even moderately large groups. A common way in which this reality gets expressed is via the domination of the group by a few vocal members. Patterns of deference or dissent based on academic prestige, educational background, gender, age, or other characteristics commonly result in power imbalances, biased allocation of resources, and failure to acknowledge, support, and integrate contributions from all team members. If the team works largely through informal coordination, the tendency toward exclusion and biased domination increases. Decisions are then more likely to be made on the basis of who eats lunch together or works out together, or whose office is conveniently located near the project leader's office. Coordination becomes even more challenging when team members are geographically dispersed (see chapter 4). Inattention to such group dynamics will ultimately undermine the effectiveness of a team, by limiting the contributions of its members.

You might think that qualitative researchers, with their focus on understanding the nuances and richness of human social behavior, would have a leg up on helping to form effective teams. Unfortunately, in this situation as in others, it is hard to see the functional and dysfunctional aspects of one's own social context and personal behavior. However, by consciously facilitating the development of "a common purpose, performance goals, and approach for which all are mutually accountable," we believe it is possible to shorten the learning curve and eliminate or lessen at least some of the bumps in the road.

How Complicated Can It Get?

Meanwhile, the following events occurred simultaneously throughout the neighborhood. . . .

THOMAS WOLFE, *LOOK HOMEWARD, ANGEL* (1929:154)

At the time of this writing, several of the contributors to this book are in the final year of a four-year, multistage, multisite qualitative research project implemented in support of a clinical research program evaluating the safety and effectiveness of an antiretroviral drug to prevent the acquisition of HIV—a strategy referred to as preexposure prophylaxis (PrEP). One trial enrolled women in Cameroon, Nigeria, and Ghana; another intended to enroll men in Malawi, but that trial was cancelled before it got off the ground. Both trial designs targeted people who were at high risk for HIV as a result of multiple heterosexual relationships. Over the course of the first three years, the qualitative research component grew to include a U.S.-based team with three PhD-level anthropologists plus master's-level staff that included a study coordinator, one to two administrative assistants, and two to four qualitative analysts. Each of the four participating field sites had a senior lead investigator and as many as twelve staff to conduct, transcribe, translate, type, and analyze data from participant observations, interviews, and focus groups. The qualitative research design included three components: a site preparedness assessment before the clinical trials began, an acceptability assessment in parallel with the clinical trials, and a trial outcomes assessment following the close of the trials at each site. Each component, in turn, included about a half dozen interview and focus group guides targeting different stakeholders in the local communities plus participant observation in local settings. All told, the project generated some six hundred individual transcripts.

Adding to the complexity was the early closeout of the trial in Nigeria for quality assurance reasons, and the suspension and subsequent closeout of the trial in Cameroon owing to controversy (Grant et al. 2005). These early trial closeouts required modifications to the original qualitative design to address locally emergent issues. We also created a media database to track local and worldwide responses to the trials in the press, on the Internet, and on listservs, in both English and French.

As project sponsor, we confronted several management challenges for the qualitative research collaboration. We needed to track staff in the United States and at each of the sites to ensure that everyone working on the project had proper training in study design, methods, and research ethics. For any given transcript we needed to know which data collection instrument was used, who conducted the interview or focus group, who took notes (if relevant), and who did the transcription, translation, and typing. We also needed to track basic demographic information for all study participants. We therefore worked with the local investigators to develop protocols for assigning identification numbers and created databases to track descriptive information for staff, for participants, and for the textual data.

Each step in the analysis of the transcripts, field notes, and media files needed to be documented. We needed to be able to combine information from all of the sites, while accounting for local differences in data collection strategies and the impact of unfolding site-specific events. We had to be flexible enough to support site-specific analysis by the local research teams, systematic enough to identify potentially contradictory results that needed explanation, and rigorous enough to know which conclusions were strongly supported by the data and which were inferential and therefore needed additional supporting evidence. Given the sensitivities and controversies associated with the clinical research, we needed to be able to verify results and demonstrate objectivity in the analysis and presentation of the qualitative data.

We also had to address the ethical dimensions of doing team-based qualitative research. For example, confidentiality is more complex when there are multiple people handling interview tapes and transcripts, and when transcripts and field notes are transmitted electronically from site to sponsor. The research included participant observation, interviews, and focus groups in settings where stigmatized sexual activity was common; thus, it was important to protect the confidentiality of not only individual people but neighborhoods and communities.

As this example demonstrates, team research is complex and presents numerous logistical, ethical, political, and methodological challenges that are not typically experienced by the lone ethnographer or that take on new twists in the teamwork context. The chapters in this book identify and discuss some of the more frequently encountered issues in larger qualitative research projects carried out by teams. The authors draw on their experience with numerous projects implemented in the United States as well as internationally, both as stand-alone qualitative research projects and as integrated, multidisciplinary endeavors.

The book is divided into three separate, yet related, sections—Research Design and Implementation, Data Preparation and Analysis, and Quality Control and Assurance. The first of these sections focuses on the front end of the research process, namely planning the project and getting it started. In chapter 2, MacQueen addresses ethical concerns for team-based qualitative research such as working with multiple ethics oversight committees, protecting confidentiality, deciding whether and how much to compensate participants in different settings, and reconciling participatory research models with nonparticipatory human subjects protections. Woodsong provides a detailed description of the range of political dimensions associated with team research in chapter 3. Using multiple real-life examples, she describes some commonly encountered political obstacles working in teams and offers constructive approaches to deal with them. Mack and colleagues, in chapter 4, describe some of the challenges associated with project preparation and logistical planning in an international setting, and provide insight into how some common problems might be avoided early on in the research process.

Once the groundwork for a research study has been laid and data collection is underway, the next step in the process is managing and analyzing the data. Chapters in the second section of the book discuss the challenges associated with preparing and analyzing qualitative data in a team setting, and provide a framework for systematizing the data management and analysis process.

Systematizing the Approach to Data Management and Analysis

Qualitative data management includes obvious tasks, such as tracking text files, and more subtle tasks, such as tracking the textual and interpretative evidence used to build an explanation of an event or theory about social and behavioral patterns. In team research, some or all of these tasks are often carried out by more than one person. Spradley (1979:102–103) long ago noted the importance of distinguishing what we observe from what we think about what we observe, warning against "the temptation . . . to create order out of other cultures by imposing your own categories"; he labeled such efforts *shallow domain analysis*. To maintain this crucial distinction between what is observed versus interpretations of the observed, and to support a richer and deeper analysis, we need to be conscious of the fundamental types of information associated with qualitative research and the processes driving the generation of each type.

A well-organized qualitative database should make it easy for all team members to understand the dimensions of each item within it. For example, who participated in the generation of the item, be it field notes, an interview transcript, or debriefing notes from a focus group? How was the item generated, for example, from an audiotape or notes or both? Who analyzed it? The database should be organized and managed in a way that will support the identification of meaningful chunks of information within each item and support linkage among different items and chunks at all stages of analysis. For example, what do the words in a particular chunk of information describe? Who is the source of the description? Who elicited the description? How was it elicited? The database should facilitate the development of analytic techniques that emphasize the discovery of patterns and relationships among items and chunks. For example, how similar is this description to others elicited in the same way or in different ways? Are some descriptive themes more likely to appear than others? Do certain themes cluster together? Do clusters of themes differ for men and women, or for people at different sites? Are some analysts more likely to see certain themes?

When working in interdisciplinary teams, the ability to provide this type of detailed information can be critical to ensure respect for and appropriate utilization of findings by colleagues who are unfamiliar with qualitative research. This is especially true if the qualitative results contradict other findings, point toward biases or inadequacies in the implementation of other research, or uncover unexpected factors that may influence outcomes. For example, ensuring adequate informed consent in low-literacy populations is a major challenge in international biomedical research (Marshall 2006, McGrory et al. 2006, Woodsong and Abdool Karim 2005). In the HIV PrEP research described above, multiple steps were taken to address these known challenges; however, accusations of inadequate informed consent surfaced during the controversies surrounding the trial. In-depth interviews with trial participants in Ghana uncovered persistent comprehension problems with regard to the experimental aspects of the trial, especially the random assignment of women to either a placebo or treatment. However, the data indicated that the nature of these problems were quite distinct from the accusations of negligence made in the press and on activist listservs. We found that some of the women interviewed believed that through the exercise of faith, God would intervene with the randomization scheme and ensure they received the experimental drug rather than the placebo. They also tended to believe that the researchers "knew" the experimental drug would be effective, despite their claims otherwise (Akumatey et al. 2006). These findings represented unexpected and important insights into the informed consent process that can contribute to future improvements in comprehension with people who hold similar values. Before we presented these potentially controversial findings at a major international conference, however, our clinical colleagues rightfully demanded strong substantiation of the results, including how the questions were asked, whether adequate probing of responses occurred, how participants were selected for the interviews, whether there were potential biases in the coding and analysis of the data, and what the frequency of particular responses among the participants interviewed was. As a result of our systematic approach to data management and analysis, we were able to rapidly address all of the questions raised.

From a data management and analysis perspective, there are two pivotal players in qualitative research: *sources*, who provide primary information, and *analysts*, who generate secondary information in the process of interpreting primary information. These are not mutually exclusive roles, as will be described later. There are four fundamental types of information associated with sources and analysts that contribute to qualitative data analysis: (1) the *characteristics of the sources* where information is sought, (2) *primary information* collected from the sources, (3) *secondary information* created to aid in the interpretation of the primary information, and (4) *characteristics of the analysts* who construct the secondary information (MacQueen and Milstein 1999).

Sources and Primary Information

Sources are not part of a qualitative database; rather, they generate the primary information in that database. Primary information exists as a result of the data collection process; it also exists independent of the analysis process. Sources can be described, for example, in terms of who or what they are, and how long they have existed or how old they are. The source providing such descriptive information may not be the same source that provides the primary information. For example, you collect a story about a long-ago event from an old woman in a market; later, another member of the research team learns from others that the old woman is the maternal aunt to key actors in the event. Deciding whether and how to track this type of complex information is an important part of developing a team-based data management system. In addition to sorting out who is a source for what information, you may need to include assessments of how reliable the information is and whether additional verification is needed before it can be used in analysis.

The use of the term *source* rather than *subject* or *participant* reflects the potential scope and complexity of qualitative research. Data collection is often interactive, with the research team playing an explicit role in the process. In team-based research, differences in interviewer style, rapport, or use of prompts may need to be evaluated carefully to ensure that they do not generate systematic bias in the types of information collected (see also chapter 11). For example, a common strategy used to generate richer data in in-depth interviews is to ask several similar, but not identical, questions about a particular topic. One of our projects included an interviewer who decided to skip a couple of the follow-up questions in several interviews. The transcripts included comments from the interviewer such as "Oh, we've already talked about this next question so I'll skip it." But the questions, though similar, were sufficiently different that they usually generated additional and richer information when included by the other interviewers on the project. Some of those interviewers acknowledged the overlap between questions by saying something like "Well, we've already talked about this but let me ask anyway in case you have something to add . . . " Quite often, there was "something to add" that was distinct from or provided greater clarity about statements made earlier.

Primary information can include published or preexisting text such as brochures, books, letters, and newspapers or graphics such as photographs, designs, and advertisements. These may have been produced by individuals or groups, and the source needs to be described accordingly. In some cases, a person cannot be identified as a source and we are forced to attribute the information to "Anonymous." Alternatively, the information may be something like a consensus or policy statement that is most appropriately identified with a named group rather than an individual, even if a primary author is known. It may be appropriate to attribute the group as well as make note of individual authors, if there is analytic value in this level of tracking. These types of decisions need to be made explicitly. Otherwise team members are likely to make judgment calls on a case-by-case basis, rendering a detailed level of analysis impossible because of a lack of comparability across cases.

As global access to the Internet increases, electronic media present a potentially rich source of data but one that is simultaneously robust and ephemeral. For the HIV prevention trial described earlier, we found the same text was often picked up verbatim from one online source and then sent out under the byline of another. In this case, the date and time of each posting became an important element of the primary information provided by each online source, as it would later help in the analysis of the global flow of information about the research. The characteristics of the sources also proved useful for understanding who the global stakeholders were and how to effectively share information with them in a timely and transparent fashion.

Like sources, primary information can also be described. This may be as simple as a table or cover sheet listing particulars such as who the sources were, when it was collected, and who translated and transcribed the information. It can also include self-referential information such as a concordance or word-occurrence list that summarizes the frequency with which words or phrases appear in the text. Word collocation matrices describe the frequency at which pairs of words occur together within a predefined textual space, for example, a certain number of lines of text or within sentences or paragraphs. Semantic networks mathematically describe the significance of recurring terms in the text and strength of relationships among significant terms. With audio and video objects, measures of voice modularity or standardized notation of nonverbal behavior can be generated. For much team-based qualitative research, interview and focus group transcripts represent the majority of primary information.

Analysts and Secondary Information

The data analyst or coder is a critical but often ignored element in qualitative analysis. The analyst cannot be disentangled from the analysis, just as the interviewer cannot be disentangled from an interview. As a result, qualitative analysis is inherently subjective. There have been few systematic attempts to understand what factors influence an analyst's interpretation of qualitative data. What are the pros and cons of having an interviewer analyze his or her own data? Does disciplinary background exert any influence? Qualitative researchers often stress the importance of rereading text multiple times as part of analysis, but is there a point where familiarity generates fatigue and an inability to perceive meaningful information? Or might the opposite occur, when meaning is ascribed where evidence is lacking? Team-based data analysis gives us opportunities to explore these types of questions. The development of descriptive information about coders can facilitate such assessments and improve our ability to obtain accurate, meaningful knowledge through the subjective process of analysis.

In contrast, a great deal has been published on the act of coding. The coding process is the primary focus of most methodological approaches, including grounded theory (Strauss and Corbin 1990), semiotic psychology (Markel 1998), symbolic interactionism (Blumer 1969, Hall 1995), and conversation or discourse analysis (Hanson 1997, Moerman 1988). Team-based research does not require the use of a particular approach to analysis, but it presents challenges for all. Managing team analysis requires an awareness of the different types of activities going on, including who is doing what and why. An earlier paper describing a systems approach to qualitative data (MacQueen and Milstein 1999) divided coding activities into two categories. *Segmenting activities* were defined as analytic actions that can be directly mapped onto text or images. Examples included defining the boundaries of a narrative passage or segment, applying codes to a segment, using tags or other marks to identify points in a text file or image, and creating hyperlinks between segments or points. Thus, segmenting activities are centered on defining or describing structure and relationships among objects in a qualitative database. *Metadata activities*, in contrast, entail the creation of data about data. Prompted by meaning discerned in the primary information, the coder generates metadata in the form of codes, comments, memos, and annotations, as well as graphical summaries of the interpreted information (e.g., diagrams, networks, clusters, and maps) capable of showing the multidimensional structure of coding patterns.

Segmenting and metadata activities take place in an iterative fashion, with feedback between the two elements. For example, a typical sequence of coder activities may include the highlighting or bracketing of a chunk of text containing semantically related terms (segmenting), the creation of a code to describe the cultural significance of the chunk of text (metadata), the establishment of a link between the code and the chunk in the database (segmenting), the creation of a memo describing related concepts described in the literature (metadata), the establishment of a link between the memo and the chunk in the database (segmenting), and incorporation of the code into a diagram describing conceptual links among related codes (metadata) (MacQueen and Milstein 1999).

One of the dangers of an iterative, feedback-driven process like qualitative analysis is that it can quickly become self-reinforcing, even when it is completely inadequate for achieving its original goals. To avoid such an outcome, corrective mechanisms need to be in place. Two management tools are essential in this regard: documentation and communication. In chapter 6, MacQueen and colleagues outline an explicit process for developing codebooks that provides checks and balances against self-reinforcing beliefs. Chapter 11, by Carey and Gelaude, provides many tips and tools for reducing bias in data collection as well as analysis.

Large, complex projects tend to generate large volumes of data. And working in a team environment usually results in the data being handled, prepared, coded, analyzed, and transferred by multiple individuals. Team-based qualitative research, therefore, requires some sort of structure to maintain data integrity and to impart a certain degree of objectivity on how data are analyzed and interpreted. Part II, Data Preparation and Analysis, covers these and other issues associated with working with data in a team setting. In chapter 5, McLellan-Lemal outlines some of the more common approaches to textual transcription and discusses key points to consider when planning and implementing transcription. By making transcription an explicit process, the transfer of data from sound to written text becomes more visible and, more important, generates more consistent textual data. Her approach has proven effective for many large team-based projects. MacQueen and colleagues illustrate the importance of structure for segmenting and coding data in chapter 6, and provide practical suggestions for how to structure, develop, and revise codebooks in the context of team research. Namey and colleagues (chapter 7), in turn, discuss some of the possibilities of how to analyze data once they have been coded. The authors describe a wide range of approaches to data reduction that are effective for large qualitative data sets typical of team and multisite research projects.

Quality Assurance

Qualitative researchers pride themselves on their flexibility and responsiveness to emergent information and conditions during the research process. One of the major challenges of team-based qualitative research is the preservation of these attributes while simultaneously ensuring an overall standard for the project as a whole. Here again, communication, accountability, and the uncovering of implicit assumptions are essential for success (Garland et al. 2006). In our team-based work we make extensive use of templates, checklists, meeting notes, and e-mail documentation as part of "norming and performing." Most evolved as tools to either solve problems or prevent their recurrence. None are etched in stone. Rather, like qualitative research in general, they are flexible and responsive, subject to constant revision and review. Some end up in the circular file as failed experiments. Others have held up well, with few changes across multiple projects.

The final section of the book, Quality Control and Assurance, covers various components of quality assurance in a team or multisite research setting. In chapter 8, McLellan-Lemal outlines techniques for ensuring good data management practices. The chapter delineates some key principles behind successful data management and also provides a critical summary of the data management capabilities one should consider when choosing among qualitative data analysis software programs. In chapter 9, Guest and colleagues describe a process and template for monitoring team-based research that have proven effective for monitoring numerous multisite projects while they are up and running. In chapter 10, we move the focus to the final stage of the research process—presenting results. Here, Guest and MacQueen argue that using guidelines in reporting qualitative research results is a further step toward ensuring quality work. In the second part of the chapter, they provide concrete recommendations for presenting results from qualitative research in a way that imparts both transparency and integrity. Finally, in chapter 11 Carey and Gelaude take a broad look at quality assurance throughout the entire research process. On the basis of extensive experience leading team-based and multisite research projects, the authors impart to the reader the lessons they have learned over the years and present approaches to minimize bias and maximize quality in the qualitative research process.

Conclusion

The approaches outlined in this book were designed to support scientific inquiry, but they will facilitate any form of systematic qualitative inquiry by a team of researchers. They support transparency in data analysis, and strive to demystify qualitative research. The chapters also offer what we hope are useful suggestions for researchers engaged in, or who plan to engage in, a wide range of team-based research projects. While the ideas and procedures presented in this book certainly are not the *only* way to go about conducting qualitative research in a team environment, they are based on years of experience doing such research, particularly in multiple sites. The information presented is based on the (too) many lessons the authors had to learn the hard way, being forced to improvise in an effort to maintain a quality effort, or in some cases salvage a failing project. By sharing these lessons and the solutions devised, we hope to minimize such problems for those who might find themselves leading or participating in a qualitative research team. At the same time we hope that others expand and improve upon what the collection of authors present in this volume, particularly as qualitative research increasingly becomes a team enterprise.

References

Akumatey, B., N. Mack, L. Johnson, and K. M. MacQueen
2006   Ethical challenges for HIV prevention trials in Africa: The cultural mean-
        ing of pill-taking and local research literacy in Tema, Ghana. Poster exhi-
        bition TUPE0429, XVI International AIDS Conference (AIDS2006),
        Toronto, Canada, 13–18 August.

Arrow, H., J. E. McGrath, and J. L. Berdahl
2000   *Small Groups As Complex Systems: Formation, Coordination, Development and
        Adaptation.* Thousand Oaks, Calif.: Sage.

Blumer, H.
1969   *Symbolic Interactionism: Perspective and Method.* Berkeley: University of Cali-
        fornia Press.

Dunbar, R. I. M., N. Duncan, and D. Nettle
1995   Size and structure of freely forming conversational groups. *Human Nature*
        6:67–78.

Fernald, D. H., and C. W. Duclos
2005   Enhance your team-based qualitative research. *Annals of Family Medicine*
        3:360–364.

Garland, D. R., M. K. O'Connor, T. A. Wolfer, and F. E. Netting
2006   Team-based research: notes from the field. *Qualitative Social Work* 5:93–109.

Gersick, C. J. G.
1988   Time and transition in work teams: Toward a new model of group devel-
        opment. *Academy of Management Journal* 31:9–41.

Grant, R. M., S. Buchbinder, W. Cates Jr., E. Clarke, T. Coates, M. S. Cohen, M.
        Delaney, P. Goicochea, G. Gonsalves, M. Harrington, J. Lama, K. M. MacQueen,
        J. P. Moore, L. Peterson, J. Sanchez, M. Thompson, and M. A. Wainberg
2005   HIV chemoprophylaxis research should be promoted, not prevented. PrEP
        trial commentary. *Science* 309:2170–2171.

Hall, P.
1995   The consequences of qualitative analysis for sociological theory: Beyond
        the micro level. *Sociological Quarterly* 38:439–467.

Hanson, R. E.
1997   Objectivity and narrative in contemporary reporting: A formal analysis.
        Symbolic Interactionism 20:385–396.

Katzenbach, J. R., and D. K. Smith
1993   *The Wisdom of Teams: Creating the High-performance Organization.* Boston:
        Harvard Business School.

MacQueen, Kathleen M., and Bobby Milstein
1999   A systems approach to qualitative data management and analysis. *Field Methods* 11(1):27–39.

Markel, Norman
1998   *Semiotic Psychology: Speech as an Index of Emotions and Attitudes.* New York: Peter Lang.

Marshall, Patricia
2006   Informed consent in international health research. *Journal of Empirical Research on Human Research Ethics* 1:25–42.

McGrory, C. Elizabeth, Barbara A. Friedland, Cynthia Woodsong, and Kathleen M. MacQueen
2006   *Informed Consent in HIV Prevention Trials: Report of an International Workshop.* New York: The Population Counsel.

Moerman, M.
1988   *Talking Culture: Ethnography and Conversational Analysis.* Philadelphia: University of Pennsylvania Press.

Rhoades, R.
2006   Seeking half our brains: Constraints and incentives in the social context of interdisciplinary research. In M. Cernea and A. Kassam, eds. *Researching the Culture in Agri-Culture: Social Research for International Agricultural Development.* Pp. 403–420. Wallingford, UK: CABI Publishing.

Rhoades, R., D. Horton, and R. Booth
1986   Anthropologist, biological scientist and economist: The Three Musketeers or Three Stooges of farming systems research? In J. Jones and B. Wallace, eds. *Applying Science in Farming Systems Research.* Pp. 21–40. Boulder, Colo.: Westview.

Senge, Peter M.
1990   *The Fifth Discipline: The Art & Practice of the Learning Organization.* New York: Currency Doubleday.

Spradley, J. P.
1979   *The Ethnographic Interview.* New York: Holt, Rinehart & Winston.

Strauss, A., and J. Corbin
1990   *Basics of Qualitative Research: Grounded Theory Procedures and Techniques.* Newbury Park, Calif.: Sage.

Tolkien, J. R. R.
1966   *The Fellowship of the Ring.* Boston: Houghton Mifflin.

Tuckman, B. W.
1965   Developmental sequence in small groups. *Psychological Bulletin* 63:384–399.

Woodsong, Cynthia, and Quarraisha Abdool Karim
2005   A model designed to enhance informed consent: Experiences from the HIV
        Prevention Trials Network. *American Journal of Public Health* 95:412–419.

Wolfe, T.
1929   *Look Homeward, Angel.* New York: Scribner.

Ethics and Team-based Qualitative Research

2

KATHLEEN M. MACQUEEN

THERE ARE TWO DIMENSIONS TO ETHICS for team-based qualitative research—professional and human subjects protections. Professional ethics include general principles and guidelines for the research disciplines, such as authorship practices and allocation of credit, intellectual rights, error and negligence, misconduct such as plagiarism and falsification of data, and conflicts of interest. The National Academy of Sciences has produced a document that outlines basic issues and standards for the responsible conduct of research (Committee on Science, Engineering, and Public Policy, 1995) that is available free on the Internet (www.nap.edu/readingroom/books/obas/, accessed September 28, 2005). Del Monte (2000) addresses professional ethics in the context of team-based research. Guidance for specific research disciplines is also generally available from professional organizations such as the American Anthropological Association, the Society for Applied Anthropology, the American Sociological Association, and the American Public Health Association. Academic and research institutions, as well as funding organizations, often have guidelines too. It is important that researchers seek out and periodically review such guidance, and not grow complacent about their professional practice. New challenges emerge with increasing globalization of research, and the limits of established standards for insuring ethical research continue to be exposed and questioned. This is especially true for interdisciplinary team-based research, where underlying assumptions and principles across different disciplines and cultures may lead to opposite conclusions about the best way to handle a problem. At a certain point, professional ethics and the politics of research intersect; many examples of this intersection are addressed by Woodsong in chapter 3.

This chapter will focus primarily on the second dimension of ethics, that is, the area of human subjects protections. *Human* means that these ethics address issues specific to research with and about people. *Protection* means that the ethics are focused on protecting people from being harmed as a result of such research. At a minimum, ethical researchers strive to leave people no worse off than they were before the research. Ideally, people should experience some improvement or benefit.

Human subjects protections are practices, guidelines, rules, and regulations that have grown out of principles for the ethical conduct of research with and about people. Historically, the Belmont Report represents the seminal document in the development of an explicit set of such principles for research in general (National Commission for the Protection of Human Subjects of Biomedical and Behavioral Research 1979). The first principle set out in Belmont, *respect for persons*, requires a commitment to insuring the autonomy of people who participate in research; if a person is vulnerable due to diminished autonomy then steps must be taken to insure that he or she is not exploited by the research. It does not mean that people with diminished autonomy cannot participate in research. If that were the case there could be no research on children or the mentally disabled or prisoners, and research on people in poverty, refugees, victims of domestic violence, and others would be severely limited. Adherence to the principle of respect for persons insures that people will not be used simply as a means to achieve research objectives and without consideration of their personal goals and wishes.

The second principle, *beneficence,* speaks to a commitment to minimize the risks associated with research and maximize the benefits that participants may experience. *Justice,* the third principle, commits researchers to insuring a fair distribution of the risks and benefits resulting from their work. Those who take on the burdens of research participation should share in the benefits of the knowledge gained. Conversely, the people who are expected to benefit from the knowledge should be among those who are asked to participate.

Increasingly, there have been calls for a fourth principle, *respect for communities*, that would confer "an obligation to respect the values and interests of the community in research and, wherever possible, to protect the community from harm" (Weijer et al. 1999:275). For qualitative research, this principle is especially relevant when community-wide knowledge, values, and relationships are a critical component of the research endeavor.

From these principles, the U.S. government developed a set of federal regulations to insure the protection of people participating in government-funded research or in research intended to lead to the licensing of medical drugs and devices (Department of Health and Human Services 2005). These regulations, in turn, have generally been adopted for all research with humans by universities, research institutes, and others in the United States, regardless of the funding source or biomedical intent. While the Belmont Report and the core set of regulations known as the Common Rule were written with all types of research in mind, they are nonetheless heavily influenced by the highly controlled and experimental contexts of biomedical and behavioral research. This has created serious challenges for qualitative researchers, who generally work in a more fluid, dynamic research context. In the sections that follow, I review those challenges through the lens of team-based qualitative research.

Does Qualitative Research Really Need IRB Review?

The U.S. federal regulations provide a great deal of flexibility with regard to requirements for much social and behavioral research and for minimal risk research. However, this is not always evident in the way that institutional review boards (IRBs) review qualitative research (Bosk and DeVries, 2004). Most qualitative researchers have at least one story about an IRB that hindered rather than facilitated the ethical conduct of research. From my own experience, the most dramatic case example centered on an IRB review of an ethnographic research project. The IRB was at a public health organization, and the research was being undertaken by an employee who was pursuing a PhD at a nearby university. The public health IRB, which did not have an ethnographer or anthropologist as a member, disapproved the research on the grounds that it was of such poor scientific quality that it would be unethical to burden people with participation. The employee, her supervisor (who chaired another IRB at the public health organization), and her academic committee were understandably upset. As an anthropologist and a member of yet another IRB at the organization, I was asked to provide an independent review of the protocol. In fact, I was impressed with the innovative design, the strategic sampling strategy, and the multimethod approach used to compensate for the potential biases that would likely result from the use of either a qualitative or quantitative approach alone. In talking with the chair of the IRB that had disapproved the protocol, it was quickly evident that no one on that particular board understood the logic of an iterative research design. After several meetings and discussions, the IRB reversed its decision and the employee/student was able to move forward with the research.

This is an extreme example; more often, the problems I have encountered are nuisances and annoyances. For example, I have had IRB members insist that I indicate the total number of participants to be included in a qualitative study even when the design explicitly relies on the concept of saturation to determine how many interviews should be conducted. Saturation is predicated on the idea that interviews should be conducted until they no longer generate any new information (Guest et al. 2006). However, since research funding is always limited, it is not always possible to attain saturation; therefore, I respond to the IRB's desire for concreteness by providing them with the maximum number of participants feasible given the funding constraints. This seems to satisfy their need for numbers.

Much of qualitative research may, in fact, be exempted from the requirements of the U.S. federal regulations if it entails research in educational settings involving educational practices, research involving educational tests (cognitive, diagnostic, aptitude, achievement), surveys, interviews, or observations of public behavior. However, such research *cannot* be exempted if (a) it identifies specific individuals (e.g., because their names, addresses, or other identifying information is collected as part of the research) *and* (b) entails a risk of criminal or civil liability, or of damage to the financial standing, employability, or reputation of those so identified (Department of Health and Human Services 2005). On the basis of my experience doing workshops with a wide variety of IRB professionals, the exemption criteria are often poorly understood and may not be used as fully as they could be. In such situations, it may be well worth the effort to meet with the IRB chair and administrator to go over the criteria and discuss their applicability to particular projects before qualitative research protocols are submitted for review. However, some IRBs may be uncomfortable with the notion of exempting any research from review and they are within their rights to refuse to allow exemptions; while the regulations allow for exemption, they do not require it. In fact, there may be good reason to require review in particular cases that otherwise meet the criteria. Except for the confidentiality concerns noted previously, the exemption rules do not consider the level of risk entailed by the research; responsible IRBs are unlikely to be willing to exempt a study perceived to carry significant potential harm for participants. For example, anonymous interviews with rape victims in an emergency room setting may meet the exemption criteria but could very well carry significant psychological risks. The risk determination is best left to an independent oversight group such as the IRB or a community advisory board. In my opinion, a researcher should never be the sole arbiter of whether a study needs independent review and oversight.

Multiple Reviews

Team-based research may present additional challenges with regard to IRB review when more than one organization is involved. Such collaborations are common among biomedical researchers and their experience is both informative and discouraging. For example, members of a tuberculosis clinical trials consortium evaluated the impact of local IRB review on the quality of informed consent forms. Each of the twenty-five sites in the consortium submitted a centrally developed consent form and protocol to their IRBs for review and the impact of the review was then evaluated. First, the evaluation team found that the median length of time for local approval of the study was 104.5 days, with a range of 31–346 days. Second, they found that the consent forms became longer and less readable as a result of the local review process, with a mean increase in (Flesch–Kincaid) reading grade level of 0.9—almost a full grade level more difficult. The local IRBs requested a median of 46.5 changes to the form (range 3–160); 85.2 percent of these changes affected wording but not meaning and 11.2 percent actually introduced errors. All told, at the end of the local review process, 66.6 percent of the consent forms included errors that were not present in the original, centrally developed form (Burman et al. 2003).

In my experience, regardless of the nature of the research, there is a relationship between the number of IRBs and the length and complexity of the ethics review process. For example, one of my projects had a very simple design where each collaborating site was to conduct approximately ten to fifteen in-depth interviews and two focus groups (MacQueen et al. in press). No personal identifying information was collected, and though the research was HIV-related we collected no data on personal behavior or HIV-infection status. The project centered on reactions to ethical aspects of a hypothetical HIV prevention trial; it was minimal risk and met the criteria for exemption under the U.S. regulations. The research was implemented at ten sites in seven countries. My home institution and the one U.S. site participating in the research exempted the protocol. Most of the participating sites in the non-U.S. settings were collaborating with U.S.-based universities; however, none of those universities used the exemption option. All of the foreign institutions reviewed the protocol as well. All told, the approvals process took about a year to complete; data collection took five months.

The length of time required to complete the reviews, the complexities of working with each site to prepare materials, and the effort needed to track all the approvals were onerous relative to the research itself. However, the actual review process at each site was relatively straightforward. The only substantive issue to arise during review was a concern on the part of several foreign ethics committees regarding our request to use oral consent rather than asking participants to sign a consent form. Since we were not collecting any identifying information, a signed consent form would actually increase the potential for a breach of confidentiality rather than increase the level of protection. In order to document the oral consent, we included verification of consent as part of the audiotaped interview and focus group process. Once we explained this reasoning and the process in more detail, all of the committees approved the study.

For some multisite projects, the review process may result in changes to the protocol in order to address local concerns. For qualitative research, this may or may not require changes to the protocol for all sites. For example, for the HIV preexposure prophylaxis research described in chapter 1 we developed a generic sociobehavioral protocol that facilitated data comparability across sites but then worked with each site to develop sampling strategies and additional questions that reflected the specific context within which they worked. As the sponsoring organization, our IRB approved the generic protocol and then reviewed amendments that reflected the evolving research process at each of the collaborating sites. At each site, in turn, the ethics committees reviewed the generic protocol and the materials specific to that site but not the materials from the other sites. For about a year, when the project was at its most complex with two sites closing early, one site on schedule, and a fourth site being added, we submitted protocols to our home IRB almost monthly. All were reviewed on an expedited basis, in accordance with U.S. regulations, and rarely took more than a week or two to approve. This in-house approval process was also coordinated with the local review processes. The paperwork was coordinated by an administrative assistant who spent as much as a day a week working with the IRB administrator, the research team, and via e-mail with the host country collaborators.

Risk and Harm: Physical, Social, Psychological

For the most part, the risks associated with qualitative research tend to be minimal and center on harms that may result from a breach of confidentiality (see below). However, some research may introduce significant psychological or social risks for participants and communities. Observations, interviews, and focus groups may uncover illegal activities, and the resulting notes and transcripts may be subject to subpoena or confiscation. Data collection itself may surface psychological trauma, for example, in the case of domestic violence or refugees from political or other forms of violence.

Research on stigmatized topics such as mental illness, HIV, or transactional sex may lead to social harms for people associated with the research, including discrimination and social isolation. Historical research may surface events, stories, and perspectives that can be damaging to the reputations of whole communities, or may perpetuate stereotypes; such costs must be considered and efforts made to mitigate negative consequences, regardless of the validity and potential contributions of the research to knowledge and the advancement of society. Very rarely, qualitative research may precipitate physical harm to participants. Extremely vulnerable people, such as women in violent relationships with controlling partners, may put themselves at risk for injury or death by telling their stories to researchers.

One of the advantages of team-based research for reducing potential harms is the ability to choose team members specifically for this purpose, in addition to those with the methodological or academic skills needed for the research. Thus, if the research includes participants who have experienced domestic violence, the team may include an experienced social worker who can be on call to provide counseling if someone experiences psychological distress during an interview, and to assist with referrals to appropriate organizations if ongoing problems are uncovered. A less extreme example is the potential to reduce social discomfort that may result for some people who prefer to talk with someone of a particular age, gender, or ethnicity. Here it is important to note discomfort may increase with similarity between the interviewer and the participant; for example, a young man may find it more difficult to discuss emotional issues with another young man and prefer talking with a woman who is somewhat older.

One way in which team research differs significantly from that done by a lone researcher is the collective responsibility for risks incurred by participants when one member of the research team makes an ethical misstep. Del Monte (2000:4) describes a situation where a report with potentially identifying descriptive information was shared by the team leader with the principal of the school where the research was conducted.

> Needless to say, some of the team members were extremely angry and upset. "We" had violated our informants' trust and broken the cardinal ethical code of social science research. To bring the story to a close, we had a final meeting in which we all expressed our anger and concern. Jenna "seemed" to understand (problematic in itself) and apologized. But apologies do not erase what occurred and do not take away the guilt that has been dumped upon the rest of us. Nothing, it seemed, could have prepared me for the violation of trust and ethics thrust upon the team because of one individual's serious misstep.

Research in what Kovats-Bernat (2002) has labeled "dangerous fields" ups the ante on risk for researcher and participant alike. Dangerous fields are contexts where violence and terror are rampant, a complex reality of negotiated power and fluid threat where the researcher is simultaneously at risk and a source of risk to others. Kovats-Bernat argues that the relationship between researcher and researched in dangerous fields must be one of *mutual responsibility* where "all participants in the research must also willingly accept the possibility that *any* involvement in the study could result in intimidation, arrest, torture, disappearance, assassination, or a range of other, utterly unforeseeable dangers" (p. 214). In his work with street children in Port-au-Prince, Haiti, Kovats-Bernat applied what he called a *localized ethic.*

> I took stock of the good advice and recommendation of the local population in deciding what conversations (and silences) were important, what information was too costly to life and limbs to get to, the amount of exposure to violence considered acceptable, the questions that were dangerous to ask, and the patterns of behavior that were important to follow for the safety and security of myself and those around me. (p. 214)

Violence, terror, warfare, and any other context where human rights abuses are at work raise important questions about the appropriateness of a given research activity. Clearly, there is a need to understand and, as Kovats-Bernat argues, demystify violence in order to address it. As with much of medical research, the risks of such research are high, but so are the potential benefits.

Benefits

When IRBs consider the potential benefits of research, they are primarily concerned with direct benefits to the participants, that is, tangible positive outcomes that accrue to the participant as a direct result of research participation. Alleviation of illness, case management that assists in solving a problem, and a video recording preserving the memories of a family member for future generations are all examples of tangible, direct benefits. Not all research projects have direct benefits. IRBs also consider potential indirect benefits to the community or society in general. These include contributions to knowledge and the advancement of science. Qualitative research tends to generate more indirect than direct benefits, unless the research team makes an explicit effort to work with communities to identify and develop appropriate tangible benefits.

Informed Consent

Informed consent is often viewed as the centerpiece of human subjects protections. The goal of informed consent is to insure that people understand what it means to participate in a particular research study so they can decide in a conscious, deliberate way whether they want to participate. Thus, informed consent is one of the most important tools for insuring *respect for persons*.

Many people think of informed consent primarily as a *form*, that is, a piece of paper that describes in detail what the research is about, including the risks and benefits. This form generally includes legalistic language and is signed by the participant, the researcher, and possibly a witness. When the risks faced by participants may be substantial, such forms are an important tool for protecting the interests of participants and documenting the steps taken by researchers toward that end. They may also be necessary for minimal risk research when the foundation for trust between researchers and participants is weak. But forms are really only one part of a *process* of informed consent. In some cases, forms may not be the best way to insure informed consent. For example, a researcher using participant observation to learn how transactions occur in a public market would find it very hard to get everyone observed in that setting to sign a consent form and would probably create unwarranted suspicion about his or her motives in the process of seeking such consent. On the other hand, if people see a stranger watching, asking questions, and perhaps taking notes, they may be even more suspicious. The consent process used by Kovats-Bernat (2002) for his work with street children in Haiti was to spend considerable time talking with the children about the research and its potential risks. He emphasized negotiation and empowering those being researched to determine whether the risks were warranted.

Many IRBs have little experience in reconciling these types of situations with the regulatory guidance for informed consent. The federal regulations specify eight required elements, including some with little relevance outside of clinical or experimental research. However, the regulations also include options for waiving irrelevant elements, for waiving documentation (i.e., for having participants sign a consent form), and for waiving individual informed consent entirely. In our international work, we have generally found that ethics committees in our collaborators' host countries are similarly accepting of such variations in the informed consent process if they are fully explained and justified.

For team-based research, it is critically important that all members of the research team understand the informed consent procedures to be used. This requires spending considerable time insuring that team members understand the purpose of the research and the study design, including why particular people and communities are being selected to participate. When a consent form is used, team members need to be able to explain the information in it in their own words. If a form is not used, for example in the case of participant observation in a public setting, then it is even more important that they be able to clearly explain what they are doing, why, and on whose behalf. In such situations the concept of respect for communities is especially relevant. It may be important to meet with community gatekeepers to explain the presence of the research team and obtain support or possibly formal permission to conduct the research. There may be public meetings where the research is described and questions are answered. Such processes are sometimes described as community consent mechanisms, but none of them is a substitute for individual-level consent. Thus, regardless of the formality of the informed consent process, the team must be respectful of autonomy by being open and honest about their objectives and acknowledging the right of people to refuse to cooperate or participate in the research endeavor.

Voluntariness

Voluntariness refers to the ability of people to decide whether and how much they will participate in research. As noted above, some forms of qualitative research such as participant observation present special challenges for insuring voluntariness because they are not conducive to individualized informed-consent procedures. This does not absolve the research team from providing means for members of the study population to opt out of participation.

People who consent to be in research maintain the right to withdraw, or to limit their participation in other ways. They may decline to answer particular questions during an interview, or decide to leave early during a focus group. If they have consented to a series of interviews they can decide to opt out of one or more. Upon completion of an interview they may request that the audiotape and notes be destroyed. These are fairly straightforward demands that are easily (if painfully) met, but others may prove challenging. What do you do if a focus group participant demands that her comments be purged from the data, when this can make nonsense of other parts of the dialog where people were responding to her? What if a participant demands the right to review the transcript from his interview and revise his responses? In such cases, the research team must still respect the wishes of the participant but in doing so may find that the resulting data are not analyzable.

If no identifying information is collected during the research, then it may not be possible for participants to withdraw consent and have their data removed from the database over the long term. Depending on the number of participants, it may be difficult for members of the research team to remember which data came from which participants after a few weeks or even days.

Confidentiality

As noted above, breaches of confidentiality represent the most common risk for qualitative research and especially for team-based research. There are several dimensions to this risk. The first is common to all qualitative research in that it is linked to the descriptive richness of the data. Even if no identifying information is explicitly collected, such as names and addresses, the content of the responses in an interview or focus group may provide personal details that make identification of the speaker obvious to another member of the community. Transcripts, whether whole or partial, could lead to identification of participants. Audiotapes, and certainly video or film, make identification even more likely. Data security is therefore essential. In team-based research, the research materials may pass through several hands, including data collectors, transcribers, translators, typists, and analysts. If there is more than one person handling the materials, a tracking system should be established so that the location of each item is always known. Electronic files and computer systems should be password protected. Paper files, including handwritten field notes, should be kept secure, with access limited to research team members on an as-needed basis. For sensitive research, where the risk of social harm to participants is significant, additional steps may be needed to remove or somehow encode potentially identifiable text if materials are to be handled away from the secure environment of a research office. Files and briefcases are notoriously susceptible to loss and theft.

If there is a risk of physical harm, that is, if the research takes place in a dangerous field, the risks associated with field notes may require compromises. For example, Kovats-Bernat (2002:216) says that he "relied at times on meticulous memorization of the details of entire conversations in order to defer the risk of having written evidence that the dialogue had taken place at all. At other times I would retreat to alleys, toilet stalls, or dark areas of cafes to surreptitiously scribble jottings onto scraps on notepaper that I kept in my boot." Even when field notes are encrypted in an effort to protect identities, it may be important to remove all copies of the notes from a dangerous field site on a regular basis to reduce the likelihood that they will end up in the hands of people who could use them to cause physical harm.

Research teams need to be acutely aware of the potential for their conversations to be overheard and to use appropriate discretion regarding their work. This includes support staff who may not be directly involved in data collection, for example, drivers, receptionists, and typists who nonetheless may be privy to information about or from participants. Lead investigators need to be prepared to take appropriate action if a team member breaches confidentiality, regardless of the intentionality of the breach. One of my African collaborators had a situation where a participant referred a field worker to another potential participant but did not give explicit permission to use his name when contacting the new person. The field worker mentioned his name when making the new contact; when the original participant heard that he had been named he became upset and complained to the lead investigator. She immediately pulled the worker from the field and reassigned her to office work. Though this was a difficult decision, it satisfied the participant and underscored the commitment to confidentiality for community members and research staff alike.

Reimbursements and Incentives

In anthropology, the issue of incentives and reimbursements for research participation has a long and complex history. Many early ethnographies contained descriptions of the demands made by the people being studied—though often portrayed as unreasonable and manipulative. Evans-Pritchard (1940:13) provided the following example of an exchange with a man called Cuol, from his 1930s study of the Nuer of the Sudan in Africa.

> *I:* What is the name of your lineage?
>
> *Cuol:* Do you want to know the name of my lineage?
>
> *I:* Yes.
>
> *Cuol:* What will you do with it if I tell you? Will you take it to your country?
>
> *I:* I don't want to do anything with it. I just want to know it since I am living at your camp.
>
> *Cuol:* Oh well, we are Lou.
>
> *I:* I did not ask you the name of your tribe. I know that. I am asking you the name of your lineage.

Cuol: Why do you want to know the name of my lineage?

I: I don't want to know it.

Cuol: Then why do you ask me for it? Give me some tobacco.

In describing his experience of doing fieldwork among the Yąnomamö of Venezuela in the 1960s, Chagnon (1968:8) stated that "it was not as difficult to become calloused to the incessant begging as it was to ignore the sense of urgency, the impassioned tone of voice, or the intimidation and aggression with which the demands were made. It was likewise difficult to adjust to the fact that Yąnomamö refused to accept 'no' for an answer until or unless it seethed with passion and intimidation—which it did after six months." By the 1970s anthropologists began to develop a more nuanced and self-reflective understanding of the power dynamics inherent in such demands. In his groundbreaking reflections on fieldwork in Morocco, Rabinow (1977) described encounters that parallel those of Evans-Pritchard and Chagnon, but he moved past a personalized view of the behavior as intentionally obstructive to his research agenda to a fuller consideration of how such exchanges reflected culturally negotiated power and relationships. The simple act of accepting a host's offer of tea, for example, carried complex implications initially unknown to the anthropologist-guest:

> As the morning passed the tea kept coming. Tea and sugar have a tyrannical and almost obsessive centrality in Morocco. Its preparation and consumption are daily rituals of generosity and exchange, but it is also economically a heavy load to bear. Who pays for how much of the tea and sugar, who owes whom from the other day or last week, and the quality of the ingredients are all constant themes of everyday life. As much as 40 percent of a poor peasant's cash income can be spent on tea and sugar. (Rabinow 1977:35)

In the twenty-first century, there is universal acknowledgement of the balance that must be struck between providing appropriate reimbursement, compensation, and inducement to research participants and avoiding coercion and exploitation. Coercion is defined as the situation where "one person intentionally uses a credible and severe threat of harm or force to control another" (Beauchamp and Childress 2001:94); as such it clearly exceeds the bounds of a fair exchange between researcher and participant. Exploitation tends to be more subtle in that it transforms what may otherwise be reasonable inducements "that ordinarily are resistible" into influences that "can become controlling for abnormally weak, dependent, and surrender-prone" persons (Beauchamp and Childress 2001:96). Inducements, as this definition suggests, are not immoral if they are subject to resistance; indeed, they are part and parcel of the negotiations common to human interaction. Inducements are the answer to the question so often raised in research where there are few or no direct benefits for the participant: why should I help you? Inducement becomes problematic primarily if there are significant risks associated with the research; we speak of *undue inducement* when the enticement is so strong as to overwhelm a person's better judgment. If both risks and benefits are minimal—as is often the case for qualitative research—then the use of large sums of money and lavish gifts to induce participation may be foolish and shortsighted, but it is not unethical from the perspective of human subjects protections. However, such inducements can be very problematic in terms of the politics of research if they promote the creation of professional research subjects or establish an expected level of compensation that makes future research in a community too expensive to conduct.

When research involves multiple sites, there may be wide discrepancies in local standards for reimbursement and other forms of compensation for research participation. In my experience, IRBs are generally accepting of such variability so long as there is a clear rationale for the levels of compensation. For example, organizations that implement multiple projects with the same population will usually want to have comparable levels of compensation for a one- to two-hour interaction. Often, reimbursements will be calculated on the basis of costs such as transportation, childcare, and a light meal or snack that might reasonably be incurred by participation. Inducements might include coupons redeemable for inexpensive but valued commodities such as a music CD, or they might include material items such as tee shirts, caps, personal hygiene items, or photographs. As mentioned previously, for some qualitative research projects a copy of a life history recording or transcript could be a valued gift for some participants and their families. For informal data collection such as participant observation and exploratory conversations and interviews, it may be appropriate or even culturally mandatory to offer a soda, coffee, or tea. Reimbursements and inducements should be explicitly discussed by the team before data collection begins, with an agreed-upon set of standards to be followed in the field by all team members. Where appropriate, these standards will also need to be in compliance with relevant IRB approvals.

Sometimes the concept of reimbursement and compensation may be viewed negatively by research participants. In one of my multisite projects, most of the research participants viewed reimbursement as a sign of respect for the value of their time. However, some high-status gatekeepers at one of the sites viewed such payment as akin to bribery. The research staff, in turn, were uncomfortable with the idea that the money set aside for the participants would be funneled back into the research funds. With the support of the relevant IRBs we came up with a compromise: we gave participants the option of either accepting the funds directly or designating a local charitable organization to which the funds would be donated. In this case, the concept of respect for communities as well as for persons proved useful.

Participatory Research: Special Issues

Many qualitative research studies are participatory, which can raise additional challenges with regard to human subjects protections. Participatory research seeks to establish a collaborative partnership between researchers and participants, often to the point where the roles are no longer separate (Chavis et al. 1983, Cornwall and Jewkes 1995, Khanlou and Peter 2005). Ideally, the research question and study design is developed as part of the partnership; however, quite often the partnership results from the researchers' efforts to gain support for a proposal in a particular community setting. Participatory research often has political and activist overtones, which may introduce significant risks as well as benefits for communities and individuals. It is frequently used to investigate and address complex problems that have both a local and a global dimension such as environmental research, public health, economic development, and human rights. Increasingly, the use of participatory research models are viewed as necessary to avoid exploitation and harm when research questions intersect with disparities in power, wealth, resources, or information.

When the distinction between researcher and participant is obscured, the human subjects protections model breaks down. The notion of protection assumes that the object of research is distinct from the observer who conducts the research. If part of the cultural learning process in participatory qualitative research includes meeting with community stakeholders and establishing an advisory board, does the university-based researcher need IRB approval to engage in that process? Or would the act of obtaining such approval undermine the very meaning of collaboration and partnership building? Should community advisory board members be allowed access to original data so they can participate in its analysis and interpretation, or would that constitute a breach of confidentiality if they are not paid members of the research staff? If community partners and IRBs differ with regard to how they believe informed consent should be obtained, how should those differences be reconciled? As participatory research models become more common, these and related issues are likely to create new challenges for the field of research ethics.

Conclusion

General ethical principles of respect for persons and communities, beneficence, and justice apply across the board for all research. Many of the ethical issues specific to qualitative research are the same for both team-based and solo projects. Human subjects protections in the United States allow considerable flexibility for addressing these issues; however, some IRBs may not understand or be willing to make use of the full range of options available. Qualitative researchers may need to make special efforts to work with their IRBs to insure appropriate levels of oversight and expertise are developed.

Team-based and multisite qualitative research requires special attention to the issues of risk, benefit, informed consent, confidentiality, and reimbursements and incentives. The administrative burdens of review and the length of time required to obtain necessary approvals may be substantial for multisite projects. Participatory research models may introduce further complexities, especially if IRBs are unfamiliar with the approaches and uncomfortable with the blurring of traditional distinctions between researcher and participant. IRBs may also be unprepared to evaluate the risks and benefits of research conducted in the context of violence, terror, and human rights abuses in general.

Ultimately, the solutions to all of these challenges lie in transparency and communication. This applies to the relationships among research team members, between researchers and IRBs, between researchers and participants, and between researchers and communities. Transparency, communication, and relationship building are not all sunshine and goodness; they are as likely to be painful, wearying, exasperating, and at times humbling. The investment of time and resources in building all of these relationships may seem high, but the costs of poor communication and the erosion of trust are likely to be even higher. If we value the relationships as well as the research, the rewards will be personally as well as professionally fulfilling.

References

Bosk, C. L., and R. G. De Vries
2004   Bureaucracies of mass deception: Institutional review boards and the ethics of ethnographic research. *The ANNALS of the American Academy of Political and Social Science* 595:249–263.

Beauchamp, T. and J. Childress
2001   *Principles of Biomedical Ethics* (4th edition). New York: Oxford University Press.

Burman, W., P. Breese, S. Weis, N. Bock, J. Bernardo, A. Vernon, and the TB Trials Consortium
2003   The effects of local review on informed consent documents from a multicenter clinical trials consortium. *Controlled Clinical Trials* 24:245–255.

Chagnon, Napolean
1968   *Yąnomamö: The Fierce People.* New York: Holt, Rinehart and Winston.

Chavis, D., P. Stucky, and A. Wandersman
1983   Returning basic research to the community: A relationship between scientist and citizen. *American Psychologist* 38:424–434.

Committee on Science, Engineering, and Public Policy, National Academy of Sciences
1995   *On Being a Scientist: Responsible Conduct in Research.* Washington, D.C.: National Academy Press.

Cornwall A, and R. Jewkes
1995   What is participatory research? *Social Science & Medicine* 41:1667–1676.

Del Monte, K.
2000   Partners in inquiry: Ethical challenges in team research. *International Social Science Review* 75:3–14.

Department of Health and Human Services
2005   *Protection of Human Subjects. Title 45, Code of Federal regulation, Part 46: Revised June 23, 2005.* Available at www.hhs.gov/ohrp/humansubjects/guidance/45cfr46.htm. Accessed October 5, 2005.

Evans-Pritchard, E. E.
1940   *The Nuer: A Description of the Modes of Livelihood and Political Institutions of a Nilotic People.* New York: Oxford University Press.

Guest, G., A. Bunce, and L. Johnson
2006   How many interviews are enough? An experiment with data saturation and variability. *Field Methods* 18:59–82.

Khanlou, N., and E. Peter
2005   Participatory action research: Considerations for ethical review. *Social Science & Medicine* 60:2333–2340.

Kovats-Bernat, J. C.
2002   Negotiating dangerous fields: Pragmatic strategies for fieldwork amid violence and terror. *American Anthropologist* 104:208–222.

MacQueen, K., E. Namey, D. A. Chilongozi, S. P. Mtweve, M. Mlingo, N. Morar, C. Reid, A. Ristow, S. Sahay, and the HPTN 035 Standard of Care Assessment Team

2007   Community perspectives on care options for HIV prevention trial participants. *AIDS Care Journal* 19(4):554–560.

National Commission for the Protection of Human Subjects of Biomedical and Behavioral Research

1979   The Belmont Report: Ethical principles and guidelines for the protection of human subjects of research. *OPRR Reports* April 18:1–8.

Rabinow, Paul

1977   *Reflections on Fieldwork in Morocco.* Berkeley: University of California Press.

Weijer, C., G. Goldsand, and E. J. Emanuel

1999   Protecting communities in research: Current guidelines and limits of extrapolation. *Nature Genetics* 23:275–280.

The Politics of Field Research

3

CYNTHIA WOODSONG

Q UALITATIVE RESEARCH IS INCREASINGLY CONDUCTED with multidisciplinary teams working in multiple country settings. These teams have the potential to effectively investigate many of today's pressing research questions. Not surprisingly though, such research is often accompanied by an array of issues that stretch beyond what is normally provided in typical research training. Included in the array of issues are those that may be conceptualized as having a "political" nature. Although there is little most researchers can do to change political issues at the country level, strategies can be developed to effectively work within political constraints that filter down to directly impact field research teams.

My focus in this chapter is to consider how political issues may arise in team research, and what one can do about it. The chapter has three sections. First, I discuss various dimensions of difference that can give rise to power and political issues that impact the conduct of field-based team research. I next consider a set of case examples that illustrate how these situations have occurred in my own field research, and that of colleagues, within the broad arena of international health. I conclude by outlining recommendations for strengthening research teams so as to mitigate political issues that could negatively affect the research endeavor.

Several naming conventions are used in this paper to facilitate discussion. The "sponsor" is the organization providing funding support for the study. "North–South" will be used rather than other common dichotomies that separate the wealthy industrialized countries from those that are not (e.g., "developed/developing," "first-world/third world"). The research dynamics discussed in this chapter center largely on issues that arise in research that is funded in the North, and led by individuals in the North, yet conducted in field settings in the South. However, similar political and interpersonal dynamics could easily occur in settings without a North–South divide. I refer to the leader of the research endeavor, usually based in the sponsor country as the "principal investigator," rather than other commonly used terms (e.g., chief of party, team leader). Terms "field-based," "host country," and "in-country" refer to research settings other than those of the principal investigator. Thus a "host-country researcher" would be a member of the research team who is based in the country where the research is being conducted. Of course, not all team research is international and problems of a "political" nature can arise in any project involving multiple team members. For example, many of the issues described in this chapter can easily surface in research conducted in poor rural areas or among marginalized populations by principal investigators based in large urban institutions in the same country.

Political issues associated with team-based research may arise at multiple levels, which can be further influenced by the background political context of multiple country settings (figure 3.1), especially for studies that are conducted with North–South research teams. In this chapter, I will not focus on country-level political differences, but rather consider how these may filter down to cultural, personal, institutional, or sponsor-level politics. For example, cultural norms for how individuals at different socioeconomic levels should be treated will influence perceptions of the appropriateness of the research approach, and potential support for the foreign-based investigator. Personal political agendas may be in conflict with those held by other members of the research team. Institutional politics arise between research teams, who may be encouraged to collaborate or to compete with other teams or institutions. Research sponsors will have political agendas that the institution hopes to further with findings from the research they support. In short, political agendas may guide the actions of all who interact with a research endeavor, in both positive and negative ways.

Dimensions of Difference

Integrated rural development projects popular in the 1970s and 1980s brought together international teams with responsibilities to jointly spearhead improvements in different sectors, such as agriculture, education, infrastructure, and health (Cernea 1985, Ellis and Biggs 2001). Here the disciplinary background of team members was usually quite diverse. Large-scale programs and projects focused on health improvements require more closely related disciplines to conduct what are frequently sequential activi-

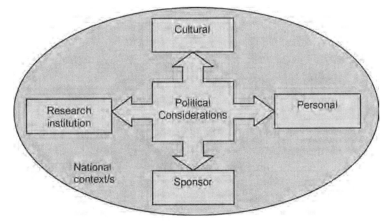

Figure 3.1.   Levels of political consideration.

ties, such as formative research, program implementation, monitoring and evaluation, and policy advocacy. Nevertheless, disciplinary proximity and more narrowly focused activities do not necessarily ensure harmonious field teams. The dimensions of difference fall along a broad spectrum of issues.

Academic/Disciplinary Differences

Some personal and institutional differences can be simply classified as arising from disciplinary backgrounds. Researchers are trained to view problems with discipline-specific lenses that influence their interpretation of the nature of the problems. Anthropologists, for example, will make different inferences than psychologists or sociologists. Similarly, health professionals may weigh priorities and issues differently than social service professionals. So-called hard sciences may be held in higher regard, and thus receive more funding support than the "soft sciences." And, of course, in many fields of research there is a marked division between those who are driven to conduct research aimed at having practical applications and those who are more focused on theory and contributing to a body of scholarly knowledge. Within any of these dimensions of difference, prestige, power, and politics may further entrench polarized positions.

Global Inequities

Debates on the North–South divide in research priorities continue to color much of health research, as does awareness of the harsh reality that 90 percent of health research centers on issues affecting only 10 percent of the world's population (Burke and de Francisco 2004). Inequities in resource support for health research are further exacerbated by constraints on human capacity to conduct high-quality scientific research. The North is seen as contributing to "brain drain," in both traditional and new ways. For example, over the past several decades, funding support from the North has been provided to strengthen research capacity in the South to counter brain drain (Bradley 2005, Ferner 2005). However, with the expansion of international research, recently strengthened researchers may find jobs in their home country as staff of North-funded projects or program offices that pay better than positions in local government, academia, or nongovernmental organizations. Research capacity may be increased, yet it may benefit primarily those who increased it and may give rise to different pay scales and expectations for in-country compatriots. This sets the stage for increased competition and tension between in-country researchers.

A less widely acknowledged, but common, phenomenon is the practice of training staff in the South to conduct data collection, then exporting data for analysis and write-up in the North. Given the prestige that accrues to peer-reviewed publication, this practice might be considered as research imperialism, maintaining dependency on foreign sources of expertise for the generation of data. Some Northern researchers now actively articulate an obligation to meaningfully involve host-country team members in analysis and write-up, yet many others do not, or do so only at a token level.

Hot Political Topics

Some research fields and scholarly disciplines are more politicized than others. Within health research, certain topical foci may be rife with politics. The field of reproductive health, and its inclusion of sexual health and sexually transmitted infections, has become particularly so. Accusations of inappropriate mingling of politics and science have been particularly acute over the past several years with regard to studies of sexual behavior and sexually transmitted infections (Woodsong and Severy 2005). Similarly, researchers may be faulted for ignoring or denying the potential political ramifications of their work. There is currently some concern in the health research community that when researchers propose to study controversial topics, those chosen for funding will reflect approaches consistent with ideologies supported by the current political powers, rather than scientific evidence (Drazen and Ingelfinger 2003, The Lancet 2003). Unfortunately, one very politically contentious topic is also one that is extremely important for improvements in health at a global level—HIV/AIDS research.

HIV/AIDS has come to dominate the broad areas of reproductive health and infectious disease. This domination is accompanied by significant increases in research opportunities, when compared with other health problems disproportionately affecting the world's most disadvantaged populations. The flow of resource dollars to HIV/AIDS studies conducted in Africa, the hardest hit region of the world, has steadily and dramatically increased since the 1990s. Many African countries heavily affected by AIDS have established their own HIV/AIDS research priorities. Foreign researchers wanting to conduct studies in these settings must ensure that the proposed research fits within the host-country's priority list, or approval to conduct the work will not be granted.

Of course, the process that countries use to establish research priorities is fraught with political issues and may suffer from a lack of transparency. Foreign researchers should carefully consider the implications of challenging a host country's priorities, as this could have further political implications. Even if there is no set research priority list, study leaders are well advised to be familiar with country-level strategies for addressing health problems, and work to develop support for host-country research objectives. Foreign researchers should also be familiar with the host-country's relevant health policies as well as policies for the protection of research participants. Finally, researchers must bear in mind that changes in the host-country political leadership, or other new developments, could cause a shift in research priorities. If this occurs, new relationships with government officials will need to be cultivated, and ongoing research efforts justified.

Sponsor's Objectives

Sponsors often have political agendas that they intend to support through the research findings. At any point in funding history, there have been "hot topics" that sponsors are keen to investigate. These topics may hold sway in funding priorities for years, or they may wax and wane quite quickly. For example, soon after the September 2001 terrorist attacks in the United States, support was offered for research on bioterrorism. Research on abortion-related topics waned dramatically with the Bush administration of the 2000s, while research on faith-based initiatives was encouraged.

Research on sexual behavior became heavily scrutinized in the early 2000s, and staff at the NIH began advising grant applicants to avoid certain topics, or at least avoid using key words in their applications that might attract unfavorable attention by those seeking to thwart funding support for controversial topics. This escalated to the development of a "Hit List" in

2003, which included a list of individuals with research portfolios on a wide array of sexual behavior, including commercial sex work, homosexuality, and substance abuse (Stewart 2003, Waxman 2003).

Sponsor support from private foundations may be seen by some as more capricious, representing the personal values of donor philanthropists. Similarly, research support provided by the private sector is usually seen as furthering financial goals. The pharmaceutical industry has been widely criticized in the popular press for providing inappropriately high incentives to researchers who will present data in a biased fashion such that products are seen in a more favorable light, as well as avoiding research on the "neglected diseases" such as tuberculosis, measles, and malaria, which cause much global suffering but do not affect people in their home country (Bradley 2005, Ferner 2005).

The United States Agency for International Development (USAID) provides research support in countries that it considers to be of strategic interest to the United States, and these, too, wax and wane with shifts in the political environment. The poorest countries are generally assured of a US-AID presence, while countries that have more resources, or are at a higher level of "development," may be included as priority countries if there is a current political threat in the region, or a significant presence of a hot topic, such as HIV/AIDS.

In summary, all sponsor organizations have strategic interests, which they work to advance through their strategic goals and objectives. It is sometimes advisable to "study up" to learn about the motivations of funding agencies and ascertain the potential political ramifications of the results of a study. Depending on the type of funding source, the sponsor agency may exercise considerable influence on the nature of how research findings will be used. Researchers should consider the larger goals and objectives of the sponsor when they agree to accept funding support. In turn, this allows the principal investigator and/or host-country research leader to make study goals clear to all team members at the initiation of a study. If the ultimate goals and objectives of a study are at odds with the personal political views of the potential team members, they may decide not to participate in the study.

Multilevel Political Interplay

As indicated in figure 3.1, political agendas and values may be interwoven in multiple arenas—cultural, personal, and institutional (both the research and sponsor institutions)—and these may reinforce tensions in research teams.

Some sources for tension may derive from cultural values accorded to attributes of a demographic nature. Age, gender, religious and/or political affiliation, sexual orientation, ethnicity, culture, or language group can mark a potential researcher in ways that transcend their research capacity and either promote them or hold them back, depending on the research topic, setting, and characteristics of the principal investigator or in-country team leader. For example, the principal investigator may be a member of a cultural group that historically has been politically opposed to that of the research team members. Even if all members of the research team do not personally follow these political traditions, it may be important to have a frank acknowledgment about this at the beginning of a study, to clear the playing field.

The interface of culture and individual-level political values can be difficult to recognize. For example, at the personal level, idiosyncratic differences such as an inclination to be a team player or highly competitive researcher may or may not be reinforced by culture. In some cultural settings, members of a certain class may be historically positioned to assume positions of leadership, and these may include positions at prestigious research institutions. Such advantages may accrue at all levels of staffing, from host-country team leader to in-country data collector. It is possible that the foreign principal investigator may be unaware of the traditional norms that effectively create a hidden hierarchy within the in-country research team. These traditions may affect who is available to serve on research teams, how they perform their role on the study, and whether or not they can be held accountable for their actions.

Case Examples

The following case examples illustrate how issues with various political twists have played out in real research settings. The examples are drawn from my own experiences as well as those of my professional colleagues. Since I have worked largely in international health research, primarily HIV/AIDS research, the examples reflect this. I label each so that I can refer back to them in the next section of this chapter. Throughout, case examples will refer to global regions rather than specific countries. Each case example highlights at least one level of political influence.

Case A: Research Institution—Local Competition

HIV/AIDS research conducted with a host-country university can easily span multiple university departments (e.g., anthropology, sociology, health behavior, community medicine), and thus such research may be accompanied by tensions between departments. A Northern-based Principal Investigator secured funding for research in a southern African country setting where she had previously worked. Her past experience was with an in-country research team housed in a different university department than the one identified for the new study. The principal investigator had maintained a collegial friendship with staff from the previous study.

The new colleagues posted job openings for multiple data collection positions for the new study, and they were quickly filled. Not long after the new study was staffed, a colleague from the other university department told the principal investigator that one applicant who secured a leadership position in the new study had recently been found unacceptable in her work with the other department. The principal investigator was reluctant to second-guess her new collaborator's hiring decision. She also suspected that interdepartment politics might be at play, and recognized that her personal relationship with staff in one department might unduly influence her actions. The principal investigator inquired about the new staff member's credentials and was satisfied that given the job description and credentials, the choice appeared to be a good match. As it turned out, the staff member in question indeed turned out to be the weakest in the team. However, the host-country collaborator who hired her found a position within the organization for which she was a better fit. Even though the poor performance weakened the study team, the principal investigator did not regret her decision to retain the questionable staff member, and steer clear of potentially divisive interdepartmental politics in the host-country institution.

Case B: Sponsor and Research Institution— Organizational Objectives

A funding agency that had spent considerable resources developing a new reproductive health technology decided to support social–behavioral research on potential users' perspectives on the new product. This decision was applauded by a network of researchers who champion such research, and the agency provided funding resources for a small study that might lead to a larger clinical trial. A principal investigator was identified and she in turn began the process of identifying potential sites to conduct both the short-term social–behavioral study as well as the larger trial. The Sponsor, however, had a specific geographic location in mind for the study, a location that the principal investigator did not consider an ideal match for the research questions outlined. Nevertheless, she traveled to the country to meet with potential coinvestigators and collaborators, including staff at the Ministry of Health, the Sponsor's in-country office, and representatives from two nongovernmental organizations.

All in-country collaborators were initially interested in the study, yet upon learning more details, they expressed reservations similar to those of the principal investigator. They agreed that the new product would likely not be well received in their populations. However, the host-country collaborators were reluctant to pass up funding opportunities, and they agreed to join the study team and contribute in whatever way they could. Upon returning to the home office, the principal investigator filed a frank assessment of the suitability of the research site for the proposed study. The Sponsor decided to postpone the research until a more suitable site and/or more resources for a multisite study could be ensured. The principal investigator did not know if the potential host-country collaborators breathed a sigh of relief or regretted losing the opportunity to do the work. However, the principal investigator's research institution was conflicted about having the funding withdrawn.

Case C: Local Context—Government Appointees

At the country level, it is not unusual for government offices to designate a person from their staff to serve in some capacity on a research team. Health research conducted with support from some government agencies requires collaboration and/or regular briefing of persons in the relevant host-country office. For HIV/AIDS research, this most often includes the Ministry of Health, but may also extend to a country's national AIDS council, as well as district-level or other local-level health and/or AIDS committees. At each step of the chain of command, and depending on the nature and pace of decentralization in effect in the country, individuals may be reconciling their own personal priorities for research with those stated by government. While it might be hoped that a project seen as high profile or high priority would have a very capable person posted to serve on the team, it is possible that this posting reflects other political agendas.

In a reproductive health study conducted in East Africa, the Ministry of Health posted a very active and highly motivated individual to work with the principal investigator on the interface between study conduct, study results, and the Ministry. At the beginning of the study she attended staff meetings and training seminars and consulted regularly with the principal investigator. However, as the study neared completion, she was reassigned by the Ministry to other pressing demands, and the principal investigator was left with the responsibility of briefing her uninformed superior. This, in turn, required another round of site visits and meetings, which negatively affected the project budget and timeline.

Case D: Research Institution and Sponsor Level— Benefits to Participants

Research team members and the larger research community may have strong feelings about how participants should be treated during the conduct of a study. The ethics approval process required of all research with human participants will yield decisions made about the relative risks and benefits of study participation, and research team members must abide by the approved protocol. They may, however, consider that some aspects of care, treatment, or referral are unfair. A frequently observed criticism is that research studies from the North take unfair advantage of impoverished or otherwise vulnerable participants in the South. A number of international ethics documents provide guidance on establishing a standard of care to be provided to research participants, but there is no clear consensus between them or among international health researchers.

Concern about the standard of care surfaced in sites about to initiate a large-scale multinational clinical trial. The trial sponsors recognized the potentially serious implications of not addressing these concerns and approved funding to conduct a study to investigate multiple perspectives on appropriate care and treatment for trial participants. A common protocol was developed by a team at a Northern institution, which then formed teams at each site and provided systematic training in data collection for the study. The teams were investigating an essentially ethical and political issue, and the views of previous trial participants, researchers, and stakeholders in the country were essential to arrive at a solution that could help pave the way for the research to be conducted appropriately. The team was highly motivated by the goal of the study, in part because many of the team members would be staff on the clinical trial. They wanted to be part of helping ensure that the study did "the right thing," in accordance with direct community-level guidance. This sub-study thus served to address concerns of the larger research community as well as those of the research staff.

Case E: Research Institution Level—Staff Selection

Principal investigators from the North usually rely on their host-country colleagues to identify staff to join research teams. In a multicountry qualitative health study taking place in East Africa, a man with a long-time association with a senior member of the in-country team leader needed a post-ing. His background did not include health research or qualitative method expertise, he was older than the other team members, and he was more ex-perienced than them (in his own field). The principal investigator had doubts that he could do the work, but he was trained along with the oth-ers. He performed quite well in the study tasks, proving the PI wrong. The PI later learned that the younger members of the team came to rely on the older man for advice on general life issues as well as help them problem-solve difficulties with data collection. Interestingly, the same dynamic oc-curred at one of the other projects sites in South America. Here, the elder individual did not perform well in his work, or as a team member. When his consulting contract expired, it was not renewed.

Case F: Cultural Level—Norms

Cultural norms for age and gender can easily influence the conduct of re-search on the topic of sexual behavior. In an HIV risk-reduction study con-ducted in an Asian country, young women were assigned to conduct interviews about sexual behavior, obtaining sexual histories from other women. The fact that some of the female interviewers were sexually inex-perienced and some respondents were older than the interviewers created problems for data capture. Young men were also assigned to interview older men, but it was considered acceptable for young men to discuss sexual be-havior with older men. These staffing assignments had been made based on the Asian coinvestigator's assessment of staff skills and with an eye to those she wanted to promote within the system. During a routine monitoring visit, staff were interviewed separately about their assessment of study progress, and they reported difficulties in conducting interviews. It was then necessary to have a frank discussion with the coinvestigator, which resulted in some of the younger and unmarried staff members being reassigned to interview age-mates only. Here it was important for the PI not to under-mine the skills of the younger women, but rather to focus on cultural norms that created barriers to data collection irrespective of skill.

Case G: Research Institutional Level—Reassigning Staff

Team members are often posted to a study because of past or current affil-iation with host-country offices. The U.S.-based methodologist providing data collection training for sites participating in a multinational study no-ticed that two of the sites included staff who were not well suited for the posts they had been assigned by the host-country research leader. Unlike

Case E and F above, problems with suitability of the team members were not associated with gender and age norms. Rather, the individuals assigned to conduct in-depth interviews simply did not have the interpersonal skills needed to be a good interviewer. When the trainer reviewed the pilot data they had collected, the data were scant and of poor quality. She met with each of them and it was clear that these individuals were rather shy and did not think of themselves as good interviewers. One even volunteered that she had not wanted the post. In both cases, it was possible to reassign these team members to other tasks (one in data management and one in analysis), and both they and the project benefited. In this way, the team was kept intact, and the host-country researcher's choice of team members was not seriously challenged.

Case H: Sponsor and National Context Level—Equal Representation

In a multinational study that required frequent face-to-face meetings, it was noted that the Northern principal investigators dominated discussions at all meetings as well as conference calls. In addition, some of the countries sent more participants to meetings than others. Finally, at one meeting, circumstances resulted in the absence of several of the Northern principal investigators, and an overall smaller number of attendees. Discussions at this meeting went at a very different pace, and were considered by those in attendance to be more inclusive of multiple views. As a result, the Sponsor requested that a new convention be established for subsequent meetings to include input from all attendees throughout the meeting, and the number of attendees was limited so that each site was equally represented.

Case I: Research Institution and Local Context Level—Stakeholder Conflicts

A multisite HIV study conducted in the North included an evaluation component conducted by a nonlocal evaluator who traveled to all the study sites and partnered with an external evaluator at each site. During an evaluation site visit conducted soon after the study started, the central evaluator began to develop a list of local stakeholders who might be contacted to inquire about their views on the study. The local study team had been working closely with an advisory committee that included representatives from a dozen local agencies, and this group formed the foundation for the list of stakeholders. However, during the course of the evaluation visit, the central evaluator became aware of a number of obvious omissions. When she inquired about them, the local principal investigator reported that the omitted groups had caused problems with other studies in the past, and the site decided to not risk their engagement in the current study. The central evaluator felt it was her responsibility to contact these groups who were clearly stakeholders in the area, and might have important information to contribute to the evaluation. After conferring with the local evaluator, who had better knowledge of local politics, a plan was developed to meet with some of the excluded stakeholders, and the site's principal investigator was notified of this. The input received was valuable, and it also revealed past political tensions between local agencies and stakeholder groups. The evaluation recommended that mechanisms be put in place to keep this additional stakeholder group informed. However, it did not presume to recommend they be added to the advisory committee.

Case J: Cultural and National Context— Media Communications

In recent years, research on a new product being developed to prevent HIV infection (topical vaginal microbicides), became the target of national and international advocacy groups. These groups claimed that studies were taking unfair advantage of their study populations, and their actions led to the closing of some clinical trial sites. Recognizing the potential for a negative advocacy campaign, a new multinational study of microbicides worked to develop a basic "script" that staff were allowed to use in discussing the study to the general public. Staff were trained in presenting this script, and coached to stick to message when presenting the overview in community settings. All requests for interviews with media and/or advocacy groups were referred to the in-country principal investigators. A media communication plan was developed for the study, which allowed for more fluid communication in country settings where the research team had good relationships with the media, and more restricted communication in settings where the team had no previous experiences on which to build. The research team had to carefully consider which local community groups should be involved in the early stages of study start-up (which is necessary to build initial support), and which groups should be approached at a later stage of research (once preliminary results were available).

Strategies for Success

The case studies above highlight some of the variety of political issues that are frequently encountered in conducting multisite, multinational, team-based research. Although there are few hard-and-fast rules for dealing with such issues, some basic tenets can be put in place at the start of a study to help ensure successful navigation of political issues that may arise. These are outlined briefly below.

Building Local-level Support

It is important to build support at the country level, community level, institutional level, and research team level to enhance the potential for successful conduct of research. At every level, it is important that individuals and the groups they represent agree that the research should be done, and they support or otherwise endorse the study. Aspects of obtaining this buy-in can be political, and the process will vary widely. We will not here discuss the process of obtaining high-level support for new studies, as this will vary with the historical, cultural, and political context of each study. We do, however, note that strong high-level support for a study can positively influence the attitudes and performance of the research team. Statements of support should be included at project initiation kickoff meetings, and individuals from influential offices could be invited to attend meetings and events associated with project milestones. Examples are included in table 3.1. Individuals with personal-level career objectives or personal values that are at odds with those of the study should have opportunities to discover this at the beginning of a study, rather than down the road.

Establishing good local support for research at the beginning of a study requires continued cultivation. This is best done through regular communications with host-country stakeholders, including those in government posts who have been assigned to liaise with the study. We have found that using a mix of informal meetings, periodic briefing sheets, and invitations to visit a research site is an effective means of keeping stakeholders informed about a study and interested in its outcome. It is important as a study progresses to keep an ear out for emergent stakeholders, as well as those who may have been overlooked in the beginning of a study, as in Case I. These individuals may have been deliberately overlooked by the host-country collaborators because of political differences that could create problems later on.

Have a Clear Scope of Work

There should be a clearly specified scope of work that will serve as a job description for members of the team. The scope of work should be as detailed as possible, and describe the range of activities planned for the dura-

Table 3.1.   Opportunities for Generating and Maintaining Support for Studies

Milestones	Groups to Involve/Target
Project conceptualization and development	Stakeholders from the participant community, members of the local research community (university, NGO, government)
Ethics review	Ethics committees
Project initiation	Community stakeholders, government offices
Mobilization and recruitment	Community stakeholders, community representatives/advisors
Preliminary results (for studies of long duration, annual or semiannual results may be appropriate)	Community stakeholders, local research community
Final results	Sponsor, community stakeholders, research communities
Presentations at local conferences	Community stakeholders, local research community
Presentations at international conferences	Community-level representatives, researchers
Publications	Peer-reviewed journals, journals published in-country
Public communications	Newsletters, public media, listservs, and websites

tion of the study. Tasks will be outlined in the study design and budget that was funded, but greater specificity will be required to more fully inform staff about what is expected. It is tempting to rehash previous scopes of work without investing sufficient time and thought to adaptations needed for a new study. For example, in-country data collectors may be required to do their own translation, transcription, and typing of interview data in one study yet not in another.

Although it is appropriate to make changes as a study progresses, expectations that adaptations will be necessary do not excuse lack of attention at the front end. Again, using the example of translation, transcription, and typing, the principal investigator may prefer to make decisions about who will do these tasks once initial data are in and it is possible to ascertain the time and skills needed. I have found it better to let staff know the full range of tasks that they may be asked to perform, and then pull back when necessary, and minimize adding work tasks once a study has begun.

The Sponsor, principal investigator, and members of a research team may all occasionally find themselves pushing beyond the specified scope of work (often referred to as "scope creep"), and when this occurs, the scope of work must be revisited. The initial scope of work should mention all tasks envisioned for the staff position as well as the degree of responsibility associated with each task. Is the staff member expected to lead or collaborate on specific tasks? Will they write initial drafts or final reports? If they are to conduct interviews, will they review the results derived from their interview data and provide written summaries? A study protocol provides a guide to the range of tasks that must be accomplished, and these can serve as a guide to development of the scope of work.

The scope of work should easily set the stage for establishing the type of background training and experience necessary to fulfill the position. It is all too often that an inappropriately trained person tries to make a case that she or he is qualified for a position, or as described in several of the cases above, a host-country collaborator may post an inappropriate person to the research team. Clarity about the required, desired, and optional background training and experience can help prevent attempts to post inappropriate staff to positions, as occurred in Cases F and G.

Provide Training and Build Capacity

Regardless of the in-country team members' background and experience, it is important to conduct training at the initiation of a new study (see Mack, Bunce, and Akumatey, this volume). This serves to help level the playing field, establish the roles and responsibilities within the team, and clarify multiple scopes of work. Training provides an important opportunity for the principal investigator, or her or his designate, to ascertain the skill set of the research team. A clear scope of work and background requirements cannot guarantee that the persons posted to the team have the skills needed. Furthermore, skilled and experienced researchers may vary in their conceptualization of the research methods to be used in a study. For example, what one investigator calls a focus group may not meet the description of another. At a minimum, all team members need to agree on the standards to be adopted for each method in the study.

Good training can provide a basic foundation; clarify the specific approach to how methods will be used in a study; and afford the team members, trainer, and/or principal investigator an opportunity to assess staff skills. Ideally, more staff than needed will be trained, to safeguard against turnover as well as to identify staff with specific strengths (or weaknesses, as in Case G above). Staff should be trained in the use of the data collection instruments to be used in the study. When possible, and when working with an experienced in-country team, it is good to train on draft (not final) instruments, so as to include the local knowledge of team members in the development of the instruments. This can result in stronger instruments and increased staff ownership of the project.

Whenever possible, in settings where there is competition for research posts, it is both practical and a goodwill gesture to open training to others in the research community. Depending on the particular type of training being provided, basic research methods training or ethics training can often easily expand to include a few more individuals. Staff from other branches of the host-country institution or other local institutions could be invited, at the discretion of the host-country collaborator. This further builds research capacity, which is invariably well received in sites with limited opportunities for research. It can also help smooth interdepartment tensions.

Develop Workplans and Conduct Site Visits

As with any research study, it is important to develop workplans for the conduct of a study and routinely monitor these plans to ensure that progress is being made. Workplans should be developed collaboratively, and made available to all on the research team. I have found it helpful to include the following categories:

- specify each task (e.g., recruitment, data collection interview, data analysis)
- study population group associated with task (e.g., focus groups among population A)
- timeline for beginning and completing the task
- identification of resources needed
- time needed of specific named staff
- equipment (e.g., tape recorder, tapes)
- funds (e.g., participant reimbursements, transport costs)
- data collection instruments (specify which one)
- person responsible for seeing the task is completed

The overall project management plan should designate how frequently progress on workplans is monitored, and how often site visits will be made. A site visit agenda should be distributed in advance of site visits (see also chapter 9 on monitoring sociobehavioral research). Throughout the study period, during these visits, activities such as individual face-to-face meetings and data review can be conducted to allow staff to demonstrate proficiency in what is needed for the study. The transparency that can be provided by a well-documented scope of work, workplans, and monitoring site visits becomes essential if staff need to be reposted to another role, or even dismissed from a study. Of course, this process is also basically fair, regardless of whether the appointment is political, and should be the model for all staff management (see also chapter 4 on enhancing team dynamics).

Consider Plans for Media Communication

In recent years, persons with media or advocacy interests have sought information from researchers in order to make reports to the popular press and/or other groups. It is increasingly important that research team members know who they can talk to, what they can say, and when they should refer outsiders to the host-country study leader or principal investigator for further information. In some studies a media plan is developed, and the rank-and-file research team members are trained on appropriate talking points as well as questions that should be referred up the research hierarchy. Research conducted among vulnerable populations or on controversial topics is vulnerable to negative media spin, and in some cases sites have been closed as a result of external pressure.

Publications and Acknowledgment

Producing publications and attributing authorship may have political aspects. At the start of a new study, it should be made clear how authorship of publications and presentations will be handled, to help avoid political insensitivities of a cultural nature. In some country settings it is common to list a courtesy author who was not intimately involved in a study, while in other settings, only those who actually work on a study expect to be included. Leading journals specify their expectations for attributing authorship, and many require an explanation for the role that each contributing author played in bringing a manuscript to the submission stage. Public thanks, including authorship and acknowledgment, can have political implications that need careful forethought. And, in some cultural settings, whom you don't include, acknowledge, or cite carries as much weight as whom you do.

Some publications allow inclusion of authors who did not contribute substantively to the research, but rather provided institutional support and leadership to the overall mission, while others require that only those who had a direct role in the research be listed. Increasingly, Northern researchers include Southern research team members in the authorship list of papers. Less common is the practice of working to strengthen the capacity of in-country research team members to make a substantive contribution to papers through mentoring or sponsoring work sessions focused on scientific paper writing.

Expectations for authorship are often explicitly addressed in contractual arrangements for the research team. Commonly, these describe expectations for "primary" papers (e.g., those that report on the studies' primary objectives), "secondary" and/or "tertiary" papers (e.g., those that use data sources from the main study, or report on ancillary findings, methods, or opinion pieces). Such policies specify those persons who must be included as coauthors of "primary" papers. Publication policies cannot ensure that political issues will not arise in determining authorship. Rather, it is incumbent on the writing team to agree upon who will be the lead author at the beginning of manuscript development. A timeline for pieces to be written by members of the research team should be set out, as well as a review and revision schedule. For team-based research, the team charged with publications should agree on who will contribute to each section, who will take the lead, who will review, and who will have responsibility for pulling together the various components. Coauthors and reviewers may hold up a publication because of their own time constraints and priorities, but it is certainly possible for a publication to be stalled for political reasons of a personal or institutional nature. To avoid delays, publication agreements can include a default approval if feedback is not received within a specified timeframe.

It is common for large studies to form a publications committee, with a protocol to be followed for submission to the committee and timeline for committee review and approval before publications or presentation abstracts can be submitted. Sponsors may also require that a representative of the funding agency review and approve publications prior to submission for publication. The funding organization may further require specific language be used to acknowledge the source of funding, as well as disclaimers to be included on all publications, indicating that the views expressed in the paper are not necessarily those of the funding organization.

Formative (also called "descriptive" or "preparedness") research is frequently conducted to guide subsequent study design and implementation. However, in large studies, such research is often not conducted with active involvement of the principal investigator. Although formative research can yield stand-alone findings worthy of publication, members of the larger research team may be loathe to allow such publications to appear before the "main" study is presented in the literature. When this occurs, by the time the main study is published, the formative research may be too dated to interest publishers; moreover, the formative team may have moved on to other projects by the time the principal investigator is ready to release the data. To forestall this problem, the formative team may request that the study publication policy specify that secondary or ancillary papers may be published in advance of primary papers.

Political whims of a researcher's institutional home may influence authorship. For example, if a particular researcher falls out of favor with, or leaves, an organization, the organization's leadership may insist that the order of authorship promotes individuals whom the institution prefers to support, while delegating the person out of favor to a subordinate role. Policies for publication and intellectual property should protect individuals from these circumstances, but a researcher who has become persona non grata may not be in a position to press his or her case.

Ensure Equal Representation

In multisite studies, it is often politic to ensure that all sites are equitably represented in team meetings and conference calls. As in Case H above, depending on the temperament of team members, it may become necessary to establish some conventions that enable all to participate fully. This principle can extend to within-site research team meetings, if necessary. One effective way to accomplish broader participation is to set a principle of going around the table, or requesting that people who already have had their say on a topic hold off additional comments until others have spoken. Meetings can open and close with remarks made by each participant, or a representative of each group at the table.

Provide Quality Ethics Training

Since all members of U.S.-sponsored research teams are required to complete basic ethics training, such training presents an opportunity to contextualize decisions made about a number of study design issues that could potentially become political. For example, consideration of the risk-benefit ratio or the standard of care provided to research participants could be discussed during ethics training associated with study start-up. In this way, all members of a research team could be better informed about the ethical integrity of the study. I have found it helpful even in studies with experienced research teams to include an ethics component in the initial study start-up training (Rivera et al. 2002, 2005). This session allows me or someone on my team to check for common understandings, and have time for discussion of ethical considerations that can improve team member support of the study. In addition, ethics issues can be integrated throughout a study's start-up training.

Summary

Issues with political dimensions may surface at multiple layers and at multiple time points during a study, and it can be difficult to predict the directions from which they will originate. For example, at national contextual levels, research efforts directed at improving health conditions are considered by some to be a political act, particularly if the research focuses on populations that have been marginalized in some way. Cultural groups may consider it unfair to target some groups for research participation and not others. At the local institutional level the appointment of particular individuals to research teams may also have political implications, both good and bad. At the personal level, the actions of individual researchers may be politically motivated to achieve an array of purposes. It is incumbent on all involved in research to be as open as possible in their political views and personal objectives and how these play out in the decision-making processes associated with conducting research.

If there are political views and objectives associated with research design and staffing of a research team, these should be made obvious to all from the very beginning. If potential members of the team are not in agreement, they should either explicitly work through areas of disagreement and develop a mutually acceptable plan for dealing with differences, or not join the study team. By adopting clear expectations for the conduct of study, roles and responsibilities of research team members, and having clear workplans and monitoring procedures, multisite studies can be more effectively completed. The recommendations in this chapter are intended to increase the likelihood of successful project completion.

References

Bradley, D.
2005 Why big pharma needs to learn the three "Rs." *National Review of Drug Discovery* 4(6):466.

Burke, M. A., and A. de Francisco
2004 *Monitoring Financial Flows for Health Research.* Geneva: Global Forum for Health Research.

Cernea, M. (ed.)
1985 *Putting People First: Sociological Variables in Rural Development.* New York: Oxford University Press.

Drazen, J., and Ingelfinger, J.
2003 Grants, politics and the NIH. *New England Journal of Medicine* 349:2259–2261.

Ellis, F., and S. Biggs
2001   Evolving themes in rural development 1950s–2000s. *Development Policy Review* 19(4): 437–448.

Ferner, R. E.
2005   The influence of big pharma. *British Medical Journal* 16(7496):858–860.

The Lancet
2003   Keeping scientific advice non-partisan. *The Lancet* 360:1525.

Rivera, R., D. Borasky, R. Rice, and F. Carayon
2002   *Research Ethics Training Curriculum*. Durham, N.C.: Family Health International.

Rivera, R., D. Borasky, F. Carayon, R. Rice, S. Kirkendale, W. Wilson, and C. Woodsong
2005   *Research Ethics Training Curriculum for Community Representatives*. Durham, N.C.: Family Health International.

Stewart, F.
2003   The war on words: Sensible compromise or slow suicide? *Contraception* 68:157–158.

Waxman, H.
2003   *Politics and Science in the Bush Administration*. Washington, D.C.: U.S. House of Representatives Committee on Government Reform—Minority Staff Special Investigations Division. (August)

Woodsong, C., and L. Severy
2005   The generation of knowledge for reproductive health technologies: Constraints on social and behavioral research. *Journal of Social Issues* 61(1):193–205.

World Health Organization
2003   *The Health Service Brain Drain: What Are the Options for Change? Global Alliance on Vaccines and Immunizations*. Geneva: World Health Organization.

A Logistical Framework for Enhancing Team Dynamics

4

NATASHA MACK, ARWEN BUNCE, AND BETTY AKUMATEY

THE CHALLENGES OF DOING TEAM-BASED qualitative research are many, whether the setting is domestic or international. At the heart of these challenges is the need to cultivate positive dynamics among the staff in order for the team to be effectively responsive to the ever-changing circumstances of the project. Without team members who think of themselves as working toward a common goal, the benefits for the project of putting minds, hands, and talents together are much diminished. In addition to sharing a team mentality, a team capable of solving problems effectively depends on all members having a well-defined understanding of their individual roles in the research process, a sense of voice within the group, and opportunities for personal and professional achievement and growth. For project managers, this means being smart about how they build the team from the beginning. It also means taking steps to be organized about how the team will accomplish project activities utilizing the strengths of each team member.

A logistics plan can serve simultaneously as a tool for cultivating positive team dynamics and furthering the project down its road. By logistics plan, we intend a well-thought-out draft specifying the activities and practicalities involved in seeing team-based research through from beginning to end. Generation of this logistics plan—and team involvement in modification of the plan, as necessary—can help project managers and the team to anticipate predictable issues before they become obstacles. This then frees them to address unforeseen problems that will inevitably arise. Rather than recommend creating a static, prescriptive document as *the* logistics plan, we see the logistics planning itself as an ongoing exercise to help project managers ensure that team efforts most effectively match the changing requisites of the project.

In this chapter, we present a framework for logistics planning that can be tailored to specific projects. Although we focus on overseas public health projects, the planning we encourage has application for domestic team-based research as well. We begin with a case study narrative of a team-based project whose challenges illustrate the utility of logistics planning. We then present four priorities in team building and team-based research that can be supported through such planning:

1. establishing meaningful relationships with people at the research site;
2. forming a cohesive research team;
3. maximizing and expanding research experience of all team members through training; and
4. keeping track of data as they are collected and processed.

For each priority, we offer suggestions for how to address, through preliminary planning, the more predictable challenges project managers and teams are likely to encounter. Our intention is to share a process for developing a logistics plan specific to the project, site, and research team, rather than present a template of procedures. Our suggestions focus on anticipating issues and problems, then developing practical solutions that are carefully designed, methodical, and appropriate to the issue or problem. We conclude the chapter with a return to our case study to reflect on our lessons learned about logistics planning during that project. Table 4.1 summarizes the common challenges and possible solutions of team-based project preparation and logistics, as detailed throughout this chapter.

A Word about the Authors

The body of the chapter reflects the perspectives of Mack and Bunce that they developed during their experiences as U.S.-based researchers working on reproductive health studies in developing countries. The case study is an account of a joint effort that was their first solo experience as project managers. The challenges of that project were particularly instructive in providing Mack and Bunce with ample opportunity to fumble through collective realization of a study across institutional, geographic, and cultural boundaries. Akumatey offers the perspective of a developing country–based researcher working on public health studies in the developing country where she grew up and currently lives, Ghana. Her insightful commentary, appearing in bold type throughout the text as "Note from the Field," was a reality check for our perceptions of what constitutes a productive, satisfying team research experience.

Table 4.1.   Creating a Logistical Framework

Recommended Actions	Purpose
Establishing relationships at the research site	
Plan site visit as soon as feasible	To begin/renew local relationships, physically meet with key contacts, and become familiar with research context
Set agenda for site visit:	To maximize the time available
▪ Identify contacts	To represent the range of people and positions relevant to project
▪ Set advance appointments	To ensure the maximum number of meetings with contacts
▪ Prepare verbal introduction of the project	To accurately represent and introduce the organization and project to contacts
▪ Create topic list cheat sheet for meetings	To ensure relevant topics for each type of meeting are discussed
▪ Identify places to visit	To gain an understanding of physical research context and facilities
▪ Schedule community tours	To gain an understanding of local cultural context, population, and recruitment areas
Forming a research team	
Determine qualifications of local project leader(s)	To ensure the person hired has all the necessary skill sets, including management
Identify and hire local project leader	Gather recommendations from colleagues in-country and at own/other research organizations; if possible meet with candidates
Determine qualifications for staff roles	To ensure that staff members have all skill sets necessary to implement the project
Identify and hire staff	Network at local level. Local project leaders may be best equipped to identify/hire local staff
Define boundaries of responsibility for all roles	To establish effective implementation of project, avoid confusion
Negotiate interface of project manager, local project leader, and team	
Maximizing and expanding team's research expertise and experience	
Schedule practical, on-site team training in methods and project implementation	To establish a shared knowledge base; require *all* team members to attend
Evaluate skills, experiences, and approaches of team members	To ensure that project responsibilities are allocated according to people's strengths
Establish training goals	To tailor training activities to specific needs of team and project

(continued)

Table 4.1.   *(continued)*

Recommended Actions	Purpose
Plan training agenda	To ensure all topics and activities are covered in the allotted time
■ Review of protocol	To ensure team's understanding of project objectives
■ Review data collection instruments	To ensure data collection guides are culturally appropriate by working with the team to discuss and refine questions
■ Practical, hands-on methods training	To ensure uniform implementation of data collection and data management methods
■ Team-building exercises requiring members to negotiate and defend group responses	To encourage team identity; to foster smooth teamwork through mutual appreciation of essential contributions of all team members
Develop training materials	To provide structure to the training and reference materials for the team; inquire about the type of equipment that the training facility will support; bring low-tech backup method; make sure tape recorders are available for training exercises
Plan for staff overturn	To provide for later training of new staff; leave training materials with team; at the beginning of training, designate staff members to train others

Creating a data management plan to track and handle data

Create data collection timeline by calculating ■ Number of data collection events ■ Time for participant recruitment ■ Amount of time needed for data collection based on number of staff ■ Time required for data processing	To set a realistic schedule for completing all research activities; to help staff pace themselves so they can keep up with the project momentum
Determine data processing requirements Consider: ■ Notes ■ Recorded data ■ Transcription ■ Translation ■ Data entry ■ Backup methods for tapes and electronic files ■ Equipment needs ■ Staff skills and time	To ensure that the team is equipped to handle a high volume of data with the necessary staff skills, time, and equipment for data processing
Create (and use!) data tracking tools Include:	To help ensure data collection goes smoothly; to keep track of data as it is

Table 4.1. *(continued)*

Recommended Actions	Purpose
▪ Checklists for data collection ▪ Tracking tools indicating stage of processing for each data collection event ▪ Progress-reporting forms for local and sponsor project management	collected; to facilitate local and sponsor review of project progress
Provide for security of electronic and physical data. Include: ▪ Staff confidentiality agreements ▪ Locked data storage ▪ Password protection of electronic files	To ensure respect of confidentiality requirements and commitments
Plan quality assurance checks. Include: ▪ Team input into data collection instruments ▪ Pilot testing of instruments ▪ Extensive data collection training Provision of feedback on transcripts throughout course of research ▪ Regular site monitoring visits from sponsoring agency	To ensure high quality of the data at all stages of the project; to ensure that in-depth understanding of the research topics may be gained through the data that is collected

Case Study

The study Mack and Bunce codirected as our first solo project was a small, qualitative study focusing on reproductive health issues. It was set in a developing country that we visited only once, about ten days before the start of data collection. Our organization's involvement in the project came through a subcontract with another U.S.-based research organization that had received government funding. The contracting organization also had a field office in the country where the study took place. This meant that we had to filter all decisions and actions through two third parties, and that we were accountable to multiple individuals and organizations located in several places.

As we were setting up the project on our end, we liaisoned closely with the staff of the contractor's country office, who were handling site coordination activities. They were to hire the principal investigator and field team, provide input during the writing of the interview and focus group questions, translate the interview and focus group guides from English to French, then to the local language, and make logistical arrangements for the training workshop that we would be conducting locally. They were also responsible for obtaining local ethics approval for the study from the country's Ministry of Health.

Collaboration and communication with the country office staff was essential for getting the project set up, but it frequently proved to be difficult.

For example, conference calls were awkward due to voice delays and interruptions in phone service. We were also so polite to one another during the calls that we were slow to conduct business. To a certain extent, e-mail proved to be the better mode of communication. For several months before the start of the study, there were frequent flurries of e-mail exchanges among all parties. Everyone was encouraged to react to everything, and indeed all had something to say. Files clogged inboxes. Sometimes there were cultural misunderstandings regarding what someone had written in their message, resulting in bruised egos. E-mail systems also went down from time to time, creating sudden unexplained silences on the Internet waves.

Collaboration was also challenging because with so many people involved in decision making, it was difficult to know when or how an activity would finally get accomplished, and who specifically had the ultimate responsibility for doing so. One example concerns the development of interview and focus group guides, which was a joint effort of all the research groups involved. Our collective goals were to ensure that the questions were culturally appropriate, effective at eliciting the information being requested by the contracting organization, and consistent with qualitative research methods. A consensus was not easy to achieve, however. Almost everyone insisted on asking questions that reflected their individual perspectives and backgrounds, but the compromise needed to create final viable guides informed by the different areas of expertise was slow to come about.

We all went back and forth making revisions so many times that version control eventually became an issue. At one point, we incorrectly concluded on our end that we at last had a final set of drafts in our hands. We asked the site to translate them from English to French, which they did. However, a couple of weeks later, more comments about a previous version of the guides trickled in from somebody. So we revised the guides again. And again. About 6 weeks before we were due to arrive for the team training workshop, all parties declared that the drafts were now truly final. The country research office then agreed to update the translations to reflect the changes, but time went by and we never got anything. When we sent e-mails every couple of weeks to remind the country office to please send us the translated updated guides as soon as they were complete, they assured us that they would. Nonetheless, upon our departure date, we still did not have the guides.

Another challenge from having so many people involved in decision making was that no one seemed to have ultimate authority. One area where this posed a problem concerned staff hires. Our involvement in hiring the local research team had been limited, but the field office kept us informed of the process by sending us the CVs of the people they hired. The principal investigator was a medical doctor, multilingual, and had prior experience in qualitative data collection. Other CVs came to us later as the rest of the field team was hired. They seemed to us a reasonably qualified group, but there were nonetheless a couple of red flags. First, there were not enough women, despite our insistence that there be a minimum number of female team members. Focus groups with local women featured questions about sexual behavior, and we preferred to have female moderators and note takers collecting this data. When we expressed concern about the gender imbalance to the country office, we were assured that more women would be hired before the project began.

The second problem we saw with the composition of the team was that one of the female hires held a post in a government office. It would be unethical not to disclose her identity to the people she interviewed because she was in a position of influence and a member of the government. At the same time, if she told them who she was it would probably influence how some people, particularly village officials and health service providers, responded to the interview questions. With the support of the domestic office of the organization that had contracted us, we wrote to the field office and clearly explained why it would be unacceptable for this person to collect any data. They resisted somewhat, but finally agreed that she would have minimal involvement in the project. They maintained that her presence was, however, required by the Ministry of Health.

We received a warm welcome from the country office staff upon our arrival at the site. They arranged for us to spend the following day meeting key officials whose support was needed in order for the study to take place. Ethics approval had already been obtained, but the staff nonetheless again sought the verbal accord of each person we visited. These included representatives from the Ministry of Health and medical personnel working in the reproductive health field. Despite the fact that we said very little at these meetings, it seemed to be important that as representatives of the foreign research team we take the time to personally greet each person identified by our local contacts.

During the week of the training, we had the opportunity to talk with local community leaders and other local people from rural and urban backgrounds. The field staff also took us to visit area health clinics. These experiences were invaluable for helping us to understand the viewpoints of the local team as we worked on the content of the interview and focus group questions. It also helped us to interpret the data that came out of those interviews and focus groups once we were back in the United States.

The team training workshop was scheduled to take place at the office of a local NGO in the area of the country where the field work would take place, some twelve hours by car from the capital city. As we were preparing for the drive, one of the staff casually mentioned that there would be no electricity where we were going. Did we have our flashlights? We had had no idea! How would we conduct the training without electricity? When we had inquired from back home whether there would be an LCD projector for PowerPoint presentations, they had told us it would be better if we brought our own. An overhead projector would be available, however, so we had printed our presentations on overhead transparencies instead. The country office had also agreed to provide a flip chart and markers. With these arrangements, we had figured that we were covered. But even though we would have been able to make do with just the flip chart, there was still the matter of our computers. How would we make do without them? The staff assured us that there was a generator at the NGO office, where we could charge the batteries.

During our initial meetings with the country office staff and research team, we were met with a few other surprises. First, we were given copies of the outdated translated draft guides that we already had. Responses to our inquiries about who would be responsible for updating the transla-tions—now a fairly urgent matter given that data collection was to start im-mediately after the training—were evasive. In order to have revised guides for the training, we finally decided to attempt the translation ourselves de-spite that we were not really qualified to do English-to-French translation. Later during the training week, all subsequent revisions to the guides—and these were numerous—became our responsibility to incorporate electron-ically. Nearly every evening following a full day of staff training, we sat sweating on the hotel balcony, working on our laptops until the batteries were dead. Then we waited in the darkness for someone to fire up the ho-tel generator, and we again worked on the guides until late in the evening. Not unexpectedly, the following day the team would find errors in gram-mar or phrasing within the updated files, and additional, extensive discus-sions would occur regarding the wording and content of the questions. In fact, discussion of the guides ended up taking so long that we were rushed to cover all of the training topics. Fatigued and exasperated about the guides by the end of the week, we turned over the task of final revisions to the local team leaders. Unfortunately, they turned out to have limited computer skills and we had to step in again to finish the job.

A second surprise was that additional women had not, in fact, been hired. The gender imbalance within the group of data collectors remained an irre-solvable issue. At the beginning of the week of training, our concerns were confirmed when we heard team members make offhand remarks about how local women would feel uncomfortable in focus groups where men were present. Later, after we made an issue of the problem, the same people argued that the situation would actually be acceptable as long as the male facilitators were not from the same village as the women in the focus group. Because data collection would take place over a very limited number of days in four different sites, it was going to be impossible to distribute the female data collectors adequately among all the female focus groups. So, we had a dilemma.

We also learned that the female government employee intended to be involved in data collection without disclosing her identity. We grappled with what to do about this all week long during the training. We tried talking to the local project leaders and to the woman herself, but we could not convince them that it was unethical. Then, to complicate matters, the woman in question turned out to be the most talented interviewer and focus group moderator of all the staff in the training. Given the gender imbalance in the team, we really did need her. Finally we all agreed on a plan whereby she would only interview one category of people deemed least likely to be bothered by her position, and she would be frank about who she was.

A couple of other things that came up during the training week are worth noting. One is that it was difficult to get the local principal investigator to remain in the training room for any length of time. He would leave at will, even though his presence was the most crucial of the whole team. This was particularly problematic during the ethics training. When he failed the ethics certification exam, we had to review the material with him again and have him retake the exam.

As for their timeline for data collection, it did not seem realistic to us. They planned to recruit participants and conduct all interviews and focus groups in two rural and two urban sites over a period of about eight days. It also turned out that data collection was going to occur during a period of religious fasting. We worried that this would have an impact on the team's ability to collect the data in the already short time frame they had set for themselves.

When the training week was over, we were not at all confident about how the data collection—or the data—would turn out. The team members had been responsive to the training, but they were much less experienced in qualitative methods than we had originally thought. Their ability to facilitate focus group discussions was especially weak. For example, they rarely probed. Surprisingly, they related in their evaluations that the most informative part of the training consisted of the formatting protocol for transcription. This was worrisome. What about the data collection methods? We were also not sure that each team member was assigned to the role for which his or her skills were best suited. Unfortunately, our efforts to suggest shifts in scope of responsibility for each team member were largely unsuccessful.

In fact, we were frustrated in general about the lack of authority we had been accorded throughout the training. Our own limited experience as project managers made it difficult to retain control over the training process. We did not even feel much a part of the team at all. Thus, we returned to the United States harboring much uncertainty about the quality of the data we would soon be receiving.

Priority 1: Establishing Relationships at the Research Site

Whether project managers will be located on- or off-site during the study, it is a priority to become familiar with and familiar to people at the site. For our projects in developing countries, we often work in places where we have never been, with people whom we have never met. It is not unusual to exchange e-mails with someone for months before ever meeting or speaking with the person. Often, we do not even know if we are dealing with a man or a woman and may feel inhibited by cultural boundaries from clarifying the issue. This is disorienting! Local social and professional roles and hierarchies are also difficult to discern over e-mail. The absence of face-to-face communication, and the resulting confusion, is particularly acute for overseas research sites. However, as written professional exchanges continue to replace verbal ones more broadly, relationships with collaborators that are exclusively electronic can be the norm just as easily when the site is across town or the next state north.

This situation calls for a "reconnaissance" trip to the site, as soon as it is feasible. Some study budgets allow project managers to make a visit to the site well in advance of study initiation. This is especially helpful in first-time situations. If a researcher is unable to make a separate initial site visit, the activities we describe below could be scheduled for just prior to data collection, during a training visit, for example. If a researcher already has some familiarity with the location or particular collaborators—as an experienced researcher might—a preliminary site visit is still useful as an opportunity to renew and build upon established relationships.

Note from the field: *This initial visit can provide an opportunity for setting up or promoting the formation of community advisory boards (CABs) as well.*[1]

Set Agenda for Site Visit

We recommend beginning the logistics planning by setting a site visit agenda. Our agenda is designed to meet two goals: (1) to form and expand relationships with people having some level of connection to the study and (2) to become familiar with the local context, both cultural and physical.

Identify Contacts

First, we have to identify the people with whom to form and expand relationships. This is not always obvious! We usually begin by listing the specific people we know we want to see. We then brainstorm to identify categories of people we consider important to meet. As a network of personal contacts is beneficial in so many situations throughout the research process, it is probably worthwhile to pursue relationships with people holding a range of positions in the project and community.

Key figures could include community leaders, stakeholders, and gatekeepers; government employees such as officials at the Ministry of Health; local public health providers; people working for local and international organizations whose aims overlap or intersect with those of our project (e.g., sponsor organization's own country office, humanitarian aid organizations, nonprofit groups, and religious institutions); and people involved in other local research activities (e.g., at a university hospital, a research laboratory, or on other local projects).

Note from the field: *It is also important to meet with relevant policymakers at this stage in the research.*

We also like to meet with members of the study population and community, in the field setting if possible. This is discussed in more detail below.

Note from the field: *A courtesy call to the traditional leaders of the local study community can create goodwill, facilitate community acceptability, and help foster lasting ties at the community level.*

Not least, we meet with hired or potential members of the research team, for example, the local principal investigator, site coordinator, research director, or the candidates for various team positions.

Existing local contacts, as well as contacts referred by our colleagues, may be able to help identify and link us with individuals in the various categories. Once on-site, we can broaden our contact list by asking each key person to recommend someone they think we should know. Another strategy we use in the field is to make a list of topic areas relevant to the project and show it to people who might be able to steer us to corresponding organizations and individuals. The goal is to create a workable itinerary that builds in flexibility for meeting additional people. Time can constrain the number of meetings we are able to manage, so it will also be important to prioritize contacts.

Set Appointments

Local contacts may be able to assist in setting up appointments, which is not always a simple matter. Forgetting to check people's availability can be a very expensive disaster, as Mack was fortunate enough not to find out. Amid the flurry of preparations for one of her first trips, it did not occur to her to contact the research team about her imminent arrival until just days before her departure. As chance would have it, all concerned were planning to be in town and were able to rearrange schedules to accommodate her. Another time, she did not remember to arrange for a courtesy visit to the country office of a prominent U.S. organization until the morning of her return flight. There again, she was lucky enough to catch someone available for a quick conversation when she stopped by the office en route to the airport.

Prepare for Meetings

Our meetings during the site visit typically range from informal meet-and-greet affairs to information meetings. Whatever the case, it helps to remember that during these meetings we serve as the face of our organization and of the research study. The impression we make may influence the person's reception and views of the project for a long time to come.

Develop Concise Explanation of the Project

When preparing for a simple meet-and-greet session, or a courtesy call, we like to develop a concise verbal explanation of the project and research goals. This is especially useful when we will be introducing the project and/or our organization to someone for the first time. It is also useful when we do not know the exact roles or stance of the people we are scheduled to meet.

Create Topic List for Meetings

For meetings in which we hope to gather information or garner support, we may also prepare an informal list of topics to address. Depending on whether it will be appropriate to take notes during the meeting, we may commit this list to memory or paper. After going through a few meetings once at the site, we will likely either revise it or find we are comfortable enough to talk through the meeting without it. In addition to addressing specific topics or questions as we converse with people, we also try to get a sense of the local politics of how different people and organizations are linked, who works cooperatively with whom, where there is a history of conflict, and the potential for misunderstandings related to study goals or procedures. Local attitudes toward research, details about the study population, the current political situation in the community or region, and any special local concerns are also of interest.

Note from the field: *As you make initial contacts, it is important to let people know that the fact that you have visited them does not imply that you are making any commitment to them about their involvement in the project.*

Once the project is underway, there will doubtless be many occasions to draw on the expertise of these contacts. Depending on their positions and circles of influence, some individuals could keep us informed of what is happening locally on the ground. Others might provide us with a cultural filter with which to interpret local events, alert us as to the key players involved in a situation and the perspectives or parties those players represent, and help us to understand the political climate of the research context. During a crisis situation, these contacts might help us decide how to respond by advising on how particular actions would be interpreted locally, communicating messages on our behalf, and so on.

Those with whom we make efforts to establish positive, collaborative relationships are the allies on whom we might eventually rely to be our ears, eyes, voice, and advocates. Our relationship with them also increases our capacity to be diplomatic in our interactions at the local level, to understand how the imminent study is likely to be viewed in the local context, and to access emerging concerns held by the study population and community.

Identify Places to Visit

To address the second site visit motivation—to become familiar with the local context—we go through a similar process as for contacts. First, we make a list of the facilities, organizations, towns, and any other locations we want to visit. Because public health projects are often housed at research centers, universities, and hospitals, these may be the most accessible places on the list. We also like to find out about other facilities where study activities will take place, including office locations where the research team will work. We may already be visiting some of the other places on our list when we go to meet with contacts. However, it may be wrong to assume that people at all the places we want to see will be amenable to ad hoc requests for tours. Local contacts can help us determine whether it is more appropriate to formally arrange for this in advance. In addition, we have learned from a sometimes cool reaction to previous tour requests that it is important to emphasize that we will not be making an evaluation of the facility or assessing the staff in any way.

Schedule Cultural and Community Tours

We will gain some familiarity with local culture and geography without much effort, as a result of spending time in a place. Nonetheless, we have probably all gone to conferences and on business trips where we see little of the hosting city and a lot of the hotel and conference rooms. After a couple of such trips when Mack was unable to describe to friends at home what some remote overseas locale was like, it seemed worthwhile to start being proactive about scheduling cultural and geographical reconnaissance activities in the site visit agenda.

Windshield Tour

Arranging for a "windshield tour" is a great way to get familiar with the site. We can gain a sense, for example, of the layout of the city, the concentration of different populations in particular areas, and the proximity of the research site to the areas where members of the study population work or reside. The times when we have chanced to get a knowledgeable and loquacious driver for one of these windshield tours, we have learned about issues ranging from transportation and housing, to beer making, to soccer rivalries.

Visit Recruitment Areas

Visiting the areas targeted for participant recruitment has proved to be one of the more rewarding reconnaissance activities on the agenda. We have ended a wearying day of meetings with a motorcycle trip to the bar district for drinks and conversation with potential study recruits. It has been inspiring to witness the warm welcome extended to outreach workers who are well known in the community because of their efforts to reduce malaria through free mosquito net distribution. We have spent time talking to the people who will be most helped by public health research breakthroughs.

For us, the psychological link resulting from experiencing the context—knowing the appearance and personalities of colleagues and collaborators, having personal contact with people having key roles at multiple levels of the community, having a visual image of the research and community setting, and first-hand exposure to the sociocultural environment—puts a project into perspective in a way that nothing else can. The site visit gives us a frame of reference for the study that will inform our approach from that point forward. The ability of project managers to share these locally based common denominators with the research team members also becomes an important initial step in constructing a team identity.

Priority 2—Forming a Research Team

A second, very obvious priority in team-based research is to form a research team. The goal of logistics planning in this regard is to forge a team that is resilient and responsive to changes in project circumstances, activities, and staff. This involves careful selection of staff, development of well-defined roles and responsibilities for all team members, and establishment of an effective system of communication. It also calls for flexibility—which is not necessarily a naturally occurring feature of group dynamics—as priorities and circumstances shift.

Building a research team can be accomplished any number of ways according to the specific circumstances, researcher, context, and project. The logistical planning we discuss here therefore reflects just one way to use a logistical framework for team building.

Identify Local Project Leader

When forming a team, the first member to identify and get to know is the person with primary responsibility for local leadership. Titles for this role vary but include local principal investigator, site coordinator, or local project manager. For larger projects, leadership roles are sometimes divided up and filled by multiple people. Choosing the local project leader(s) is one of the most important logistical decisions project managers will make. Local project leaders will be highly influential in the research process and in local team dynamics. Their personal motivation and expertise can therefore have a substantial impact on the ultimate quality of the data.

Note from the field: *Specific guidelines may be needed to minimize conflicts when top leadership roles are split among two or more individuals. For example, if the person controlling the funds for the project is different from the person leading the research, there may be confusion regarding appropriate allocation of funds for project activities. Decision-making authority may also be unclear.*

Determine Qualifications of Project Leaders

To help ensure the best possible hire for leadership positions, we determine and outline the qualifications and qualities the local project leader should have. Academic qualifications, subject expertise, and proven field experience depend on the nature of the specific project. Personal characteristics desirable for this position include being reliable, proficient, and engaged in the research. Managerial and administrative skills are crucial. As team leader, the person must be able to relate well to other people and gain the respect of the team members. Ideally, the person knows when to provide team members with the opportunity to express their opinions but also when to exert authority and make decisions. Outside the team, a good project leader interfaces well with other local and nonlocal researchers, key community stakeholders, and the study population.

Note from the field: *Project leaders will be capable of working independently but also willing to ask questions and ask for help when needed.*

Determine Staff Roles and Responsibilities

To ensure the best possible hires for all other project staff, we create a complete list of staff roles as well. We also define the knowledge base and skill set necessary for each role, and the approximate percentage of a forty-hour week that each one will involve. We prefer a division of labor in defining roles, distributing tasks among team members rather than having all members perform all jobs.

Hire Project Leader

Once we have outlined what we are looking for in a project leader, we'll want to find out whether anyone with this impressive list of qualifications exists and, moreover, is interested in the job. Soliciting recommendations from colleagues is one effective way to identify candidates. Another option is to write an advertisement of the position for local distribution in newspapers and job databases, and more global distribution on listservs, informal e-mail networks, and Internet sites. Local research agencies are another resource. Working with agencies may involve a bidding process in which the winning organization will supply the whole team.

In developing countries, the pool of candidates for the project leader position can sometimes be small owing to lack of qualified personnel, conflicting time commitments of personnel who are qualified, and the inherent instability of contract work. On more than one occasion, we have received e-mail pleas from overseas colleagues asking for help getting into a more stable employment situation. Colleagues also commonly take on contract jobs as supplementary employment, which sometimes results in time crunches.

We find that it is of benefit to build some flexibility in the project activities timeline for this reason. The pervasive concern of compensation in developing countries is important to consider when discussing contractual agreements, pay schedules, study startup dates, duration of the study, and employment policies during unplanned study suspension or closure. Another important issue concerns the avenues through which contracts and compensation must be routed in order to hire the person (Garland et al. 2006).

For project managers attempting to make a hire from a distance, it can be difficult to assess how well a given candidate meets the criteria. A curriculum vitae only portrays a person's accomplishments; missing are the character traits that may indicate how well someone can manage research activities and get along as team leader. If we are able to make a pre-study site visit early enough in the research process, we try to arrange to meet a candidate or two at that time. If we do not have this luxury, we have to rely on CVs and cover letters, recommendations from colleagues and local contacts, and perhaps a telephone conversation. After identifying a potential hire, it is a good idea to make inquiries both in-country and at other research organizations to see if anyone can comment on the person's previous work and performance.

Hire Other Staff

Networking with people at the local level is usually the most effective way to fill other staff positions. It is possible that some or all research team members will have been hired before or during the search for a local project leader, such as when a candidate is better suited for a nonleader position. If not, once the project leader is hired, we would discuss with that person the remaining team roles, the qualifications desirable for each role, and the possibilities for finding qualified people locally. When working internationally, we have found a task-oriented approach to defining roles within the project to be more effective than specifying a combination of skills that one person should possess. Local project leaders, having a better understanding of how people are trained in their cultural setting, will know best how to assemble a group of people who collectively possess the skills needed for the project.

Define Responsibilities of Project Manager and Local Project Leader

Once the team has been hired, forging a positive and productive team dynamic will depend on establishing clear boundaries of responsibility for each person, including decision-making authority within the project. (We address negotiation of team member roles further under Priority 3.) For project leaders, one aspect of defining our role includes deciding how directly we will be involved in the day-to-day operation of the project. If we live at some distance from the site, our participation in on-site activities will evidently be limited. In that case, we have to consider the degree to which we want the site to apprise us of everyday events, with whom local decision-making authority should lie, and potential communication issues. Other points to consider include how autonomous the local leader will be. How autonomous does that person want to be, and how well is he or she qualified to do so? How much mentoring, if any, is needed, and at what stages of the project?

Note from the field: *The line between working independently as the local project leader and working as a team player in the larger project context is sometimes difficult to grasp. There is a need to define the autonomy of the local leader vis-à-vis the foreign team. For example, it will be very useful for the local team leader to understand the specific aspects of the study that can be addressed without consultation with or approval from foreign team members, in order to save time or facilitate prompt action when necessary.*

Negotiating and differentiating our role from the role of local project leaders helps avoid violating boundaries of responsibility and authority. Achieving a balance in this regard can be quite challenging and requires ongoing effort. We have written many an apologetic e-mail after inadvertently offending someone by a remark, a request to review a document (misinterpreted as an approval requirement), and cultural misunderstandings.

One example that comes to mind occurred when a high-level administrator at an organization having local oversight for one of our studies had been asked to hire a social scientist to fill a newly created position. The weeks wore on following this request, and partly as an effort to keep ourselves from forgetting about the issue of the hire, we wrote to ask if we could see the CVs of the top candidates once the pool had been narrowed. It was as much an attempt to make up for our silence about the issue as anything. The administrator, a person with whom our relationship had been untroubled up to then, became livid. Via e-mail, he very clearly let us know that we were being patronizing by not trusting his group to select a qualified candidate. This was a decision that they were fully capable of making without our help. We repaired the damage with an apology that was apparently accepted, and the relationship continued on without further issue. However, we were more mindful of his realm of authority and competence after that.

Note from the field: *An issue that often arises as projects come to a close is our right to publish analyses of the data we have collected. Clarifying publication rights in a logistics plan can help avoid conflicts later on.*

Other authors have mentioned the need to discuss from the project outset the issues of publication rights, the possibility and need for mentoring in results write-ups, procedures for routing eventual manuscripts for review, and opportunities for local project leaders and other staff to attend conferences (Fernald and Duclos 2005, Garland et al. 2006). That we had not mentioned these issues in the draft of this chapter prior to Akumatey's note from the field is revealing of how long-distance project managers can sometimes be unaware of concerns that are of high importance to the field team.

Determine Interface of Project Manager, Local Project Leader, and Team

Upon initial face-to-face interaction with the local project leader and research team members, we begin trying to assess the degree of structure, guidance, and instruction that they expect from us. Each site, project, and research team has different expectations and needs. Some teams want procedures laid out step by step, whereas others prefer to focus on objectives and then work out the details themselves. We find that this varies from site to site and project to project, depending on the educational style of the particular country, the nature of the staff's research experience, and individual personalities.

For example, we had one research team in which all team members, regardless of their role in data collection, sat around a large table and took turns reading each study document aloud. They discussed each point thoroughly until everyone was satisfied that they agreed with its purpose and relevance. They liked to be sure that each person clearly understood the objective of each research activity, the intent of each question in the interview guides, and so on. On the other hand, they never wanted to spend time during our site visits discussing how they would arrange the research activities logistically. Theirs was an experienced research site with many research procedures already established. When it came to writing a report of the data later, they then did need more help from us. They had kept assuring us by e-mail that they were working on it until one person finally confessed that they were not sure what they were supposed to do. They then asked for guidelines specifying the exact content, format, and length of the report we were looking for. On our end, we had not had anything so specific in mind when we requested a final report. We learned from working with this team that we should have asked them directly about the level of structure that would be most helpful to them rather than trying to figure it out through observation and guessing.

Another way to plan logistically for project manager–local project leader–research team interactions is to outline strategies for making ourselves overtly approachable to the project leader and research team and receptive to their contributions. Equally important is to outline strategies for demonstrating our own humility, and indicating our willingness to also approach them with our comments and questions. Strategies include asking each and every team member to report on his or her research activities during group meetings, soliciting team members' expert opinions regarding culturally specific issues or questions related to data they have collected, and consulting individuals for project-related questions outside of team meetings. Another strategy is to get in the habit of phoning team colleagues frequently so that infrequent, individual conversations do not take on undue importance. We make every attempt to provide the local project leader and team with opportunities to ask questions. We also make a point to openly encourage them to share their expertise and perspectives with us.

In international settings, we have found that local ideas of authority and hierarchy often preclude disclosure of opinions and ideas to "outsiders," who are often perceived as high-ranking. If a problem arises at the site, the staff may not always inform us in a timely manner if they believe we might not be interested, or if they worry about putting their own competence into question. Not only does good communication prove important for ensuring that we learn of local issues and problems as they arise at the site, but it also encourages the local team to participate in shaping the research early on. For example, if there are things about the research design, questions, instruments, study population, and so on that do not correspond well to local conditions, it is ideal if the local project leaders and team feel comfortable discussing these issues candidly.

Priority 3: Maximizing and Expanding Research Expertise and Experience of All Team Members through Training

Most team-based research, including that conducted domestically, yields results of best quality when team members have individual specialties representing a diverse range of disciplines and skills (Rhoades 2006, 1986, Rhoades et al. 1986). In developing country settings, solid representation of local cultural expertise is especially important. For this reason, we advocate strongly for hiring local research teams.

Internationally and domestically, working with local research teams has many practical advantages. Local staff can draw on their own cultural knowledge and therefore work more efficiently and effectively than nonlocal researchers. It is logistically more feasible to conduct the research if staff live near the data collection site already, as well as more affordable than if budgets have to include per diem for nonlocal researchers to spend extended periods at the site.

The research itself also reaps benefits when conducted by people who are either very familiar with or who are members, at some level, of the community. Local researchers usually have a keener understanding of how things work in the local context and may have stronger interest in the research activities. Members of any team are likely to have a greater sense of ownership and personal investment in the work when they have contributed to decision making during the research process. These have positive effects on the quality of work the team does and consequently the results.

Being aware of any limitations team members have will help maximize these benefits. For example, in developing country contexts, finding people who have research expertise requiring formal training is sometimes problematic. This is due to local economic constraints that can severely limit people's opportunities for formal education and professional development. Finding qualified personnel can also be challenging because it is difficult to evaluate a person's skills, formal training, and experience from a distance, especially if a CV is the only documentation.

Another common circumstance in overseas settings is that researchers have a more quantitative than qualitative research background. Sometimes, they may have no experience at all in one or more qualitative method. As Carey and Gelaude mention (chapter 11, this volume), it is also often the case that staff have used a form of a particular qualitative method, but toward different ends. For example, many types of research and health-related activities involve interviews. However, the goal of interviewing patients as a health counselor is to dispense information and provide counseling, whereas the objective of qualitative interviewing is to collect information from participants without influencing what they say. Another distinction that can make a big difference in the nature of the data collected concerns the degree of flexibility in the interviewer's use of the interview guide, including wording, order, and number of questions. Those people with quantitative experience may continue to prefer a more structured, versus interpretive, approach to interviewing, other data collection, and analysis even after taking qualitative methods training (Garland et al. 2006). None of these issues should prove impossible to handle as long as the project manager addresses them through training early in the life of the project and monitors the interviewers regularly.

Also having a potential impact on research activities are differences in worldview. In international contexts, approaches to public health research sometimes differ in style and perspective from those of U.S. researchers. For example, when working in Latin America on a qualitative study about HIV risk behaviors among youth MSM (men who have sex with men), Mack noted that the local researchers integrated their scientific and Catholic backgrounds into their data collection styles, reflecting an approach that was more openly religious than is the norm among American researchers. She has made similar observations among research teams in West and southern Africa, where religious and spiritual beliefs were regularly evoked in the context of data collection activities. Mack has also observed conflicts arising over differences in perspective regarding social responsibility, such as when local research practices involved a humanitarian component that U.S. researchers viewed as incompatible with scientific studies. For example, after one study site was closed prematurely, the local principal investigator implored U.S. researchers to continue to provide clinical trial participants with the health services from which they had benefited during the study, at least for as long as the study would have lasted. "They are demoralized," he said. "Please give them something. Anything!" Unfortunately, the researchers were unable to do so due to expenditure restrictions on study sites that were officially closed.

When hiring and training research teams, we try to be aware of any gaps in experience, the possible challenges these gaps may present, and how we can contribute to improving the capacity of the staff. We also try to find ways to be respectful of local cultural perspectives and practices without compromising the research objectives. The above example illustrates the complexity involved in this, but each lesson learned helps us plan more effectively for the next study. In our recommendations for planning a pre-study team training workshop, we take all of these factors into account.

Schedule Team Training

Training the research team is indispensable for every new project, even for teams who have worked together in the past. When to schedule the training workshop varies according to the specific situation and project budget. One possibility is to schedule it during the project manager's reconnaissance visit to the site. Ideally, we like to hold the training soon after the research team has been assembled but not far in advance of the data collection start date. In this way, the team can start implementing the data collection techniques while the information is still fresh. For example, if we schedule the training workshop about two weeks before data collection officially begins, that gives us one week to go through the training activities and a second week to practice piloting the data collection techniques and instruments. By the third week, the team is ready to launch research activities.

Our trainings generally last three to five days depending on the number and types of methods to be used in the project. We usually ask the local project leader to help coordinate dates and staff to ensure everyone's availability. We also ask someone at the site to facilitate reservation of training facilities, including coordination of lunch and break time refreshments. These should be scheduled according to local practice, not the foreign visitors' expectations.

We prefer that all team members attend the training, regardless of each person's background, level of expertise, or role in the project. As we learned from the example cited in the case study, it is best to establish this early on by stating attendance as a requirement. The entire team's involvement in initial meetings is an important stage in team building. As Fernald and Duclos (2005) point out, it helps everyone to understand the purpose of the project, the methods, data collection activities, roles and responsibilities, and any specialized vocabulary that will be used. Group attendance and participation in training for all roles, to the extent possible, also allows the flexibility to have staff fill in for each other if necessary.

In cases where qualitative research is being conducted in parallel with a clinical trial, we would encourage members of the clinical staff to participate in at least part of the social–behavioral team training as well (and vice versa). A lesson learned in the past from training two such teams as separate entities is that we lose an opportunity for building relationships and cohesion within the overall project team, which can be difficult to make up for later. Of course, some local project leaders will have already thought of this. For example, at the start of a behavioral team training at a West Africa site, Mack was emphasizing the importance of working closely with the clinical team when the people present informed her that half were themselves clinical staff members. What was more, they wanted to know why she kept referring to the two teams as so distinct. "We don't work that way. Here, we are one."

Note from the field: *A joint training session for both teams prior to project takeoff will enhance subsequent collaboration and reduce the possibility of distrust in regards to research endeavors. Such a meeting will spell out areas for which collaboration will be needed and the form it will take. If there are separate protocols, the respective project leaders can share and discuss them thoroughly prior to presenting them to the teams in order to identify areas of potential conflict.*

Establish Training Goals

When we plan our training workshops, we seek to meet several goals. First, we want to begin forming social cohesion and build a shared sense of mission. Mutual recognition among team members of the importance of each person's role in rendering a study successful can lead to greater respect for all jobs and as a consequence improved teamwork. Appreciation of all contributions can be fostered through training exercises in which team members discuss a hypothetical issue that could come about during the study (e.g., an ethical dilemma), debate approaches to solving it, and defend their solutions.

A second goal is to assess each team member's strengths and qualifications beyond what we already know from the CVs. This assessment by the project manager and local project leader will happen over the course of the whole workshop. However, by about the end of the first day, we like to have at least a rough idea of the learning curves people will have in terms of understanding the project objectives and effectively utilizing the data collection methods. We can then tailor the workshop activities to meet their needs. Some of this staff assessment will be unnecessary in cases where we have worked with the team members previously (Garland et al. 2006). It should be possible to have already defined the responsibilities and scopes of work for each person prior to team training. Local project leaders may appreciate having the scope of work in written form for easy referral. They can always revise it later, during or after the training workshop as the distribution of responsibilities among the staff gets refined.

A third goal of the training is to provide all staff with an equivalent minimum knowledge base for the study objectives and methods. To meet this goal, we design most of the training activities to utilize the actual study protocol and instruments, if possible. Topics essential to cover include the study design and objectives, specific data collection methods, operation of data collection equipment, recruitment issues, data management logistics, and research ethics.

Plan Training Agenda

When planning the agenda, we like to start by listing and clearly defining all activities that the project will require. We then try to figure out the best way to cover all of these activities and the practice they require over the total number of training days. Scheduling regular coffee/tea breaks and lunch as we create the agenda helps to divide up the day for the various activities.

We usually begin the workshop with a thorough review of the study protocol so that everyone understands what the research is intended to accomplish and how this will be done. Then for the majority of the workshop we focus mostly on data collection methods. For each research method, we recommend providing a basic explanation of what the method is and the type of information we can learn from it; practical, hands-on instruction in how to use the method; real or sample instruments for each method; and practice exercises. It might also be important to brainstorm about and pilot strategies for recruiting participants for each method. Ethical issues concerning confidentiality will be important points of discussion throughout the workshop, but we may or may not decide to provide full research ethics training. In the latter case, we make other arrangements for the team to receive this training (and certification, if required) prior to data collection. Data management is another important training topic (see below and chapter 8).

To cover what is typically a large amount of material in a concentrated period of time, a teaching style that emphasizes practice of the methods over lecturing is usually most effective. In our experience, the workshop is an inappropriate setting for presenting highly theoretical concepts that would require time for people to mentally absorb. Instead, information on theoretical issues could be provided to interested staff as supplementary material or in a list of suggested readings. Sessions dedicated to in-depth discussion on these topics could be scheduled apart from the practical training in the event that this is desired or deemed necessary. Practice exercises can take place both in and outside the classroom. Our exercises typically include extensive role-playing, class presentations, self-critiques, peer critiques, hypothetical situations similar to the real project, instrument piloting (e.g., of interview guides), and practicing data management procedures. Sample training exercises can be found in Mack et al (2005).

The workshop is also a good opportunity to revise data collection instruments. Typically, we have already developed drafts of the instruments as part of the protocol approval process, but the team's input will be essential for bringing them to their final versions. We usually begin with group review of the instruments, during which we make a first round of edits. During the discussion, we try to find out if the team understands the intent behind each question, if the wording makes sense to them, and, especially, if the questions are culturally valid. How would they go about eliciting the same information if they were designing the question? How well will these questions translate? What additional questions or topic areas can they suggest? We then have the team to pilot the instruments. During piloting exercises, the team simultaneously practices the research methods and tests the instruments for comprehensibility, cultural appropriateness, and effectiveness. We then review the instruments again to note new issues they identified during the piloting.

Note from the field: *If possible, the field team should be encouraged to translate and back-translate the guides verbally during role-play to ascertain clarity of meaning.*

This exercise can be invaluable. It helps the study overall by ensuring that the instruments (and data) are culturally relevant and valid. It also helps to balance team dynamics in offering a forum for all the team members to express themselves as cultural experts rather than have the trainers always represent the voice of authority. One word of caution is to not let the discussion of data collection instruments, which can generate very animated and lengthy discussions, overwhelm methods training.

Once we have created a tentative agenda for the training, we then send it to the local project leader for feedback to ensure that we are covering their needs. When creating the agenda we try to be realistic about how much we can accomplish each day. However, we usually end up adjusting it on a day-by-day basis according to how the training plays out. The team may end up needing more instruction or practice in one area than in another. There may be personal emergencies, problems with infrastructure, and so on. It is important to be flexible in how training goals are met.

Develop Training Materials

After we have planned the training agenda and know how we will train on each data collection method, we make a list of the equipment we will need. This includes both teaching equipment and data collection supplies for the staff, such as notebooks, pens, tape recorders, tapes, and batteries. It is a good idea to inquire about the type of equipment the training facility can support, the reliability of the infrastructure, and computer compatibility. It can be very frustrating to show up with training information on a diskette only to find that none of the local computers has an appropriate disk drive. Likewise, there is no use in bringing overhead transparencies if the overhead projector is broken or without a power source, in preparing a computer presentation with small print if there is no LCD projector, or in planning to show a video if the recording format is unsupported. We have been surprised to find that in some developing country settings, newer technologies are more readily available than old ones; it is therefore best not to make assumptions. Planning for at least two ways of presenting material—including one very low-tech way—can be a lifesaver. For example, flipcharts and markers are usually a reasonable request and can always serve as backup.

Training materials to develop include teaching tools and materials to distribute to the team. The latter might be copies of the study protocol and instruments, instructional materials, and any standard operating procedures that have already been developed (e.g., for data management). Many of these materials can be prepared and mailed or shipped in advance. This is especially useful for international travel, when lost luggage could delay a training workshop for several days. Certificates of completion of training are important in many international settings. We usually bring a few extra hardcopies of all materials in case more people attend the training than was anticipated. We also bring electronic versions.

Instructional materials for methods ideally take a format that is easy to follow during the training and easy to refer back to in a field setting. No matter what the team's range of research experience, it can never hurt to include how-to instruction and basic background information on the methods. A team member may have extensive experience in specific research methods, but the approach for the current project may be somewhat different. (This can sometimes require negotiation and tactful presentation of alternate viewpoints during the workshop in order not to be critical of a person's previous training and experience.) Two potentially useful manuals for training in practical qualitative methodology are *Qualitative Methods: A Field Guide for Applied Research in Sexual and Reproductive Health* (Ulin et al. 2005) and the more team-oriented *Qualitative Research Methods: A Data Collector's Field Guide* (Mack et al. 2005).

Note from the field: *It is possible that the number of qualified applicants for staff positions may exceed the actual number required for the project. In that case, it does not hurt to train two or three more field people beyond those hired. This will facilitate replacement if a staff member decides to leave the project.*

Develop Procedures for Training Staff Hired Later

As Akumatey notes above, most projects that go on for any significant length of time will experience staff overturn. Some data collectors will leave the job, other full-time data collectors might be hired later, and new people could be hired to cover specific tasks such as transcription or translation.

Project leaders will need to be able to train staff who are hired subsequent to the training workshop. To prepare for this eventuality, they might proactively discuss with project managers during the initial training what subsequent training sessions would need to include. It is a good idea to plan to leave training materials at the site for this purpose, including any PowerPoint presentations and overheads. In addition, confidentiality issues will require particular attention in the context of staff turnover, both for outgoing and incoming staff members. New staff members may require ethics training, and project leaders will need to remind old staff that their pledge of confidentiality remains binding even after their involvement with the project has ceased.

Priority 4: Tracking and Handling Data as It Is Collected

If one of the advantages of doing team-based research is an increased capacity to collect large amounts of data, the flipside is that there is that much more data collection activity to monitor and data to sort out. The volume of data coming in can be overwhelming. There will also likely be multiple types of data to manage. How can we keep track of the data as they are collected? What will we do with the data once we have it? How will we ensure that their quality is high?

We try to avoid problems related to a high volume of data by creating a data management plan. When creating the plan, we consider several factors: (1) the data collection timeline; (2) data processing requirements; (3) data security; and (4) quality assurance. Here we only touch the surface of data management issues. (See chapter 8 in this volume for a more detailed treatment of the subject.)

Data Collection Timeline

The data management plan takes into account how long data collection should take relative to the overall project timeline. What needs to happen in order for the team to collect the data in the time allotted? To determine this, we calculate how many data collection events (e.g, structured observations, interviews, focus groups) will occur; the time required to recruit participants and set up these data collection events; how long it will take to do the actual data collection given the size of the research team; and the time it will require to convert each type of data from raw to analysis-ready form. For example, it takes approximately four to twelve hours to turn out a transcript from a sixty- to ninety-minute tape recording, depending on the quality of the recording, the efficiency of the transcriptionist, the type of data collection instrument, and the languages involved.

Data Processing Requirements

Once the raw data has been collected, it will need to be processed in the field in preparation for eventual analysis. When creating our data management plan, we think about how the project manager and the research team will keep track of all the data as it is collected and then as it passes through the various stages of processing. Below we identify some of the tasks involved in processing data in the field.

a. *Handwritten notes* from observations, interviews, and focus groups, as well as handwritten field notes, focus group note-taker notes, and focus group debriefing notes will need to be typed into computer files.

b. *Recorded data* from interviews and focus groups should be transcribed, translated, and entered into a computer database, if this technology is available. Researchers sometimes prefer to do transcription by hand first, and then type (or have someone else type) the transcripts into an electronic file. In either case, the person who collected the data should review the transcript for accuracy before it can be considered final.

c. A *transcription format protocol* for typists to use to render transcripts uniform as they enter data into a computer file typically features rules for font size and type, spacing, and speaker identification. That is, the text within every file must be formatted in exactly the same way. These conventions are tailored to the requirements of the data analysis software package. This means that the project manager (or someone) must therefore select the software in advance of data collection. Adherence to a transcription protocol saves much time and effort for those who will be manipulating the data later.

Transcription machines make transcription significantly easier, but the cost of these machines may make them a luxury item if they have not been included in the budget. At the least, sturdy tape recorders capable of withstanding frequent manual stops and starts are essential. McLellan-Lemal provides an in depth discussion of transcription issues and processes in chapter 5 of this volume.

d. *Translation guidelines* will depend on the type of data analysis planned. In many cases field staff may elect to translate directly as they transcribe, rather than transcribe verbatim and then translate, in order to save a step and time. If appropriate, this can be a cost-effective option and may be especially practical in the case of data collection in unwritten languages. However, this also means that there will be no exact written rendition of the oral recording and certain nuances and cultural distinctions may be lost. If it is decided to translate and transcribe simultaneously, the team should decide ahead of time how to deal with idioms and proverbs that will not make sense when directly translated.

e. A plan for *data entry* will save much confusion. In addition to a formatting protocol as mentioned above, it should include conventions for naming computer files. These names should ideally allow for easy identification of the type of data collection event without opening the file. For example, we would want to be able to distinguish between an interview with a health care provider, an interview with an injection drug user, and a focus group with pregnant women. For example, SAHPI03 (South Africa, Healthcare Provider, Interview No. 3).

f. *Centralization of data into one database* should occur once each file is in final form. The database itself should be secure, and it is a good idea to password-protect the files in the interest of confidentiality and data security. Tapes and transcripts should also be kept in a locked storage facility. Creating sign-out sheets for data packets will help to keep track of items removed for processing or review.

g. *Backup copies* of all data are essential. A designated team member should make backup tapes of recordings before tapes are submitted for transcription. This means that the site will need a double cassette deck with dubbing features (preferably high-speed). Tabs on the cassettes should be punched out to prevent tape erasure, re-recording, and accidental dubbing. If initial transcription is being done by hand, it is necessary to make a photocopy of the handwritten transcript before it goes to the typist. Thus, if something happens to the original transcript before it gets typed, the recording will at least not have to be transcribed again.

h. It is a good idea to find out what *computer equipment*, if any, is already available at the site and what needs to be provided. When evaluating and planning for computer equipment, consider software compatibility, Internet connection speeds, and computer literacy of the research team members. Know that although computers are becoming widespread in much of the world, not everyone knows how to use them. Because computer literacy is a highly desirable skill for many people in developing countries, providing computer training can be a very valuable contribution to capacity building.

i. *Data collection and data tracking checklists, forms, and templates* help keep track of what we need to do in order to accomplish the work, what has already been done, and where the data are located. *Checklists* are useful for ensuring that data collectors know what to take with them to the field (e.g., proper recording equipment, question guides, informed consent forms) and what to bring back to the office (e.g., cassettes, signed forms, field notes, question guides). We recommend creating *progress report* templates the team can use to report their data collection and processing activities to the project manager. We usually choose to have the staff complete these on a daily or weekly basis; however, monthly reports probably leave too little time for correcting errors and adjusting procedures. Finally, *data tracking forms* help project managers and the team to be organized. The level of detail on the forms should conform to the degree of detail desired by the research team; some teams prefer to document every single step of data processing, whereas others are more comfortable with fewer steps. Some teams work best with a form they create, perhaps working from a sample we provide. Others may simply prefer to use a template. We might choose to track a single event on each form, or make it more of a log sheet for tracking multiple events.

j. As we begin to compile a list of tasks related to data tracking, we assess the *staffing needs* for processing the data according to schedule. It helps to outline all staff roles and decide who will have which responsibilities, including transcription, typing/data entry, translation, data management, and/or office management. Also, someone will need to keep up with all tapes, notes, hardcopies, and backups, and someone will need to be in charge of data security, sign-out sheets, and equipment inventory. If we elect to have a data manager staff position, we outline their on-site responsibilities and discuss how these will interface with sponsor expectations.

Data Security

Data security refers to safe storage of the electronic and physical data (computer files, cassettes, transcripts, and notes). It also refers to confidentiality. We recommend that all staff members sign confidentiality agreements prior to the launch of the study and that these agreements be kept on file. All new staff members, even those hired for specific tasks such as data entry, must sign a confidentiality agreement prior to beginning work. All physical data, both originals and backups, should be stored in a safe place (e.g., a separate room at the local organization's headquarters) under lock and key. Electronic data should be stored in a centralized location, and files should be password-protected, with access only for those directly connected with the research.

Quality Assurance

A study is only as good as the data that comes out of it. Attention to data collection strategies and quality at every step of the process will ensure rich understanding of the research topics. This is especially true for qualitative research, in which the goal is to gain in-depth comprehension of specified topics and processes rather than to provide circumscribed answers to structured questions.

Quality assurance begins with protocol and guide development. Issues related to the timing and methods of quality checks should be thought out in advance, included in the work plan, and communicated to all members of the team before data collection begins. This will help prevent team members feeling criticized or singled out when there are comments to be made.

Data collection training is another key component in ensuring quality data. Data collectors who feel invested in the project and have a full understanding of the goals of the research, as well as a sound grasp of methodology, will have the skills to elicit a much richer picture of the research topic than those who do not feel as comfortable with the study. The training session should include extensive role-play and/or pilot testing of the instruments, with feedback from both other team members and the trainers. If interviews are tape recorded, data collectors should listen to their own interviews and note their strengths and weaknesses. Plenty of time should be allowed during the training for questions concerning the aims of the study, methodology, and any other issues that arise, to ensure that the staff are as comfortable as possible with their roles.

Even if study instruments have been pilot-tested, initial transcripts should be reviewed before succeeding interviews are conducted. Often team members will critique each other's transcripts in the field before they are turned in to the designated project leader or manager for review. Feedback should remain mainly positive, and provide concrete suggestions and examples for alternate ways of eliciting information, following up on participant comments, and explaining study components. It can also identify problems with translation or transcription that, if caught early, can be fixed without much trouble. This early and continuing review also allows for identification of emergent themes that may be important to a full understanding of the subject and that can then be incorporated into subsequent interviews. Ideally this feedback should be done for as many interviews as possible throughout the course of the study; at a minimum the first three interviews from each data collector should be reviewed, as well as spot checked for the duration of the study. Although this continuing review requires a significant time expenditure, it will ultimately make a huge difference in data quality.

Another issue related to quality assurance is that of project monitoring. In our work, staff from the sponsoring agency plan to visit the site(s) at key times in data collection activities—not so early that the research team has not had sufficient time to work out the kinks, but not so far into the project that mistakes and oversights will have a substantial impact on data quality. These regularly scheduled visits serve as a check that the research is proceeding as planned and that all protocols are being followed.

Prior to the visit, monitors prepare a list of activities and documentation to check on; this list covers research procedures, confidentiality and informed consent, budget, data storage, equipment, and questions to ask staff. Any deviation from protocol or timeline is discussed with the PI and relevant study staff. The decision as to who should be involved in resolving the issue will depend on the type and seriousness of the deviation. Guest et al. provide a useful framework for monitoring qualitative research in chapter 10.

In sum, handling large amounts of data is made simpler with a data management plan. This plan ideally accounts for the data collection timeline, data processing requirements, data security, and quality assurance. It also takes into account local realities and staff capabilities. This allows us to monitor the quality of the data as well as keep data organized in preparation for eventual analysis.

Case Study, Revisited

At the beginning of this chapter, we left off the description of our training trip with our concern about the research team's preparedness and willingness to collect the data ethically and systematically. Indeed, when we received the transcripts, our fears were confirmed that things had not quite gone according to plan. Why had things not come together despite significant effort expended on all sides?

One major reason was that our research team was not especially cohesive. The scattered nature of our group dynamics had been established at the instrument development phase of the project, when there were so many people involved in decision making that it was unclear who was ultimately responsible for what. The dynamics continued on in this way straight through implementation of data collection. During the training, we felt discounted at times, not really part of the team. Among the entire group, none of our roles was well defined. Tasks were distributed ineffectively. At the same time, concerns related to politeness and cultural sensitivity made it difficult for us to directly address each other about problems that arose. It was as if we were operating according to a politically correct egalitarian model, when a clear hierarchy of authority and responsibility would have served us much better.

Some of the problems with data collection had to do with staff composition. The local office had hired mainly people in high-level positions, including professors, government officials, and longtime NGO employees. This had both positive and negative ramifications. Although the range of their experience and backgrounds enriched the discussions of methodologies and cultural relevance, the staff also had their established ways of doing things. This made them less likely to set aside preconceived notions and be open to new ways of approaching data collection. This was apparent in the resultant transcripts, which varied tremendously in quality.

A probable reason for the sometimes poor data quality was ineffective time management on our part during the training. The time we spent revising the interview and focus group guides as a group was excessive compared to the time we spent practicing the data collection methods. Although the process of instrument revision definitely improved the cultural appropriateness of the instruments, it came at the cost of the staff's proficiency in methods. In retrospect, we should have cut short the guide revision process and spent more time in hands-on practice and role-playing.

The disorganized state of the data once it came into our hands reflected ineffective distribution of responsibilities among team members. This made it clear how important it is to identify a motivated, capable person to be responsible for overall data management from the outset. In this case, the local team leaders were in charge of data management, but they really should not have been. They were very competent in subject and cultural matters, but they were not detail-oriented, as became clear during the problems with guide translation. When we realized this, we tried to suggest that the role be transferred to a team member who did have the requisite skills. Owing to local ideas of hierarchy and proper organizational structure, however, we were told that it would not be appropriate to give control of data tasks to another team member. We did not insist, but as predicted, data management was a problem. Despite extensive training on the various forms, checklists, and timelines for data submission, we did not receive the transcripts and attendant information and forms in a correct and timely manner, or even updates, making it difficult for us to tell what was happening on the ground.

In addition, despite hands-on training with a transcription protocol, transcripts arrived incorrectly formatted and had to be reformatted before they could be entered into the software program and analyzed. We also ran into a problem with translation; the person conducting much of the translation and all of the final quality checks "cleaned up" and synthesized the data, apparently with the intention of making it easier for us, as foreigners, to understand. This inevitably led to issues with bias and the ultimate "truthfulness" of the data by the time it reached us, which in turn had serious implications for analysis.

Geography also played a role in the difficulties of data management. The research was conducted in a region far from the city where the coordinating office was located, making data transfer difficult. To complicate matters more, the local investigator was not an employee of the sponsoring organization and so did not have dedicated space at the office. The result of all of this was confusion regarding data storage, transfer, and security. No data were lost, but the less than ideal conditions created some disorder and delays in getting the transcripts and accompanying information to us.

Quality assurance was also an issue with this study. From previous experience, Bunce was aware of the substantial improvement that early and continuing review of transcripts can make in the quality of data received. However, there was pressure from the sponsoring organization to get results quickly in time to inform their planned intervention. Also, the local team insisted on an abbreviated timeline because of staff schedules (most of them were from other areas of the country and had other jobs and families to return to) and religious holidays. In practical terms, this meant that we did not get a chance to review and comment on any of the transcripts until data collection was already complete. Problems that would have been caught and corrected earlier, including confusion regarding the intent of questions and a lack of in-depth probing on the part of the interviewers, instead persisted throughout all of the interviews and focus group discussions.

In retrospect, many of these problems could have been avoided if we had stood firm on certain key points, such as insisting on a longer timeline. This would have allowed us to catch and correct errors in data collection and transcription early on in the process. In response we could have provided feedback to the data collectors that would have significantly improved interview content. After all, data of good quality are the most important outcome of any research study.

Conclusion

Laying the groundwork for putting the research team together and preparing them for the research activities are essential for successful multisite team-based projects. The project manager and team's ability to anticipate potential areas of concern and to create procedures to deal with these issues is a key strategy for working toward a successful study.

The logistics planning for this begins with establishing relationships with people at the research site through a site visit. Logistics planning also involves hiring the research team, assessing their backgrounds and training needs, creating a tailored training workshop on site, and working with the team to define distribution of responsibilities. Comprehensive staff training will ensure not only that the team has the necessary skills to complete the research, but also that they feel involved and committed to the study. Development of systematic, feasible procedures for data management is also important.

Emphasizing a spirit of collaboration from the very beginning, and providing for multiple avenues of communication between team members and between the field team and researchers at the sponsoring agency, will set the stage for a smooth research process and provide support in case of problems. While nothing will entirely prevent the difficulties that inevitably arise in international team-based research, logistics planning for the four priorities will prepare a solid team base.

Note

1. A CAB is a group of influential people selected to represent the community at multiple levels. Their purpose is to act as advisors, as opposed to decision makers, during the research process (Ulin et al. 2005).

References

Fernald, D., and C. Duclos
2005   Enhance your team-based qualitative research. *Annals of Family Medicine* 3(4):360–364.

Garland, D., M. K. O'Connor, T. Wolfer, and F. E. Netting
2006   Team-based research notes from the field. *Qualitative Social Work* 5(1):93–109.

Mack, N., C. Woodsong, K. MacQueen, G. Guest, and E. Brelsford
2005   *Qualitative Research Methods: A Data Collector's Field Guide*. Research Triangle Park, N.C.: Family Health International.

Rhoades, R.
1986   Using anthropology in improving food production: Problems and prospects. *Agricultural Administration* 22:57–78.
2006   Seeking half our brains: Constraints and incentives in the social context of interdisciplinary research. In M. Cernea and A. Kassam, eds. *Researching the Culture in Agri-Culture: Social Research for International Agricultural Development*. Pp. 403–420. Cambridge, MA: CAB International.

Rhoades, R., D. Horton, and R. Booth
1986   Anthropologist, biological scientist and economist: The three musketeers or three stooges of farming systems research? In J. Johnes and B. Wallace, eds. *Applying Science in Farming Systems Research*. Pp. 21–40. Boulder, Colo.: Westview.

Ulin, P., E. Robinson, and E. Tolley
2005   *Qualitative Methods in Public Health: A Field Guide of Applied Research*. San Francisco: Jossey-Bass.

DATA PREPARATION
AND ANALYSIS

II

the dead speakers
we can hear
but the dead listeners
can not be retrieved

ANSELM HOLLO, *IN THE LIBRARY OF POETS' RECORDINGS*

5

Transcribing Data for Team-based Research

ELEANOR MCLELLAN-LEMAL

RESEARCHERS FREQUENTLY INVEST A GREAT DEAL OF TIME figuring out how qualitative data are to be collected and analyzed, but less on the procedures for preparing, transforming, and managing it. Take for example a case of six investigators, geographically dispersed across different cities, collaborating on a qualitative study that requires each to conduct forty individual interviews and twelve focus groups. They make no effort to minimize any potential variability in how text is transcribed from the audiotape or digitally recorded data. Some investigators opt to transcribe verbatim, some decide to paraphrase and summarize responses, while others transcribe only those speech passages they think are relevant to the interview guide questions. Different steps are also taken to prepare transcripts: one investigator hires a professional medical and legal transcription service, two opt to commission the work to several university students, two prepare the transcripts themselves, and one assigns the task to a clerical staff person. While all use the same word processing software to prepare the transcripts, formatting varies greatly between sites (and within sites, in some cases). Some use participant names to identify who is speaking, some assign ID numbers, and some create a new paragraph (insert a hard return) whenever there is a change in speaker but do not include any identifiers.

Three hundred twelve transcripts later, the team faces the challenge of using a team-based approach to analyze hundreds of pages of textual data using a qualitative data analysis (QDA) software program. The software program has not yet been selected. Four of the six investigators have computer-assisted QDA software experience that ranges from taking part in a two-day training workshop to year-long data collection; however, none are familiar with the same software program. Some of the QDA programs have strict file requirements, including file types accepted (plain text, rich text, etc.) and formatting of document header, margins, and font size, while others are more flexible. Although fictional, this account is hardly uncommon. Data preparation, transcription in particular, requires careful planning so that it supports data analysis and interpretation.

Transcripts generally refer to text records prepared from audio or video recordings. However, written materials, such as diaries, observation records, field notes, meeting minutes, conference proceedings, historical documents, or letters and other types of correspondence that are transformed into typed-out records can also be classified as transcripts. Currently, the transformation to a text record is done via an electronically prepared document using a word processor, HTML (Hyper Text Markup Language), or XTML (Extensible Hypertext Markup Language).

Newcomers to qualitative research frequently make the mistake of characterizing transcription as a technical, mundane clerical task (Bucholtz 2000, Lapadat and Lindsay 1999, Mishler 1991, Powers 2005, Roberts 2003). They fail to consider how transcription may influence their ability to analyze and interpret the textual data. Academic discipline, methodology, theoretical orientation, qualitative data analysis software, researcher experience, timelines, and resources all ultimately influence transcription decisions and preferences (Bloom 1993, Lapadat and Lindsay 1999, Mishler 1991). If transcripts are incongruent with the theoretical and interpretative positions of the researchers, they may hinder the researchers' ability to extrapolate or assign meaning to the textual data. Moreover, if transcripts contain too many details about speech patterns, nonverbal communication, or background noise, text can become difficult to read, making interpretation problematic (Ochs 1979).

Fitting the question of how transcripts need to be prepared into the context of team-based research introduces additional challenges. As the opening account demonstrates, coordination is imperative and can be accomplished only if specific procedures and guidelines are laid out in advance. If you have no prior experience in team-based qualitative research or in developing and implementing transcription protocols, you may be asking yourself, "What could be so hard about producing a transcript?" "Don't you just type what you hear?" You could certainly just go about this task without further thought, but then what happens when you end up with transcripts that vary greatly in terms of content, format, and file type? What happens if the transcript does not match what was said in an interview or focus group discussion?

The goal of this chapter is to examine the role that transcription plays in data collection and to offer practical guidance on preparing transcripts that meet your theoretical and analytical needs. The linguistic and computer science literatures provide excellent information regarding conventions for converting voice to text. Because teams undertaking qualitative research are often multidisciplinary and may not include linguists or computer scientists, transcription needs to be presented from a consumer perspective.

Some researchers prefer to use audio, video, and handwritten data in their original or "raw" form/medium and forgo transcription entirely. This approach is seldom feasible or practical for researchers working in a team, especially if the team is geographically dispersed or a large amount of data has been collected. When the group is geographically dispersed, analysis is likely to be handled via conference calls or e-mail, or by post. There are three challenges with trying to listen jointly to audio recordings during a conference call. First, the audio recording will come from a separate electronic device; hence, sound quality is likely to be poor. Focus group recordings, in which people are simultaneously talking or carrying on side conversations, may create audio confusion even when sound quality is good. Second, to solely listen for extended periods of time is difficult for most of us. Personal observation and experience suggest that multitasking is very common during conference calls. Even note-taking activities can cause you to miss information or mishear something stated. Lastly, stopping and starting the recordings can inhibit the team's ability to take into account a complete description or response. Moreover, if the team needs to discuss what something may mean, there is the danger that "preanalytic closure" may result (Miles and Huberman 1994). Preanalytic closure can lead to over- or underinterpretation as well as misinterpretation of information or taking it out of context.

Handwritten data need to be photocopied or scanned to be shared with team members. If the handwritten data are not properly labeled or numbered, team members may find it difficult to work efficiently with the data. Moreover, legibility may also be a factor. Only the person authoring the document may be able to read and navigate through it. In addition, the document may be crafted such that it is difficult to discern if what was observed represents emic (insider) or etic (detached/scientific observer—outsider) descriptions.[1] The amount of data that need to be reviewed can encumber either of these approaches. To consistently analyze and interpret a large volume of data, a coherent system for presenting and organizing information is needed. Where multiple researchers are involved, it is essential to apply the same rules for preparing a transcript. Standardized transcripts assist researchers in focusing on analysis instead of forcing them to spend time deciphering an idiosyncratically prepared collection of transcripts. Moreover, the approach for standardizing transcripts is informed by the theoretical and analytical approaches selected to guide the research questions and data collection methods.

Regardless of the data source and the technology applied pre– and post–data collection, if the intent is to create a textual record for qualitative data analysis, researchers undertaking team-based projects need to consider how to best bridge conceptual elements with the practicalities of producing transcripts appropriate for their analytical needs. Since most team-based qualitative projects involve individual and focus group interviews, the emphasis of this chapter will be on the preparation of transcripts generated from audio recordings. Attention will not be given to the technology or tools used to collect the data. In addition, comparisons will not be undertaken on the differences between analog and digital audio recordings or audio and video data collection. Film production and photography have long traditions in ethnographic research. Some qualitative research, in particular marketing-oriented and observational research, relies heavily on videotaping. Visual methods, however, are still fairly novel in team-based research.[2] Concerns about the anonymity of respondents, added cost, and the possibility that the camera can influence respondent behavior are a few of the reasons that this data collection technique has been used infrequently.

Approaches to Transcription

Transcription in qualitative research must take into account what is transcribed—the interpretative process—as well as how it is transcribed—the representational process (Bucholtz 2000, Green 1997). A transcript can be prepared verbatim (i.e., recorded word-for-word, exactly as said), partially verbatim, summarized, or translated from one language to another. Moreover, it can undergo an editing process, whereby a complete or partial verbatim transcript is stripped of repetitions and filler words (e.g., huh, mhm, uh huh, ah) and transformed into a smooth, easy-to-read record. Transcripts may include phonetic, phonemic, prosodic/intonation, paralinguistic utterances, nonverbal utterances, noises that occur while data collection is taking place, pauses, repetitions, speech overlaps, and other descriptive or analytical annotations, such as time, speaker identification, or cross references (Bird and Liberman 1999, Mergenthaler and Stinson 1992). Edwards (2003) indicates that from a minimalist perspective there are five distinct potential categories of labeling events within a transcript:

1. Words (standard word forms available in the dictionary, truncated words, numbers, decimals, and percentages, pronounceable acronyms, spoken letters, etc.)
2. Utterances
3. Vocalizations that are not words (laughs, coughs, sighs, etc.)
4. Nonvocalized sounds (paper rattling, pencil tapping, doors slamming, telephones ringing, etc.)
5. Silence (absence of any of the four other types of events for brief or extended periods of time)

Decisions about how to handle these five labeling events will be important in developing transcription guidelines for your team.

The qualitative transcript is typically characterized as serving an orthographic or linguistic approach. At one extreme, orthography focuses on written or symbolic representation of language or the sounds of language, such as spelling (e.g., there, their, or they're). At the other extreme, linguistic approaches focus on the phonemic and phonetic aspects of a language (e.g., gonna vs. going to). Bucholtz (2000) refers to these two extremes as *naturalized* and *denaturalized* transcription styles.[3]

Naturalized Transcription

Naturalized transcription captures as much detail as possible for every utterance and favors written discourse conventions. It attempts to provide an account of the "real world" (Oliver et al. 2005) with verbatim depiction of speech as its aim (Schegloff 1997). Naturalized transcription is generally associated with conversation analysis (CA), discourse analysis (DA), and discursive psychology (DP) and supports language as *talk of social action* (Bucholtz 2000). Hence, naturalized transcription relies on the use of linguistic shorthand/symbolic notations. The Jefferson Transcription System and the International Phonetic Alphabet are often used in conversation analysis to help "reveal the sequential features of talk" (ten Have 1997). Table 5.1 displays the notations used in the Jefferson Transcription System.

Denaturalized Transcription

A denaturalized approach focuses on the distinctive features of oral language. It too attempts to produce a verbatim transcript. However, instead of noting accents, vocalizations that are not words, or nonvocalizations, attention is

Table 5.1.   Jefferson Transcript Notation

Symbol	Name	Use
[text]	Brackets	Indicates the start and end points of overlapping speech
=	Equal sign	Indicates the break and subsequent continuation of a single utterance
(# of seconds)	Timed pause	A number in parenthesis indicates the time, in seconds, of a pause in speech
(.)	Micropause	A brief pause, usually less than 0.2 seconds
. or ↓	Period or down arrow	Indicates falling pitch or intonation
? or ↑	Question mark or up arrow	Indicates rising pitch or intonation
,	Comma	Indicates a temporary rise or fall in intonation
-	Hyphen	Indicates an abrupt halt or interruption in utterance
>text<	Greater-than/less-than symbols	Indicates that the enclosed speech was delivered more rapidly than usual for the speaker
<text>	Less-than/greater-than symbols	Indicates that the enclosed speech was delivered more slowly than usual for the speaker
°	Degree symbol	Indicates whisper, reduced volume, or quiet speech
ALL CAPS	Capitalized text	Indicates shouted or increased volume in speech
text	Underlined speech	Indicates that the speaker is emphasizing or stressing the speech
:::	Colon or colons	Indicates prolongation of sound
(hhh)	hhh in parentheses	Audible exhalation
· or (.hhh)	High dot	Audible inhalation
(text)	Parenthesis	Speech that is unclear or in doubt in the transcript
((text))	Double parentheses with text italicized	Annotation of nonverbal activity

Source: Jefferson 1984:ix–xvi.

given to accurately depicting the meanings and perceptions created or articulated during the data collection (Cameron 2001, Oliver et al. 2005). A denaturalized approach is typically used in ethnography, grounded theory, and critical discourse analysis. Bucholtz (2000) cautions that the denaturalized transcript must be attentive to possible social and political stereotyping that can occur if the interviewee's speech is presented in a particular manner.

Practical Considerations and Technological Dimensions

Regardless whether a naturalized or denaturalized approach will be used, it is necessary to recognize that when we talk about producing a verbatim transcript, the audio recording tools that are used gives us incomplete accounts of the interaction (Green et al. 1997, Kvale 1996, McLellan et al. 2003,

Mishler 1986, Poland and Pederson 1998). The "emotional context, non-verbal communication, and the 'messiness'" of natural conversation are impossible to capture in an audio recording (Poland 1995). Even the highest-quality audio recording equipment will not fully account for all verbal communication during a one-on-one interview. Focus groups create additional challenges. People talk at the same time, they interrupt one another, they shake their heads to indicate yes or no, they talk too fast, they speak too softly, they mumble, they stammer, they do not articulate complete thoughts, their accents influence how they pronounce words, they trail off at the end or whisper, and so on.

While technology, such as voice recognition software and digital recording,[4] may help alleviate some of the burdens of transcription, researchers must still play a substantial role in finalizing the transcript. Researchers may then need to incorporate information about nonverbal communication or speech patterns that are contained in handwritten notes or head notes[5] into transcripts. Qualitative interviews are often conducted in settings where acoustics are less than optimal and background noises often compete with verbal and nonverbal utterances. Hence, digitally produced audio are not pristine recordings that permit the transcriptionist to produce a written document that is free of inaudible notations or word errors.

Who Transcribes?

Atkinson and Heritage (1984) encourage us to view transcripts as "research activities." Does this then mean that only researchers involved in collecting or analyzing qualitative data should perform transcription? The answer depends on theory, analytical procedures, values and political views, how the data were collected, the sensitivity of the data, the audience, and required transcription style (Lapadat and Lindsay 1999, Roberts 2003). Budgets and timelines may also be considerations. Thus, in addition to considering what and how to transcribe, careful thought needs to be given to who will perform the transcription. What is included or excluded from a transcript is seldom determined entirely by the quality of the original data source/medium. As demonstrated by Tilley (2003), a transcriptionist may make spur-of-the-moment decisions (that probably go undocumented) that may influence format, content, and analysis. For example, in transcribing audiotaped interviews, the transcriptionist may encounter speech overlaps (e.g., persons simultaneously talking), problems in identifying speakers or differentiating between speakers, difficulty deciphering a speaker's comment, or uncertainty about where to insert punctuation. The transcriptionist may develop personal strategies to address these challenges, especially if no transcription protocol is present or if the one provided is vague. A transcript may then end up heavily peppered with "inaudible" inserts and incorrect speaker assignment that can limit text interpretation as well as the ability to accurately determine convergent and divergent experiences or points of view. Moreover, if the transcriptionist relies on what he thinks was said (e.g., uses his own logic/knowledge base or relies on prior comments and explanations to fill in the blanks), misinterpretation or overinterpretation is likely to occur.

Transcribing your own data is an incredibly valuable experience provided that you have both the time and adequate skills. If you have never transcribed, the task is bound to be challenging and labor-intensive. The mechanics seem fairly straightforward. Set up the equipment, press on a foot pedal to play, rewind, or fast-forward, and begin typing. More than likely you will listen to the recording for a few seconds, type a few words, rewind, listen again, and possibly type out a sentence or two. You may find that listening to and accurately typing out text at a consistent pace usually requires several passes, and that transcribing requires three to four times more time than it took to collect the data. If unfamiliar symbols and notation are required, you may spend a couple more hours editing the transcript. As your transcription proficiency increases, you ultimately reach a point where you can shift your focus from the mechanics of preparing a transcript to the conceptual advantages, especially familiarity with the text and preliminary identification of recurrent concepts. An added bonus of transcribing your own interviews is that it gives you the opportunity to assess strengths and weaknesses in your interviewing skills as well as determine how well the interview guide worked.

Taking time to transcribe during data collection, however, means that data collection is likely to occur at a slower pace. If an interviewer conducts an hour-long interview and then takes the next three hours to transcribe it, it is unlikely that there is enough time or energy to conduct a second interview the same day. For one person to recruit, travel to, prepare for, conduct and transcribe thirty interviews on an eight-hour workday schedule, a minimum of three time-intensive months would be required to collect and prepare the data for analysis. If transcription was delayed until data collection was completed, it is highly likely that data collection could be finished within a thirty-day period. The transcript preparation and verification process, however, would take an additional three to six months. On the other hand, a team composed of two interviewers and two transcriptionists could easily conduct the thirty interviews and complete transcription for analysis within forty-five to sixty days.

If you are not prepared to do your own transcription, the next logical step is to identify what will be required to assign this task to someone else. Transcription guidelines, appropriate background and training of transcriptionists, confidentiality protections, plus strategies for verifying the accuracy of transcripts may come to mind. Conventions need to be established to guide the transcriptionist on how to handle "prosodic and paralinguistic features such as intonation, quality, rhythm and so on, other non-verbal phenomena such as coughs and sighs, turn taking and other features of context which are relevant" (Roberts 2003). In team-based research these decisions should be based on how notation will enhance an understanding of specific comments or concepts introduced by a speaker. The more the transcript needs to look and read like naturalized text, the more need there may be to have a researcher undertake the transcription, because knowledge of linguistic notation may be required.

The person or persons undertaking transcription must receive detailed training to ensure that they understand both the structure and layout of the transcript as well as the rules for recording the conversation. Minimally, transcriptionists should receive instructions regarding inclusion or exclusion of the five types of labeling events previously presented. Once prepared, transcripts should be inspected to ensure that they are consistent with the transcription conventions. If they meet these criteria, they should be reviewed against the original recordings for accuracy. Both of these features are discussed in more detail.

Formatting Considerations

In general, transcription guidelines should be designed to optimize a systematic but flexible means of organizing and subsequently analyzing textual data. Standardized transcripts make it easier to verify that content is correct and to perform a basic assessment of comparability, complexity, and volume of data (McLellan et al. 2003). My first data reduction step typically involves examining the text to determine if all interview guide items were covered in all the interviews by the various interviewers on the team (chapter 7 in this volume addresses data reduction techniques for large qualitative data sets). To facilitate such an assessment, each transcript includes unique labels that identify each speaker (i.e., a source ID). Figure 5.1 provides an example of a transcript containing unique speaker labels for each speaker. Because I also want to check the interviewing style (e.g., asks leading questions, fails to probe, presents open-ended questions as close-ended ones, or delivers an analytical summary for every comment made by the respondent) of each interviewer to gauge if and

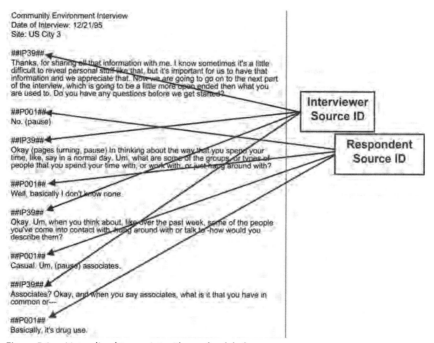

Figure 5.1.   Naturalized transcript with speaker labels.

how it influences what is or is not said by a respondent, more than a generic label of INTERVIEWER is required. The transcripts can be coded by the interview guide question to complete this assessment; however, my preference is to create a macro in Word for each interviewer source ID. A macro is a programming command used to automate a task or set of tasks. If a transcript contains all the correct labeling, a macro saves a great deal of time and avoids errors that result from cutting text manually. A macro can then be created to automatically remove all respondent-related text from a transcript and create a new file. Figure 5.2 displays a text file containing only the interviewer's text. Intra- and inter-interviewer performance can readily be assessed, including the possible influence of interviewer-generated probes or lack of them.

The presence of multiple interviewers in team-based research as well as the possibility that the person analyzing the data was neither involved in data collection nor transcription require a careful balance between rigor and flexibility. Flexibility is important because it allows you to include supplemental information that is necessary to accurately interpret specific text. For some researchers, this would mean adding contextual information (e.g., type and frequency of interruptions, beliefs and practices regarding

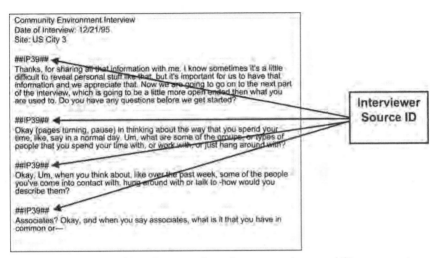

Figure 5.2.   Extraction of interviewer text for performance and comparability assessments.

personal space, mixed-gender interaction, and historical context), vernacular translation, or linguistic emphasis that may not necessarily be included in the verbal exchange that appears in the transcript.

In team-based research, ongoing discussions on how to handle special information need to occur and, where necessary, transcription guidelines modified so that all transcriptionists present such information in a similar manner. Regular meetings can help in this regard, particularly early on in the transcription process. If team members are geographically dispersed, frequent monitoring (both remote and in situ) can improve reliability and consistency immensely (see chapter 9). Agreeing on emergent conventions and tackling the issue of consistency up front can save a lot of time and resources later on. Trying to compare transcripts prepared with different understandings of how the raw data should be represented can present significant challenges; ensuring consistent interpretation of transcription guidelines addresses this problem. Preparing a transcription protocol or format is the first step in this process.

A universal transcription format that would be appropriate for all types of qualitative data collection approaches, settings, or theoretical frameworks does not exist. However, there are transcription conventions that do lend themselves to replication, especially for team-based research. Such conventions include, but are not limited to, instructions on

1. How to organize and physically lay out a page, including line spacing, line numbering, use of columns, margin widths, and so on.

2. What demographic or other personal data about the persons interviewed that may be relevant to the analysis (e.g., age, ethnic background, culture, sex, gender) to include in a header or face sheet. *Note that some qualitative data analysis software programs require that this be set up in a specific manner.*

3. How pronunciation should be handled, including if nonstandard, colloquial spelling or "eye dialect" (i.e., looks like it sounds) is appropriate.

4. What paralinguistic and nonverbal information should be included, as well as the symbols or marks that will represent such information.

5. How basic units (utterances, turns, tone units, etc.) of a transcript will be identified.

6. How to note verbal stresses, overlapping talk, and pauses.

7. How to assign unique symbols (i.e., only represents one category of information) and other notations, and how to verify that they are applied consistently.

8. Which accent marks (diacritics) are familiar and easy to use.

9. Whether speaker identification tags are to be used and how such tags will be created, if appropriate.

10. What the procedures are for annotating technical notes about the type of recording equipment used, the quality of the audio recording, background noise, length of time of interview, time lapses for pauses, and any disruptions in recording, such tape changes, end of interview, or turning off of the recording equipment during the interview.

11. How confidential and sensitive information should be handled.

12. What the procedures are for verifying accuracy of transcripts against audio recordings as well as steps for storing or disposing of audio recordings after transcript verification has been completed.

In preparing transcripts, it is also important to keep in mind that even the most proficient transcriptionist misses a word or two or transcribes some phrases slightly different from what was actually said (Weiss 1994). Therefore, it is necessary to proofread all or a random selection of transcripts. Ideally, the interviewer conducting an interview should proofread its corresponding transcript. This entails reading through the transcript while listening to the audio recording. If it is not feasible to have interviewers proofread the transcripts, someone other than the person who transcribed it should complete this task. To make sure that the person selected to transcribe the interviews is the right person for the job, proof-reading should happen as soon as an initial transcript from one interview is produced. I once worked on a rapid qualitative assessment project in which three to five interviews were being collected daily by each of the six interviewers on the team. Because there was no way the interviewers could undertake transcription while data were being collected, a transcriptionist was hired. This person was amazingly fast and could easily produce five to six transcripts during an eight-hour period. Unfortunately, her listening skills were not equal to her typing skills. When the interviewers selected transcripts to proofread, they found that the error rate was alarmingly high. What she was hearing did not correspond to most of what the interviewees and the interviewers were saying.

If only a subset of the transcripts is to be proofread, it is similarly important that the first two or three transcripts prepared by a transcriptionist undergo careful review. Otherwise, problems may go unnoticed until analysis is well underway, at which point it may be difficult and time consuming to correct transcription errors. Unless a formatting problem is present, there may be no obvious indication that a transcript does not accurately reflect what was actually said in an interview. Therefore, this is an important reason to always check the transcript against the audiotape. If a researcher decides on proofreading a selection of transcripts, it is important that the tapes be retained for reference. The disposal or destruction of audio recordings should take into account proofreading time. If the maximum life of an audio recording is one year, the data management plan should be designed to get transcription and proofreading completed within that time span. Most of the team-based projects I currently am involved with require that audio recordings be submitted for transcription within twenty-four hours of being collected. The transcription service is contracted to provide a transcript within seven business days. Any audio recordings that present a problem must be reported within three business days. This rapid transcription phase, however, is followed by a much slower proofreading period. Interviewers tend to be involved in multiple projects, so proofreading is predominately handled by the data analysts because it provides them an opportunity to hear the data before focusing on them exclusively as written text. The proofreading phase takes six to eight months for a large data set (hundred-plus individual interviews or thirty-plus focus groups). In the event that unanticipated delays in proofreading occur, the life of an audio file should be planned for eighteen months instead of twelve months.

Training of transcriptionists and persons verifying the accuracy of transcripts must be specific to the transcription conventions. All persons handling audio recordings and transcripts should be thoroughly familiar with the specific procedures for preparing a transcript and documenting exceptions (Kelle et al. 1995, MacQueen and Milstein 1999). Measures should also be taken to ensure that the transcription guidelines have been applied consistently across interviews.

Translation

When interview data are collected in a language other than the primary or common language of the research team, translation is usually required. If the researchers are fluent in the data collection language and no technological constraints are present (e.g., software program recognizes the writing system/alphabet used), there is no need for translation provided that analysis is based on the cultural perspectives of the respondents (Barnes 1996). Translation adds a layer of complexity to the transcript preparation process because it inevitably involves some interpretation. It is unlikely that word-for-word translations are appropriate; hence, meaning-based translations must be undertaken, especially given that "not all concepts are universal and that not all words or phrases are translatable" (Esposito 2001). The respondent's language is referred to as the source language and the translation product (in this case a transcript) as the target text. Figure 5.3 demonstrates the translation task.

Steps should be taken to ensure that the meaning-based translation is accurate; however, back-translation is not recommended. In addition to the significant amount of time and resources required to undertake such a task, back-translation of qualitative data is more complex. Translating one

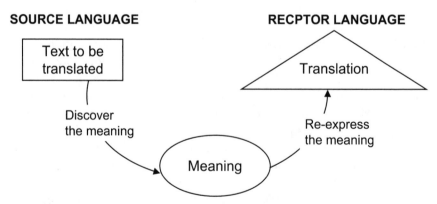

Figure 5.3.   Overview of the translation task (from Larson 1998).

written language into another written language is not comparable to taking a spoken language and transforming it into a different written language, especially if the translation is meaning-based. Moreover, the goal would be to compare the back-translation to the audio recording. If we take into account idiosyncrasies and nuances in the spoken language as well as colloquial expression, it is unlikely that we would find a perfect match between the two. In the end we would have to make a meaning-based comparison of the back-translated transcription to the spoken language and in the process further remove ourselves from the raw data.

Conclusion

The transcript is a representation and interpretation tool that helps qualitative researchers examine interview data orthographically or linguistically. While no single transcript format meets all qualitative data analysis needs, team-based research benefits if attention is given to development of transcription guidelines and procedures for verifying adherence to these guidelines. Transcription is more than a technical, clerical task; it is theoretical. What is transcribed, what is not transcribed, and how the transcript is structured very much influence the analysis process.

Perhaps the most important aspect of transcription, particularly in a team setting, is consistency. Establishing a transcription protocol is critical to this end. That said, qualitative data analysis is typically inductive and the analysis/transcription process needs to be flexible enough to allow team members to regularly share insights and information about the data and the ongoing transcription process.

Finally, a key to a good transcript is making sure that the end result allows the research objectives to be met with as few problems as possible and with the most efficient use of resources. Requiring too much detail can become unnecessarily burdensome. Conversely, not having enough information in a transcript can lead to difficulties when it comes time to interpret the data. Matching the transcription process to the research objectives is, therefore, essential. And, if in doubt, err on the side of including more detail; doing so can save countless hours of retranscribing.

Notes

The findings and conclusions in this chapter are those of the author and do not necessarily represent the views of the Centers for Disease Control and Prevention.

1. The terms *emic* and *etic* were coined by linguistic anthropologist Kenneth Pike in 1954. *Emic* is derived from the linguistic term *phonemic*. Phonemic involves

analysis of how sounds are interpreted and perceived by the speaker. Consequently, Pike defines the emic perspective as focusing on intrinsic cultural distinctions meaningful to a given society (or cultural subgroup). *Etic* is based on the term *phonetic* and involves analysis of how sounds are interpreted. The etic perspective then focuses on extrinsic concepts and categories that have meaning for scientific observers.

2. Transcription of video data is covered in Christian Heath and Jon Hindmarsh, "Analyzing Interaction: Video, Ethnography and Situated Conduct," in *Qualitative Research in Practice*, edited by Tim May (London: Sage, 2002).

3. For a more detailed comparison of naturalized and denaturalized transcription, see Daniel G. Oliver, Julianne M. Serovich, and Tina L. Mason, "Constraints and Opportunities with Interview Transcription: Towards Reflection in Qualitative Research," *Social Forces* 2005; 84(2):1273–1289.

4. For additional information regarding digital recording and transcription, see Lisa M. Givens, "Mini-disc Recorders: A New Approach for Qualitative Interviewing," *International Journal of Qualitative Methods* 2004; 3(2): article 5. Retrieved 15 July 2005 from www.ualberta.ca/~iiqm/backissues/3_2/pdf/given.pdf; David Brown, "Going Digital and Staying Qualitative: Some Alternative Strategies for Digitalizing the Qualitative Research Process," *Forum Qualitative Socialforschung/ Form: Qualitative Social Research* [on-line journal], 2002; 3(2): 29 paragraphs. Retrieved 15 July 2005 from www.qualitative-research.net/fqs-texte/2-02/2-02 brown-e.htm; Alan Stockdale, "An Approach to Recording, Transcribing, and Preparing Audio Data for Qualitative Analysis," Education Development Center 2003 (September). Retrieved 15 July 2005 from caepp.edc.org/QualAudio.pdf; Alan Stockdale, "Tools for Digital Audio Recording in Qualitative Research," *Social Research Update* 2002; 38. Department of Sociology, University of Surrey. Retrieved 14 July 2005 from www.soc.surrey.ac.uk/sru/SRU38.html.

5. For information regarding head notes, see Simon Ottenberg, "Thirty Years of Fieldnotes: Changing Relationships to the Text," In *Fieldnotes. The Makings of Anthropology*, edited by Roger Sanjeck (Ithaca, N.Y.: Cornell University Press, 1990), pp. 139–160.

References

Atkinson, J. M., and J. C. Heritage
1984   *Structures of social action.* Edited by J. M. Atkinson and J. C. Heritage. Cambridge: Cambridge University Press.

Barnes, Donelle M.
1996   An analysis of the grounded theory method and the concept of culture. *Qualitative Health Research* 6(3):429–441.

Bird, Steven, and Mark Liberman
1999   A formal framework for linguistic annotation. MS-CIS-99-01, 1–48. University of Pennsylvania, Linguistic Data Consortium.

Bloom, Lois

1993   Transcription and coding for child language research: The parts are more than the whole. In J. A. Edwards and M. D. Lampert, eds. *Talking Data: Transcription and Coding in Discourse Research.* Hillsdale, N.J.: Erlbaum.

Bucholtz, Mary

2000   The politics of transcription. *Journal of Pragmatics* 32:1439–1465.

Cameron, Deborah

2001   *Working with Spoken Discourse.* Thousand Oaks, Calif.: Sage.

Edwards, Jane

2003   The ICSI meetings corpus: Transcription methods at Hong Kong. Available at mail.cse.ohio-state.edu/pipermail/cse888-r04/2005-June/000011 .html. Accessed August 25, 2006.

Esposito, N.

2001   From meaning to meaning: The influence of translation techniques on non-English focus group research. *Qualitative Health Research* 11(4):568–579.

Green, Judith, Maria Franquiz, and Carol Dixon

1997   The myth of the objective transcript: Transcribing as a situated act. *TESOL Quarterly* 31:172–176.

Jefferson, Gail

1984   Transcript notation. In J. Maxwell Atkinson and John Heritage, eds. *Structures of Social Action: Studies in Conversation Analysis.* Cambridge, UK: Cambridge University Press.

Kelle, U., G. Prein, and K. Bird

1995   *Computer-aided Qualitative Data Analysis.* Thousand Oaks, Calif.: Sage.

Kvale, S.

1996   *Interviews: An Introduction to Qualitative Research Interviewing.* Thousand Oaks, Calif.: Sage.

Lapadat, Judith C., and Anne C. Lindsay

1999   Transcription in research and practice: From standardization of technique to interpretive positionings. *Qualitative Inquiry* 5(1):64–86.

Larson, Mildred L.

1998   *Meaning-based Translation: A Guide to Cross-language Equivalence.* Lanham, MD: University Press of America and Summer Institute of Linguistics.

MacQueen, Kathleen M., and Bobby Milstein

1999   A systems approach to qualitative data management. *Field Methods* 11(1):27–39.

McLellan, Eleanor, Kathleen M. MacQueen, and Judith L. Neidig

2003   Beyond the qualitative interview: Data preparation and transcription. *Field Methods* 15(1):63–84.

Mergenthaler, Erhard, and Charles H. Stinson
1992   Psychotherapy transcription standards. *Psychotherapy Research* 2(2):125–142.

Miles, M. B., and A. M. Huberman
1994   *Qualitative Data Analysis: An Expanded Sourcebook* (2nd ed.). Thousand Oaks, Calif.: Sage.

Mishler, Elliot G.
1986   *Research Interviewing: Context and Narrative*. Cambridge: Harvard University Press.
1991   Representing discourse: The rhetoric of transcription. *Journal of Narrative and Life History* 1:255–280.

Ochs, Ellinor
1979   Transcription as theory. In E. Ochs and B. B. Schieffelin, eds. *Developmental Pragmatics*. New York: Academic.

Oliver, Daniel G., Julianne M. Serovich, and Tina L. Mason
2005   Constraints and opportunities with interview transcription: Towards reflection in qualitative research. *Social Forces* 84(2):1273–1289.

Poland, Blake D.
1995   Transcription quality as an aspect of rigor in qualitative research. *Qualitative Inquiry* 1(3):290–310.

Poland, Blake D., and Ann Pederson
1998   Reading between the lines: Interpreting silences in qualitative research. *Qualitative Inquiry* 4(2):293–312.

Powers, Willow R.
2005   *Transcription Techniques for the Spoken Word*. New York: Altamira.

Roberts, Ceila
2003   Part One: Issues in Transcribing Spoken Discourse.

Schegloff, Emanuel
1997   Whose text? Whose context? *Discourse & Society* 8:165–187.

ten Have, Paul
1997   Methodological issues in conversation analysis. Available at www2.fmg.uva .nl/emca/mica.htm.

Tilley, Susan A.
2003   "Challenging" research practices: Turning a critical lens on the work of transcription. *Qualitative Inquiry* 9(5):750–773.

Weiss, R. S.
1994   *Learning from Strangers: The Art and Method of Qualitative Interview Studies*. New York: The Free Press.

6

Team-based Codebook Development: Structure, Process, and Agreement

KATHLEEN M. MACQUEEN, ELEANOR MCLELLAN-LEMAL,
KELLY BARTHOLOW, AND BOBBY MILSTEIN

O NE OF THE KEY ELEMENTS in qualitative data analysis is the systematic coding of text (Miles and Huberman 1994:56, Strauss and Corbin 1990:57–60). Codes are the building blocks for theory or model building and the foundation on which the analyst's arguments rest. Implicitly or explicitly, they embody the assumptions underlying the analysis. Given the context of team research and the propensity for multiple interpretations of codes among two or more analysts or researchers, it is important to establish an explicit and systematic procedure for codebook development. On the one hand, qualitative researchers must often explain basic methods such as this in clear terms to a wide range of scientists who have little or no experience with qualitative research and who may express a deep skepticism of the validity of the results. On the other, a codebook development strategy for team-based projects must be responsive to the logistics and challenges of developing a codebook by two or more persons who may be located at widely dispersed sites. For large projects, using more than one coder is often the only reasonable way to handle the sheer volume of data generated. For team research, multiple coders provide an important mechanism for assessing the reliability and validity of the coded data through intercoder agreement measures (Carey et al. 1996, Thompson et al. 2004). The standardized structure and dynamic process used in our codebook development strategy reflects these concerns.

Ryan and Bernard (2003:85) identified four tasks associated with text analysis: (1) discovering themes and subthemes, (2) winnowing themes to a manageable few (i.e., deciding which themes are important in any project), (3) building hierarchies of themes or codebooks, and (4) linking themes into theoretical models. While a codebook is obviously an outcome of the third task, its structure and content also reflect decisions related to all of these tasks. Nor are the tasks undertaken in a simple linear fashion; the coding process is iterative. Thus the tasks may not always be clearly distinguished during coding, which can lead to fuzzy coding practices if care is not taken. For example, a theme that emerges from a careful reading of text and a theoretical construct intended to explain how that theme supports or hinders social interaction might be inadvertently combined into a single code definition. Coding for the theme would then be influenced by each coder's on-the-fly interpretation of the validity of the theoretical construct for a particular instance of the theme in the text. Or one coder may focus on the theme while another focuses on the theoretical interpretation. Either approach could result in widely divergent coding of the same text.

This chapter describes (1) how a structured codebook provides a stable frame for the dynamic analysis of textual data, (2) how specific codebook features can improve intercoder agreement among multiple researchers, and (3) the value of team-based codebook development and coding.

Developing a Codebook Format

Our codebook format evolved over the course of several years and a variety of team-based projects. The conceptual origins took shape in 1993 during work on the CDC-funded Prevention of HIV in Women and Infants Demonstration Project (WIDP) (Cabral et al. 2004), which generated approximately six hundred transcribed semistructured interviews. One research question pursued was whether women's narratives about their own heterosexual behavior could help us understand general processes of change in condom-use behavior (Milstein et al. 1998). The research team decided to use the processes of change (POC) constructs from the Transtheoretical Model (DiClemente and Prochaska 1985, Prochaska 1984) as a framework for the text analysis. However, the validity of the POC constructs for condom-use behavior was unknown, and a credible and rigorous text coding strategy was needed to establish their applicability and relevance for this context. To do this, the analysts had to synthesize all that was known about each POC construct, define what it was, what it was not, and, most important, learn how to recognize one in natural language. Several years earlier, O'Connell (1989) had confronted a similar problem while examining POCs in transcripts of psychotherapy sessions. Recognizing that "coding processes of change often requires that the coder infer from the statement and its context what the intention of the speaker was," O'Connell (1989:106) developed a coding manual that included a section for each code titled "Differentiating (Blank) from Other Processes" where "Blank" was the name of the process being explored. Milstein and colleagues used O'Connell's "differentiation" section in a modified format in their analysis of condom behavior-change narratives. They conceptualized the "differentiation" component as "exclusion criteria," which complemented the standard code definitions (which then became known as "inclusion criteria"). To add further clarity to the process of coding POCs, examples from the qualitative data were added to the differentiation criteria.

The final version of the analysis codebook contained five parts: a code name or mnemonic, a brief (one-line) definition, a full definition of inclusion criteria, a full definition of exclusion criteria to explain how the code differed from others, and example passages that illustrated how the code concept might appear in natural language. During the code application phase, information in each of these sections was supplemented and clarified (often with citations and detailed descriptions of earlier work), but the basic structure of the codebook guidelines remained stable.

A similar codebook format was used in an analysis of brief open-ended responses to a question about perceived exposure to HIV, which was included in a standardized survey of 1,950 gay and bisexual men enrolled in the CDC Collaborative HIV Seroincidence Study (MacQueen et al. 1996). For this project we needed a codebook that would facilitate coder recognition of discrete events and specific behaviors as well as the ability to distinguish statements of fact (e.g., a partner who was *known* to be HIV-seropositive) from statements of perception (e.g., a partner who was *thought* to be uninfected). The structured codebook format was subsequently used as a key element in data management and analysis for a number of research studies (e.g., Guest et al. 2005, MacQueen et al. 2001). In addition, our codebook format has been incorporated into software applications for qualitative data management and analysis such as CDC EZ-Text (Carey et al. 1998) and AnSWR (CDC 2004).

Codebook Structure

The codebook structure has evolved to include six basic components: the code, a brief definition, a full definition, guidelines for when to use the code, guidelines for when not to use the code, and examples. Table 6.1 illustrates how the components were operationalized for a code we developed as part of an analysis of emic representations of "community" (MacQueen et al. 2001).

Table 6.1.   Example of a Codebook Entry

Code: MARGIN

Brief Definition: marginalized community members

Full Definition: Community groups that are negatively perceived as socially and/or physically outside the larger community structure. In marginalized groups, boundaries are imposed by others to keep "unfavorable" groups from participating in or interacting with the mainstream community groups

When to Use: Apply this code to all references to groups of individuals that the larger community has marginalized. These individuals or groups may be referred to as outcasts, extremists, and radicals or explicitly described as peripherals, strangers, outsiders, ostracized, bizarre, etc.

When Not to Use: Do not use this code for reference to community groups institutionalized for health or criminal reasons (see INSTIT) or for groups that have voluntarily placed themselves on the outer boundaries of community life (see SELFMAR).

Example: "Then you got the outcast blacks—drug dealers, junkies, prostitutes."

Although the structure is simple and stable, the process of building the codebook is complex and dynamic. While all qualitative data management and analysis software programs include tools for documenting and managing the coding process, many offer little more than a blank text box for typing whatever information strikes the analyst as relevant. On the one hand, this allows great flexibility in how codebooks are developed and maintained. Given the exploratory nature and often unpredictable content of qualitative data, flexibility and openness are needed especially in the early stages of coding—what Ryan and Bernard (2003) describe as the tasks of identifying and winnowing themes and subthemes. On the other hand, there is a point where the analysis must shift to the tasks of representing the thematic structure of the data and linking that observed structure to one or more theoretical models. The transition from empirical observation to interpretation and model building is chock-a-block with subjective pitfalls for all research. How can we demonstrate a link between the volumes of data we collect and the elegant models we develop to represent and explain the patterns and relationships observed in the data? We have found that use of a structured codebook fosters a reflexive approach to documenting the necessary links throughout the coding process. The structured codebook continually prompts us to ask whether, how, and why this chunk of information is similar to or different from other chunks of information in the database. Note that we use structure as a prompt, not a constraint. For example, we generally do not use all five of the components of the structured definition consistently in the early stages of codebook development, particularly when we are exploring the definitional boundaries of themes and subthemes. Nonetheless, the definitional structure serves as a reflexive guide: What evidence in the textual data are we drawing on to identify the expression of a particular theme? Are there criteria we can use to distinguish closely related themes? How is a theme expressed in the vernacular of different populations?

If you are using software for qualitative analysis that lacks easy-to-use options for developing a structured codebook it may be worthwhile to use a spreadsheet or database program as part of data management. There are practical advantages to using a spreadsheet or database for team-based codebook development. First, it facilitates a systematic approach by providing a template that prompts for key components. Second, it facilitates the production of multiple versions of the codebook, for example, a simple listing of the codes with brief definitions for quick reference and a full version with all components for detailed reference and comparison of coding guidelines. Third, it is easy to revise selected components in the codebook and then print only the modified codes and their definitions (rather than the whole codebook). Fourth, use of a date field makes it easy to generate reports that list coding guidelines that were changed after a particular date. Fifth, the codebook can be output in a wide variety of formats including ASCII text files and other database formats. Some of these formats may then be imported directly into qualitative analysis programs. Sixth, the fact that the codebook can be detached from other parts of the analytic database means it can easily be modified, copied, and replaced.

Most qualitative analysis software programs now allow the analyst to define links between sets of codes and add new dimensions to the relationships among codes. For example, hierarchical relationships can be defined such that a single code is linked to a series of related codes. Hierarchical relationships can be used to create families of codes (Muhr 1994) that can be aggregated, reviewed, and analyzed at increasingly general levels. Thus, the scale of analysis can be easily and systematically modified. Alternatively, codes may have multiple, nonhierarchical links to other codes and thus form relationships that are best summarized as a network. Both hierarchical and network linkages can then be portrayed graphically (see Namey et al., this volume).

In our approach, the codebook functions as a frame or boundary that the analyst constructs in order to systematically map the informational terrain of the text. The codebook may or may not reflect "natural" boundaries for the terrain, but it always reflects the implicit or explicit research questions and theoretical constructs. It forces the analysis team to place assumptions and biases in plain view. The codes, in turn, function like coordinates on the map frame; when applied to the text, they link features in the text (e.g., words, sentences, dialog) to the theoretical constructs. The adequacy of answers to research questions can then be assessed in terms of the sensitivity and specificity of the codes, the richness of the text, and the validity and reliability of the links established among them. From this perspective, the central challenge of systematic qualitative analysis lies within the coding process.

The Coding Process

As Bernard (1994:193) points out, a code can be used as an encryption, indexing, or measurement device; we focus on using index codes to tag text for retrieval and measurement codes to assign values to text such as the frequency, amount, or presence/absence of information (Bernard 1994, Bernard and Ryan 1998, Seidel and Kelle 1995). In both cases, the code adds information to the text (rather than reducing the text) through a process of interpretation that simultaneously breaks the text down into meaningful chunks or segments. Thus, the coding process must include explicit guidelines for defining the boundaries of the text associated with a particular code. How the text is segmented is influenced by the data collection strategy and the way that strategy structures the resulting text. Data collection strategies generally fall along a continuum from minimally structured (e.g., transcribed interviews) to maximally structured (e.g., brief responses to open-ended survey questions).

With large databases composed of transcribed structured or semistructured interviews and focus groups we find it useful to begin by coding text according to the specific research questions used to frame the interview; we label this type of index coding as Stage 1 or *structural coding*. The purpose of this step is to make subsequent analysis easier by identifying all of the text associated with a particular question and associated probes. The code inclusion criteria can include linguistic cues that signal the coder to apply structural codes to text that is out of sequence with the original interview structure. This is important for situations where respondents spontaneously return to earlier topics or make a cognitive leap to a topic that the interviewer intended to cover later. With regard to segmenting the text for structural coding, we find it useful to include within each segment the full elicitation from the interviewer and the full response from the participant, including all dialog between the interviewer and participant that flows from the elicitation. This preserves both the flow of the interview and the full context of the discussion on a particular topic. Structural coding can be straightforward when interviews or focus groups follow a highly structured format. Or it can be complex and highly dependent on linguistic cues if the topics are covered in a more free-flowing dialog. Structural coding generally results in the identification of large segments of text on broad topics; these segments can then form the basis for an in-depth analysis within or across topics.

We have found that code definitions that incorporate substantial references to professional jargon tend to encourage the use of coders' preconceptions in the analysis, making it difficult to distinguish the text (or "voice") of the respondent from that of the analyst or researcher. In contrast to structural coding, we therefore attempt to use respondents' own terms and semantics to guide the construction of codes and their definitions for in-depth analysis. In addition, the use of linguistic cues to assist coders in correctly applying codes to text tends to reduce the potential for misinterpretation and omission of relevant information.

For example, in one of our projects we created three socioeconomic-class status codes (poor, middle class, and rich) to measure the salience of socioeconomic class for the way individuals perceived the structure of their community. However, these codes did not capture the more subjective viewpoint of the participants, who often described the financial status of others relative to their own, for example, richer, poorer, "those with more money." The research-driven codes and definitions also led the coders to make implicit assumptions about education, employment, access to resources, and basic living conditions that were not always supported in the text. We therefore eliminated the original research-driven codes with their implicit assumptions about social conditions and used a single code to capture all references to income levels and socioeconomic class, with additional codes to capture explicit references to homelessness and employment status.

Text segmentation during in-depth analysis is less straightforward than during structural coding. A coded segment could be as simple as a text marker or tag placed over a word or phrase, with the boundaries of the segment free-floating; in this case the segment can be continuously redefined during analysis to include only the word, a set number of lines above and below the word, or the full text document. Alternatively, rules for bounding segments can be established a priori, for example, through use of textual units such as sentences or grammatical guidelines such as requiring the inclusion of subject references. Since qualitative analysis software programs differ with regard to the amount of flexibility allowed for defining segments, the research team needs to consider this issue early. Segmentation and software choice also have implications for the way text is transcribed for analysis (see the chapter on transcription by McLellan-Lemal for further discussion of this issue).

With brief responses to open-ended questions on standardized surveys, there is generally little need to develop structural codes because the data are prestructured by question and participant. Here the goal is to code the text in such a way that the information can be combined meaningfully with a quantitative database. The codes are used primarily to signal the presence or absence of particular pieces of information. The open-ended responses can then be summarized in a 0/1 matrix where the rows are labeled with participant identification numbers and the columns with the codes; the cells are filled with either a 0 (to indicate that the information was not present) or a 1 (to indicate that it was present). For example, table 6.2 presents a matrix for a hypothetical group of responses to a question concerning how persons think they may have been exposed to HIV. It would also be possible to attach values to the codes, for example, the MULTPARTS code could be valued to reflect the total number of partners that a person reported (provided that information is available from the data).

To facilitate quantitative analysis of open-ended responses, it is generally advisable to limit the total number of codes to be used. However, this can easily be done by collapsing code categories together through data transformations performed on the matrix. The final code categories can be built into the coding process through the use of hierarchical codes and code families. Such a strategy is preferable to limiting the content of the

Table 6.2.   Examples of Coded Responses from a Structured Survey Question, "How Do You Think You Were Exposed to HIV?"

ID	Response	Codes				
		ANON	MULTPARTS	ANAL	EJAC	PERCEV+
101	"Had anal sex with a guy I think was infected and he ejaculated."	0	0	1	1	1
102	"Had a lot of partners; some of them I don't know. I'm worried about HIV in ejaculate."	1	1	0	1	0
103	"Been exposed to ejaculate from two or three different partners."	0	1	0	1	0

ANON = Exposure from anonymous partner(s)/contact(s)
MULTPARTS = The number of partners is stated as greater than one
ANAL = Anal sex that is unspecified as insertive or receptive
EJAC = Ejaculation occurred, participant reports exposure to ejaculate
PERCEV+ = Respondent perceives or suspects that partner(s)' HIV status is HIV+

codebook a priori only to find that the resulting codes are too crude to permit a meaningful analysis.

Between the two sets of examples discussed above (transcribed interviews and open-ended survey questions) lie a range of other possibilities. For example, rather than record and transcribe interviews verbatim, researchers may take notes and then organize their notes according to specific research topics. Although the elicitation is relatively unstructured, the resulting text is highly structured and pre-segmented by research topic. Another possibility would be the collection of open-ended responses on a single question across multiple waves of structured interviews with the same individuals. The responses from each wave could be compiled into a single textual response for each individual that permits segmentation by recurrent themes as well as by interview wave. The analysis of other types of text such as field notes, diaries, and newsletters each present their own challenges and possibilities. The issues of data collection and text segmentation as elements in the coding process are complicated and deserve further systematic exploration.

Refining the Codebook

Before coding an entire data set, we systematically evaluate the utility of the codes and the coders' ability to apply the codes in a consistent manner. The steps in this process begin with the development of an initial code list derived from etic concepts, emic themes, or both (figure 6.1). Usually, one or two team members take a lead role in developing the list, which is then reviewed by all members of the research team (figure 6.1), who have also reviewed the raw data. Once there is agreement on the scope and level of detail for the items in the list, the team leaders begin the process of codebook development. Definitions are proposed and reviewed by the team, with an emphasis on achieving clarity and explicit guidance for code application.

When the team is comfortable with the code definitions, two or more coders are given the task of independently coding the same sample of text. The results of their coding are then compared for consistency of text segmentation and code application. If the results are acceptable and consistent, the coding continues with periodic checks for continued intercoder agreement. If the results are unacceptable and inconsistent, the inconsistencies are reviewed by the coders and team leader(s). The codebook is reviewed to determine whether the inconsistencies are due to coder error, for example, misunderstanding of terminology or guidelines. We view these as

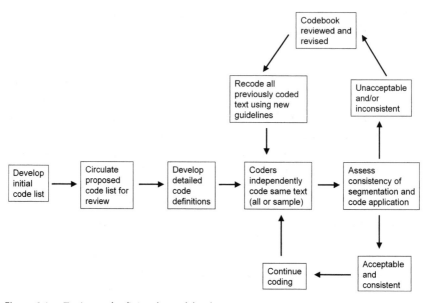

Figure 6.1.   Testing and refining the codebook.

training errors and they are generally handled by the coders and team leader(s). Other inconsistencies are due to problems with the code definitions, for example, overlapping or ambiguous inclusion criteria that make it difficult to distinguish between two codes. These types of problems are generally discussed by the whole team, as they have implications for the interpretation of the text. Once the problems are identified and the codebook clarified, all previously coded text is reviewed and, if necessary, recoded so that it is consistent with the revised definitions. Intercoder agreement is again checked, to ensure that the new guidelines have resolved the problem. This iterative coding process continues until all text has been satisfactorily coded.

There are a variety of ways that intercoder agreement can be assessed; a comprehensive discussion of intercoder agreement and reliability can be found in Carey and Gelaude's chapter in this volume. For transcribed interviews, we generally prefer a detailed segment-by-segment review that includes assessments of consistency in defining the beginning and end of segments as well as the application of codes within segments. All inconsistencies are noted, discussed, and resolved. When only a subsample of the text is coded by multiple coders, this strategy may not capture all coding errors. In particular, it is prone toward the loss of pertinent text, that is, text that is not captured by any code. Erroneously captured text, in contrast, is more likely to be spotted during the course of either coding checks or subsequent analysis. As noted previously, we also use kappa to statistically assess the level of intercoder agreement. This approach is useful for identifying coder error, as long as the error is not due to systematic mistraining of all coders. It is also helpful for identifying poorly defined codes, which tend to be applied erratically.

A more common measure, and one that is easy to use by teams with all levels of expertise during early codebook development, is percent agreement. This technique simply measures the percentage of text segments or units that are coded the same way by pairs of analysts. If agreement is poor, for example, below 85 percent, the team should examine the coding and identify problematic areas. The codebook may need to be renegotiated and revised, or a particular analyst might need to develop a better understanding of the existing codes. The following exercise provides details of such a process.

Percent–Agreement Exercise

Once the team has developed an initial set of codes, intercoder checks can be conducted by having all team members code the same text without consulting each other. Their codes can then be compared to assess agreement on the codes assigned to the text. This does not require any special software. In fact, if there are team members with limited or no experience doing qualitative analysis, or if you are analyzing text in the field with limited access to computers, a paper-and-pencil approach can be very effective as a training tool. The percent-agreement exercise outlined here was developed as part of training for international research projects with teams that had a range of qualitative analysis experience. It has proven useful for demonstrating the need for clearly defined codes and for illustrating the idiosyncratic ways that analysts may interpret poorly defined codes.

As noted previously, the way that text is segmented for in-depth analysis is subjective and it is therefore to be expected that some coders will tend to segment larger pieces of text than other coders. This "lumping" and "splitting" is not generally a cause for concern, as long as the same essential information is coded similarly. For example, if one coder included an entire paragraph and another coded only one sentence in that paragraph using the same code, this is likely to be acceptable agreement. However, if the coders coded the paragraph segment and the embedded sentence segment differently, there is no agreement.

The first step in conducting this intercoder agreement exercise is to decide which coded text will serve as the master for intercoder checks. The text taken to be the master may be the one coded by the project leader, the lead analyst, or it could be selected by a coin toss. The master text is not necessarily correct; it simply provides a base for comparison. A second analyst's coded text is then compared to the master text, segment by segment, and the codes applied are counted as being in agreement or disagreement with the master.

Let's say we want to compare the work of analyst A to the master. Using the coding-agreement template in table 6.3, percent agreement is calculated as follows:

- On the coding-agreement template, write down the name of the file being coded.
- In the column marked "Code," write down the names of each of the codes in the codebook. Enter the codes alphabetically so they will be easier to find. Use as many sheets as necessary; number the pages and include the file name on each page.
- Look at the first code applied to the master text and find it in the first column on the coding-agreement template. Now look at the same text coded by analyst A. Was this same code applied to similar text on analyst A's coded text? If yes, make a tick mark in the column labeled "Agree" next to the code. If no, make a tick mark in the column labeled "Disagree."
- Still looking at the same text, check to see if analyst A applied a code that is not on the master. If yes, find that code on the coding-agreement template and make a tick mark in the column labeled "Disagree."

Table 6.3.   Intercoder Agreement Template

Master Coder: _____

Comparison Coder: _____

Total Agree: _____

+ Total Disagree: _____

Total No. of Codes: _____

Overall Percent Agreement: _____

Code	Agree	Disagree	Code Total	Agreement
Code #1	Total:	Total:		
Code #2	Total:	Total:		
Code #3	Total:	Total:		
Code #4	Total:	Total:		

- Now look at the second code on the master and find it on the coding-agreement template. Once again compare the master with analyst A's coded text, making a tick mark for each code that agrees or disagrees, as appropriate. If there is any uncoded text on the master that was coded by analyst A, make a tick mark in the column labeled "Disagree" for those codes.
- Continue the comparison process until all of analyst A's codes have been compared to the master's.
- On the coding-agreement template, count the number of ticks in each "Agree" and "Disagree" cell and write the total in the cell. Add the number of "Agree" and "Disagree" totals; this is the total number of times the code was applied by both the master and analyst A. Write this total in the column marked "Code Total."
- For each code, divide the "Agree" number by the "Code Total" number. This is the percent agreement for that code. Write that number in the column marked "Agreement."
- Now total all of the numbers in the column marked "Agree"; write this total in the appropriate space at the top of the first page of the coding-agreement template. Do the same for the numbers in the column marked "Disagree"; again, write this number at the top of the first page. Add the total number for "Agree" and the total number for "Disagree"; this is the total number of codes applied by both the master and analyst A. Write this number in the appropriate space at the top of the first page.
- Divide the Total Number Agree by the Total Number of Codes Applied; this is the Overall Percent Agreement. Write this number in the appropriate space at the top of the first page.

If the Overall Percent Agreement is 85 percent or greater, then Analyst A and the master are in good agreement. If it is less than 85 percent, they should look at the percent agreement for individual codes to identify those codes where there is substantial disagreement, review the text where they disagreed about whether a code should be applied, discuss how they are each using the codes, and revise their coding strategies as needed. If revisions to the code definitions are necessary to improve agreement, this should be done in consultation with the rest of the analysis team. Each of the analysts should then independently code another interview and conduct another coding-agreement analysis, repeating this process until they are able to achieve 85 percent agreement. Intercoder checks can be repeated periodically to ensure that agreement is maintained.

Some Practical Suggestions

We have learned eight practical lessons from our experience with team-based codebook development and application.

1. Assign primary responsibility to one person for creating, updating, and revising a given codebook. This will ensure that the codebook is consistent, and it will minimize ambiguities due to differences in vocabulary and writing styles. Require all members of the coding team to clear all coding questions and clarifications with the codebook editor. Make certain that the codebook editor has the basic competence for the task.

2. Schedule regular meetings where the coding team reviews each code and definition in the codebook. It is easy for a coder to develop a set of implicit rules without realizing that the codebook no longer reflects his or her actual coding process; in addition, this evolving process may or may not be shared by other members of the coding team. Without regular review sessions, the codebook can quickly become obsolete and useless as an analytic tool.

3. Establish a coding process that consciously seeks to enhance intercoder agreement. One way to do this is to create a codebook that someone can learn to use within a few hours. For the most part, coders can reasonably handle thirty to forty codes at one time. If the codebook contains more than forty codes, the coding process needs to be done in stages. Separate the codebook into three or four related components or domains and have the coders apply one set of codes to the entire data set before moving on to the next set.

4. Develop a written plan for segmenting text at the same time the codebook is being developed. Segmenting complex text into smaller natural units, such as a line or a sentence, may be helpful. If you are segmenting less than a sentence, it may be better to utilize a word-based content analysis strategy than a codebook strategy. Of course, the word-based strategy can evolve into codebook development.

5. Establish intercoder agreement measures early in the process of codebook development. Decide a priori how much variability you are willing to permit with regard to both segmentation and code application, and how you will assess that variability. Make sure the coding team understands and agrees with the criteria, and that coding will not be considered final until those criteria are met.

6. When defining codes, do not assume that anything is obvious; always state specifically what the code should and should not capture. This

includes defining common abbreviations and "shorthand" references that may occur in the text. Include all such information in the full definition of the code and explanations for its use. Things that seem obvious to coders at a certain place and time can be totally obscure in another context, even to the same coders.

7. Don't clutter the codebook with deadwood: throw out codes that don't work, and rework definitions for codes that are problematic. Some codes may capture the specificity of a single response rather than general patterns and themes. It is best to eliminate these types of codes from the codebook or expand their usage. A single generic code (e.g., UNIQUE) can be designed to capture all unique responses on a given topic. The codebook should be a distillation, not a historical document. If maintaining a history of the codebook development process is relevant, then develop a separate strategy for that purpose.

8. Finally, accept the fact that text will need to be recoded as the codebook is refined. Recoding should not be viewed as a step back; it is always indicative of forward movement in the analysis.

Conclusion

The interdisciplinary team-based approach to qualitative analysis that we often use in our research projects has provided us with both the incentive and the resources to develop explicit guidelines for and documentation of our methods. For coding, this has led to the generation of a basic structure for organizing codebooks that is also flexible enough to meet the needs of a variety of coding situations. When combined with an informed discussion of the coding process, the use of a flexible yet standard structure facilitates coder training. It also enhances the analyst's ability to transfer skills from one project to another, regardless of variability in the particular software tools used.

Note

An earlier version of this chapter appeared in *Cultural Anthropology Methods* 1998;10(2):31–36.

References

Bernard, H. R.
1994   *Research Methods in Anthropology: Qualitative and Quantitative Approaches* (2nd ed.). Walnut Creek, Calif.: AltaMira.

Bernard, H. R., and G. Ryan
1998   Qualitative and quantitative methods of text analysis. In H. R. Bernard, ed. *Handbook of Research Methods in Cultural Anthropology*. Pp. 595–645. Walnut Creek, Calif.: AltaMira.

Cabral, R. J., D. Cotton, S. Semaan, and A. C. Gielen
2004   Application of the transtheoretical model for HIV prevention in a facility-based and a community-level behavioral intervention research study. *Health Promotion Practice* 5(2):199–207.

Carey, J. W., M. Morgan, and M. J. Oxtoby
1996   Intercoder agreement in analysis of responses to open-ended interview questions: Examples from tuberculosis research. *Cultural Anthropology Methods* 8(3):1–5.

Carey, J. W., P. H. Wenzel, C. Reilly, J. Sheridan, and J. M. Steinberg
1998   CDC EZ-Text: Software for management and analysis of semistructured qualitative data sets. *Cultural Anthropology Methods* 10(1):14–20.

Centers for Disease Control and Prevention
2004   *AnSWR: Analysis Software for Word-based Records, Version 6.4*. Atlanta, Ga.: Centers for Disease Control and Prevention.

DiClemente, C. C., and J. O. Prochaska
1985   Processes and stages of self-change: Coping and competence in smoking behavior change. In S. Schiffman and T. A. Wills, eds. *Coping and Substance Abuse*. Pp. 319–343. New York: Academic.

Guest, G., E. McLellan-Lemal, D. Matia, R. Pickard, J. Fuchs, D. McKirnan, and J. Neidig
2005   HIV vaccine efficacy trial participation: Men-who-have-sex-with-men's experience of risk reduction counseling and perceptions of behavior change. *AIDS Care* 17:46–57.

MacQueen, K. M., K. L. Kay, B. N. Bartholow, S. Buchbinder, D. J. McKirnan, F. Judson, and J. Douglas
1996   The relationship between perceived exposure to HIV and actual risk in a cohort of gay and bisexual men. Poster presentation at the XI International Conference on AIDS, July 7–12, Vancouver, BC, Canada.

MacQueen, K. M., E. McLellan, D. Metzger, S. Kegeles, R. Strauss, R. Scotti, L. Blanchard, and R. Trotter, II
2001   What is community? An evidence-based definition for participatory public health. *American Journal of Public Health* 91(12):1929–1938.

Miles, M. B., and A. M. Huberman
1994   *Qualitative Data Analysis* (2nd ed.). Thousand Oaks, Calif.: Sage.

Milstein, B., T. Lockaby, L. Fogarty, A. Cohen, and D. Cotton
1998   Processes of change in the adoption of consistent condom use. *Journal of Health Psychology* 3:349–368.

Muhr, T.
1994   *ATLAS/ti&Computer Aided Text Interpretation & Theory Building, Release 1.1E. User's Manual* (2nd ed.). Berlin: Thomas Muhr.

O'Connell, D.
1989   Development of a change process coding system. Ph.D. dissertation, University of Rhode Island, Kingston.

Prochaska, J. O.
1984   *Systems of Psychotherapy: A Transtheoretical Analysis* (2nd ed.). Homewood, Ill: Dorsey.

Ryan, G. W., and H. R. Bernard
2003   Techniques to identify themes. *Field Methods* 15:85–109.

Seidel, J., and U. Kelle
1995   Different functions of coding in the analysis of textual data. In U. Kelle, ed. *Computer-aided Qualitative Data Analysis: Theory, Methods, and Practice.* Pp. 52–61. Thousand Oaks, Calif.: Sage.

Strauss, A., and J. Corbin
1990   *Basics of Qualitative Research: Grounded Theory Procedures and Techniques.* Newbury Park, Calif.: Sage.

Thompson, C., D. McCaughan, N. Cullum, T. A. Sheldon, and P. Raynor
2004   Increasing the visibility of coding decisions in team-based qualitative research in nursing. *International Journal of Nursing Studies* 41:15–20.

Data Reduction Techniques for Large Qualitative Data Sets

7

EMILY NAMEY, GREG GUEST, LUCY THAIRU, AND LAURA JOHNSON

You have your way. I have my way. As for the right way, the correct way, and the only way, it does not exist.

FRIEDRICH NIETZSCHE

WORKING WITH DATA COLLECTED through a team effort or in multiple sites can be both challenging and rewarding. The sheer size and complexity of the data set sometimes makes the analysis daunting, but a large data set may also yield richer and more useful information. In this chapter, we explore strategies for combining qualitative and quantitative analysis techniques for the analysis of large, qualitative data sets. *Large* is a relative term, of course, and many of the techniques described here are applicable to smaller data sets as well. However, the benefits of the data reduction techniques we propose increase as the data sets themselves grow in size and complexity. In our selection of techniques, we have taken a broad view of large qualitative data sets, aiming to highlight trends, relationships, or associations for further analysis, without deemphasizing the importance of the context and richness of the data themselves. This perspective also brings focus to the multiple interpretive lenses that a group of researchers brings to team-based analysis.

Throughout the chapter, we use examples from some of our research to illustrate the use of the methods discussed. In doing so, we identify the strengths and weaknesses of each method and suggest ways in which an appropriate technique may be chosen for a given research question and its corresponding data set.

Approaches to Data Analysis

During the past few decades, qualitative research has greatly benefited from theoretical and methodological developments in data analysis (see, e.g., Bernard and Ryan 1998, Dey 1993, LeCompte and Schensul 1999). Analyses typically fall into one of two categories: content and thematic. In content analysis, the researcher evaluates the frequency and saliency of particular words or phrases in a body of original text data in order to identify keywords or repeated ideas. In addition to simple word counts, content analysis can be expanded to include associated attributes of keywords and other semantic elements, such as synonyms, location in the text, and surrounding words or phrases (Dey 1993:59).

Content analysis techniques are valued for their efficiency and reliability. With appropriate software, large numbers of text files can be quickly scanned and keywords tallied. And since the original, "raw" data are used, there is minimal interpretation involved in the word counts, resulting in greater reliability. The primary drawback to content analysis is that context is usually not considered or is highly constrained, limiting the richness of the summary data produced.

Thematic analysis, in contrast, is more involved and nuanced. Thematic analysis moves beyond counting explicit words or phrases and focuses on identifying and describing both implicit and explicit ideas. Codes developed for ideas or themes are then applied or linked to raw data as summary markers for later analysis, which may include comparing the relative frequencies of themes or topics within a data set, looking for code co-occurrence, or graphically displaying code relationships.

Reliability is of greater concern with thematic analysis than content analysis because research analysts must interpret raw text data in order to apply codes, and because interpretations may vary across analysts. Strategies for monitoring and improving intercoder agreement, and therefore reliability, add to the time required for thematic analysis, but the investment is well worth the context-rich coded data produced (see chapters 6 and 11, this volume).

Both content and thematic analysis can be data-driven, as in grounded theory (Glaser and Strauss 1967, Kearney et al. 1994, Wright 1997), or theory-driven (Krippendorf 1980, Weber 1990). In a data-driven approach, the researcher carefully reads and rereads the data, looking for keywords, trends, themes, or ideas in the data that will help outline the analysis, *before* any analysis takes place. By contrast, a theory-driven approach is guided by specific ideas or hypotheses the researcher wants to assess. The researcher may still closely read the data prior to analysis, but his or her analysis categories have been determined a priori, without consideration of the data.

Theory-driven approaches tend to be more structured, and for this reason may be considered more reliable, in the sense that the same results are likely, regardless of the coder. Conversely, data-driven approaches may be considered to have greater validity because they are more flexible and open to discovery of themes or ideas not previously considered, resulting in theory that is "grounded" in the data. Fortunately, neither approach is so rigid as to prevent borrowing from the other, to maximize the findings of an analysis and to balance reliability and validity. Theory-driven analysis does not preclude the analyst from uncovering emergent, data-driven themes, which may then be added to the analysis, and similarly data-driven analyses may generate theories to explain emergent structure. The techniques presented below span both content and thematic analysis and are applicable to both theory- and data-driven approaches. The examples presented, however, are primarily drawn from data-driven thematic analyses.

Framing the Analysis

Large qualitative data sets generally encompass multiple research questions. Hence, very few, if any, analyses of such data sets simultaneously involve *all* of the data that have been collected. From the outset, researchers need to delineate the boundaries of a given analysis with a comprehensive analysis plan. This plan can include guidelines for data set reduction, including whether all the data will first be coded in an exploratory analysis, whether they will be partitioned in a way appropriate for theoretical analysis and hypothesis testing, or whether some data will simply not be included in specific analyses. Eliminating data not relevant to the analysis at hand—or extracting the data that *are* relevant—is usually the first, and arguably the simplest, form of data reduction. As Miles and Huberman (1994: 11) explain,

> Data reduction is not something separate from analysis. It is *part* of analysis. The researcher's decisions—which data chunks to code and which to pull out, which evolving story to tell—*are all analytic choices*. Data reduction is a form of analysis that sharpens, sorts, focuses, discards, and organizes data in such a way that "final" conclusions can be drawn and verified.

In cases where the larger data set was compiled from more than one type of data collection instrument (e.g., semistructured in-depth interviews, structured focus groups, and pile-sorting activities), the researcher needs to make a decision about the type of data she or he will select from the larger data set. She or he may choose to analyze data from only one type of instrument, or from several different instruments. As described by Patton (1990), this form of "triangulation" across different data collection strategies during data analysis can be particularly helpful when dealing with large data sets. The researcher may also need to frame the analysis in terms of the sources of data or the categories of participants from whom the data were collected (MacQueen and Milstein 1999). This may require limiting the analysis to one or two sites of a multisite project, or limiting the number of subgroups included in the analysis (e.g., including only data relevant in terms of select participant characteristics regardless of site).

The researcher's primary guide in all of these data reduction decisions is a clearly defined analysis objective, accompanied by an analysis plan. The objective may be based on the research questions addressed in the project or it may be determined on the basis of specific reporting or publishing goals. In the analysis plan, the researcher also defines the level of the analysis—whether exploratory, descriptive, hypothesis testing, or comparative in nature—and chooses data accordingly. These initial data reduction decisions are critical to choosing an appropriate strategy for the ensuing analyses.

Analytical Techniques

In this section, we summarize the basic steps, strengths, and weaknesses of several analytical techniques for large qualitative data sets. The techniques do not comprise an exhaustive list; rather, on the basis of our experience in the field, we highlight some of the techniques we have found useful when working as a team in multisite research studies. In addition to these techniques, the fundamental step of reading and rereading text data files is still essential for adding context to theory-driven analyses and for identifying themes for data-driven analyses.

Structural Coding

One effective method for making large qualitative data sets more manageable, for either content or thematic analysis, is to develop and apply a series of "structural" codes to the data. As described by MacQueen et al. in chapter 6 of this volume, the term *structural code* refers to question-based, rather than theme-based, codes. This approach works for data collected using structured or semistructured interview or focus group guides that have discrete questions and probes that are repeated across multiple files in a data set. Each discrete question and its associated probes are assigned a code that is then applied or linked to the question and subsequent response text in each data file. Sets of questions that comprise a conceptual domain of inquiry can also be given a structural code.

Namey and colleagues, for example, worked on a project that included semistructured interviews with participants in an HIV prevention clinical trial. The trial was testing a drug for HIV prevention, and the interviews were designed to gather information on trial participants' experiences throughout the research process. Questions were grouped within different domains of inquiry: *Demographic Information, Trial Experience, Acceptability and Knowledge of the Study Drug,* and *Sexual and Contraceptive Practices.* Within each domain, questions were given code names. These code names included a prefix for the domain and an identifier for the question topic. For example, within the *Trial Experience* section, participants were asked, "How do you feel about the HIV counseling sessions you received at the study clinic?" The code developed for this question was *TE_Counseling.* In each interview transcript, the code was applied to the section of text that included both the interviewer's question and the participant's response. Each question and respective response was coded this way. Once all of the data were structurally coded, the analysis team could easily sort through the data by question or domain to contextualize the data included in specific analyses (e.g., an analysis on trial experiences). Data from related questions could be easily consolidated and extracted from the full data set for further analysis.

Structural coding, as illustrated above, acts as a labeling and indexing device, allowing researchers to quickly access data likely to be relevant to a particular analysis from a larger data set. This makes analysis of copious data more efficient. Structural codes are also helpful for pulling together related data for development of data-driven thematic codes, but because they are developed without consulting the data, these codes are neither data-driven nor thematic in nature. Rather, as summarized by MacQueen et al. in chapter 6 of this volume, structural coding usually results in the identification of large pieces of text on broad topics that form the basis for an in-depth analysis within or across topics.

Frequencies

As noted in the description of content analysis earlier in this chapter, counting the frequency of a word or a phrase in a given data set is often a good starting point for identifying repeated ideas within a large body of text (Ryan and Bernard 2000:776), and gives an idea of the prevalence of thematic responses across participants. Simple keyword searches or word counts within a data set can allow a quick comparison of the words used by different subpopulations within an analysis (e.g., Ryan and Weisner 1996), or can be useful in developing a thematic codebook. So depending on what is being counted, frequencies can be part of either content or thematic analyses. The example provided below illustrates the advantage of simple keyword quantification as a potentially effective way to make decisions about what to include in or how to structure thematic codebooks.

In a study conducted in three West African countries, Namey and colleagues collected information on the experiences of people living with HIV/AIDS using semistructured interviews. One of the objectives of the research was to find out how people with HIV cope with the disease in resource-poor settings. The analysis was exploratory and focused on a short series of structurally coded questions in which respondents had been asked about their coping strategies. The analysis team compiled a list of the coping strategies identified by respondents as they read through the relevant structurally coded segments from forty transcripts from the three sites. In considering how to best code the strategies thematically, the team was faced with the following question: "Should a codebook be developed for each of the sites, or should the codebook be shared across all three sites?"

The team decided to use the MS Word search function in a qualitative data analysis (QDA) software package to answer the question. With researcher-defined parameters for the search, the program allowed them to identify the number of times each of the keywords associated with coping strategies appeared in the data sets from each of the sites. Examples of keywords used included *family*, *faith*, *doctor*, and *support group*. The search was limited to the segments of text structurally coded as part of the domain *Coping with HIV*. Within these segments, the frequency of the predetermined keywords was compared across the three sites. On the basis of this comparison, the researchers determined that the three sites were sufficiently similar to be analyzed using a single, shared codebook.

As the example above shows, word counts and keyword searches often require that researchers know what words to search for. Prior knowledge of the data is often essential, and accuracy of language is a concern. The data from the example above were originally collected in French, Pidgin English, and several local African languages, before being translated into English for analysis. The use of one specific word or another as a marker for an idea becomes less certain here, particularly without context to assist in checking meaning.

In the above example, the researchers focused the word count on the small section of text that was already known to relate to coping with HIV. This decision was made to avoid tallying uses of the common terms *family* and *doctor* that may have appeared in other contexts. However, the approach excluded any discussion of coping strategies that may have arisen spontaneously in other parts of the interview.

Another limitation to the use of content analysis is that keywords are acknowledged only as part of a simple word count, without taking the words' context into account. In the above example, both negative and positive mentions of *family* or *doctor* were counted equally, and without regard for whether the word actually described a coping strategy. This distinction would need to be made subsequently in a thematic codebook, after context from the transcripts was considered. Alternatively, "keyword in context" reports may be used to create a concordance that provides a certain number of words before and after the keyword, thus providing the context with which to interpret keyword frequencies (Ryan and Bernard 2000). The QDA Miner with WordStat and MaxQDA with MaxDictio software packages offer these and other content analysis capabilities.

Assessing the frequency of themes (i.e., code applications), rather than words, helps to incorporate context into the analysis, and is another helpful and fairly simple analytical technique. Different QDA software packages have different capabilities for creating code frequency reports, which list the number of times each of the codes from a selected thematic codebook is applied within a given data set. Some programs allow analysts to count the total number of files with the code applied, or the total number of times the code was applied across all files. These frequencies can also be tabulated without using software, though this can be quite time consuming.

Generally, we suggest determining frequencies on the basis of the number of individual participants who mention a particular theme, rather than the total number of times a theme appears in the text. We base this on the assumption that the number of individuals independently expressing the same idea is a better indicator of overall thematic importance than the absolute number of times a theme is expressed and coded. One talkative participant, for example, could express the same idea in many of her or his responses and thus significantly increase the overall frequency of a code application. However, the choice of frequency report ultimately depends on the analysis objective. In some cases the number of times a code was applied within each file—across different domains, for example—may be the best indication of the breadth or pervasiveness of a coded theme.

If coding has been done systematically using clearly defined codes, a code frequency report can help identify which themes, ideas, or domains were common and which rarely occurred. In this way, the number of times a code is applied can be used as an indication of the salience of a theme or an idea across files, domains, or questions, depending on the analysis objective. Coding frequencies, like word counts, can also be compared between different sources or subpopulations within the data to explore similarities and differences among these. When using code frequencies, it is important to keep in mind that the codes represent interpretive summaries of data, rather than the primary data themselves. This is another reason to monitor the reliability of the code application process.

Code frequency reports can also be helpful for managing data and for revising codebooks. For example, a code that tends to appear numerous times within a data set may need to be refined and, if any subthemes or subconcepts are identified, the analyst may need to create subcodes that describe these in more detail. Conversely, a code that rarely occurs may need to be redefined or eliminated from the codebook altogether. The "standard of care" example described below illustrates the use of code frequency reports.

MacQueen et al. (2007) used code frequency reports to frame their analysis of data about locally acceptable standards of care related to HIV prevention clinical trials. Key informants, health care providers, and potential clinical trial participants at ten sites in seven countries were identified to participate in semistructured interviews or focus groups. These respondents were presented with the description of a hypothetical clinical trial, and were then asked to evaluate three scenarios about ways to care for people who might become HIV-positive during the course of a clinical study. After each scenario, the participant was asked whether she or he considered the scenario fair treatment. In total, 130 individual interviews and twenty focus group discussions were conducted and transcribed. Predetermined codes of *fair*, *unfair*, and *mixed* (elements of fairness and unfairness together) were then applied to participants' responses to each of the three hypothetical care scenarios in the transcripts.

To determine the number of respondents who felt that a given scenario was fair, unfair, or of mixed fairness, the analysis team generated code frequency reports for each of the three codes and for each scenario, using AnSWR software (CDC 2004). In addition, more focused code frequency reports were generated to find out whether there were differences in response to the three scenarios across the different categories of respondents. In other words, key informants were compared to health workers, who were in turn compared to potential trial participants. In this way, the research team used the code frequency reports to identify the perceived level of fairness for each of the scenarios according to the type of respondent. In subsequent analyses, the team examined participants' specific reasons for considering the scenarios fair or unfair.

Co-occurrence

Code co-occurrence is defined as the application of two or more codes to a discrete segment of text from a unique respondent (Guest and McLellan 2003). For instance, a paragraph of text about strategies for coping with HIV extracted from one respondent's interview transcript may contain references to "family," "faith," and "doctors." Each of these references is a separate idea that requires a separate code. The paragraph would be coded with all three codes, which are then said to co-occur in this text segment.

Code co-occurrence reports often provide helpful information in understanding how thematic domains, concepts, or ideas are distributed within a data set, beyond simple frequencies. Patterns in data sets can be identified by examining co-occurrences such as correlation between code items, themes, respondents, or events (LeCompte and Schensul 1999). Some QDA software packages frame these types of reports in Boolean terms, allowing the analyst to search for the intersection of Code A AND Code B, or Code C NOT IN Code D. Again, which report is most helpful will depend on the analysis objective.

As with code frequencies, it may be instructive to look at the total number of times any two codes co-occur within individual data files as well as across the entire data set. For example, a unique pair of codes may co-occur hundred times within a data set of fifty files, but all one hundred co-occurrences appear within a small number of individual data files only. Alternatively, a pair of codes might co-occur only twenty-five times, but be distributed across twenty-five different files within the data set. For this reason, it is often important to look at these two reports, code frequency and code co-occurrence, together, before giving weight to one co-occurrence or another.

In the "standard of care" example described above, MacQueen and Namey used code co-occurrence reports to help address why some categories of respondents considered certain hypothetical scenarios for treatment to be fair and others unfair. They created thematic codes describing different benefits or limitations of treatment (e.g., *drug access, counseling, long queues at the medical center,* or *poor service*), and looked at all of the co-occurrences of these codes with the fairness codes mentioned earlier (*fair, unfair, mixed*). The resulting co-occurrence report, when subdivided by scenario, indicated respondents' perceptions of benefits or limitations of research-related care in relation to their assessments of fairness. Again, the researchers used this information as a guide for reviewing and reorganizing the text data for interpretation.

Graph-theoretic Data Reduction Techniques

While traditional thematic or structured coding can be a first step in ordering large data sets, the richness of the various codes applied to the data, coupled with the possibility of having multiple salient themes, requires additional consideration. In particular, as summarized by Miles and Huberman (1994:69), analysts are often faced with the following questions: "How do all the codes and themes relate to each other? What is the big picture, and how does it relate to each theme or code? Where does one begin to tell the story?"

To answer some of these questions, graph-theoretic techniques, also referred to as semantic network analyses, may be used to identify complex semantic relationships in bodies of text (Barnett and Danowski 1992, Danowski 1993, Osgood 1959). Using co-occurrence matrices as input, these techniques graphically depict the relationship between semantic items, such as words or codes. The development of various software programs for the statistical analysis of qualitative data has allowed matrices to be analyzed with increasing sophistication (Borgatti 1996b, Doerfel and Barnett 1996, Schnegg and Bernard 1996, Weitzman and Miles 1995). The most common graph-theoretic techniques, discussed in more detail below, include multidimensional scaling and hierarchical cluster analysis.

The techniques described in the previous section are useful for reducing and/or guiding analysis of large amounts of text, although these approaches result in a lot of detail and require piecing together interpretations from multiple, distinct reports. Cluster analysis and multidimensional scaling (MDS) techniques provide a broader, more holistic perspective. These methods are designed to identify the "structures" of categories that fit a collection of observations. Rather than starting with a priori or emerging categorical structures and filling them with data, these techniques allow the analyst to identify the "natural groupings" within the data set. As such, these approaches constitute an important technique that can help generate hypotheses about relationships between concepts or ideas or confirm initial ideas about how the data fit together (Johnson and Wichern 2002).

Hierarchical Clustering Techniques

Hierarchical cluster analysis is an agglomerative methodology that identifies clusters of observations in a data set (Aldenderfer and Blashfield 1984). As described by Anderberg (1973), at its most elementary level, cluster analysis "sorts data into groups, such that the degree of natural association is high among members of the same group and low between members of different groups." In other words, a cluster analysis is a statistical method for grouping "like" things together. Before performing a cluster analysis, the analyst first needs to display qualitative data using similarity matrices. A similarity matrix is a table of scores that express numerical distances—or likeness—between data points. These matrices can be binary (using zeros and ones to indicate simply whether two data points are similar or not), or they can be valued (using a range of values to indicate the degree or strength of similarity). These matrices can be composed of data from various sources, including direct word counts, pile sorts, or code frequencies, depending on which item of analysis best addresses the analysis objectives. Table 7.1 below provides examples of two code-by-code matrices, the first binary, and the second a valued matrix, based on the aggregate binary matrices of several individual respondents.

Using these similarity matrices as input, cluster analysis allows a researcher to see patterns in large data sets. Moreover, a refined context can be created by careful selection of the words or codes to be included in a similarity matrix. If the words or codes are limited to those that appear

Table 7.1.   Examples of Individual and Aggregated Similarity Matrices

A. Code by Code Similarity Matrix, Individual Case (Binary Matrix)

	Code A	Code B	Code C	Code D	Code E
Code A	—	0	1	1	0
Code B	0	—	1	0	0
Code C	1	1	—	0	1
Code D	1	0	0	—	0
Code E	0	0	1	0	—

In this matrix, we have used QDA software to determine whether (yes = 1, no = 0) specific codes co-occurred in the text file associated with one particular participant. Codes A and B, for example, did not co-occur, while Codes A and C did.

B. Code by Code Similarity Matrix, Aggregated Cases (Value Matrix)

	Code A	Code B	Code C	Code D	Code E
Code A	—	2	15	12	1
Code B	2	—	4	6	0
Code C	15	4	—	8	11
Code D	12	6	8	—	0
Code E	1	0	11	0	—

This matrix displays the sum of several individual matrices for the same codes assessed in Matrix A. Rather than determining simply whether the selected codes co-occurred, this matrix tells us the number of individual participant files in which two codes co-occurred. Codes C and E, for example, were found to co-occur in eleven participant files.

within a particular domain or structural-level code segment, a bounding context can be used in interpretations of the resulting clusters. The example below illustrates the use of hierarchical cluster analysis in an integrated analysis of a multisite qualitative data set.

Guest et al. (2005) used hierarchical cluster analysis to examine the risk reduction counseling experience of men participating in an HIV vaccine trial. Seven respondents were selected from each of five U.S. sites, for a sample of thrity-five men in total. Responses to two questions about risk reduction counseling experience were coded with forty-six thematic codes using AnSWR QDA software. The researchers created a binary matrix in which the rows represented each of the thirty-five respondents and the columns represented each of the forty-six codes developed. Rather than determining the number of times the code was applied in the interview, the matrix was designed to identify only the presence of the code in each respondent's transcript, thus obviating the potential numerical bias that would occur if, for example, a code was repeatedly applied to a single respondent's interview. The initial matrix was produced in AnSWR, and then the resulting file was imported into ANTHROPAC (Borgatti 1996a) to conduct a hierarchical cluster analysis. For a detailed account of the procedures used, refer to Guest and McLellan (2003).

Figure 7.1 depicts the resulting dendrogram of a cluster analysis of men's risk reduction counseling experiences within the context of HIV vaccine trial

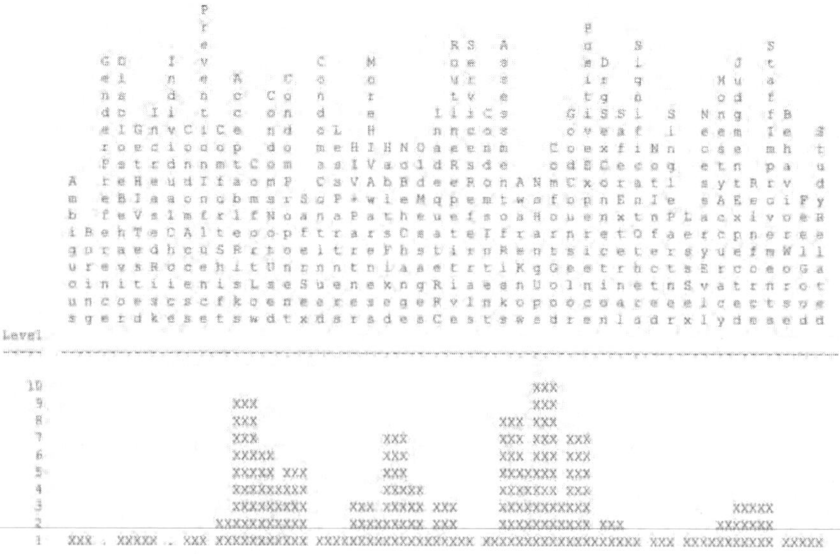

Figure 7.1. Hierarchical cluster analysis of thematic data.

participation. The figure illustrates broad clusters that break down into several smaller clusters. In this analysis, the unit of observation is the code, and the unit of analysis is the respondent. This means that all numbers, such as levels in the cluster, salience, and frequency counts, are references to the number of unique respondents. Within a cluster, there are codes that occur at a low rate or level and others that occur at higher levels. Codes grouped at higher levels suggest co-occurrence as well as high frequency within the text. Put another way, codes that occur at a high rate signify themes that lots of men talked about; codes in the same cluster signify different themes that tended to come up together in an interview. The dendrogram thus provides a starting point from which to develop a more comprehensive interpretation of the data.

As shown in figure 7.1, the coded data split into three main clusters. Two of these clusters are further divided into subclusters. To determine the cutoff level for defining a cluster, the research team compared the cluster tree diagram to code frequency and salience reports derived from the coded data in AnSWR. At level 4 (see bottom left of figure 7.1), Guest and McLellan found that more than 20 percent of respondents provided information associated with a code contained within a cluster. The tree diagram displays notable breaks in clusters for codes with a salience of level 4 or less, supporting the chosen benchmark.

From this predetermined cutoff point, Guest and McLellan filled in the details to build a "narrative" that was grounded in the data. They added relevant quotes from text, compared findings to the literature, and confirmed their interpretations with saliency and frequency tables. For example, the cluster on the right in figure 7.1 included several codes related to the level of rapport men reported as part of their risk reduction counseling experience. The codes comprising the cluster third from the left—No Hang Ups and Comfort Good codes—indicate a relationship between men's ability to talk freely about sexual behavior and comfort with the risk reduction counseling. The coded text corroborated and added context to this clustering, by providing the evidence from interview transcripts that men were accustomed to talking about their sexual behaviors with others and/or being part of a research project.

Similarly, in the cluster analysis, risk assessment questions were frequently connected to an increased self-awareness of risk behavior (subcluster on the left: Assessment of Risks and Aware Know codes), while in the text data, explicit vocalization of risk behavior was reported to be an eye-opening experience. The subcluster on the right includes the related elements of a positive trial experience and having a good counselor (Positive Experience and Good Counselor codes), which is supported by text describing the comfort and ease engendered by good rapport with a nonjudgmental and sincere counselor. In this way, the researchers moved between the cluster analysis and the text data to summarize their findings, demonstrating the creation of a narrative structured by the clustered configuration of the data and interwoven with quotes or details from the qualitative data.

Cluster analysis can also be used for text-based content analysis. Newly developed software, such as IN-SPIRE (Pacific Northwest National Laboratory 2004), can handle extremely large data sets (an estimated million words per hour), and using sophisticated clustering techniques can produce three-dimensional outputs of data configurations.

Multidimensional Scaling

Multidimensional scaling (MDS) is another useful graph-theoretic technique that is based on similarity matrices. Schiffman et al. (1981) describe MDS as "a powerful mathematical procedure which can systematize data by representing the similarities of objects spatially as in a map." For a set of observed similarities (or distances or proximities) between N pairs of items, MDS techniques allow the researcher to find a representation of the items in the fewest possible dimensions in space, such that the distances between the points match as well as possible the original distances or proximities (Johnson and Wichern 2002).

A classic heuristic for explaining MDS can clarify this explanation. Think about creating a map using only a set of distances between various geographical locations. Given only the distances between all pairings of ten cities from around the borders of the United States, any MDS program (in SPSS, Systat, or SAS, for example) would draw a reasonable outline map of the country. This capacity of MDS to create visual, spatial representations of relationships among data points is particularly useful for more abstract data, like themes or ideas, which have no material or geographic representation. Ideas that are judged to be closer to each other according to the distance between them (similarity) are represented as points that are close to each other, and locations that are judged to be far from each other are represented as points that are distant, just as on a map (Schiffman et al. 1981). This "map" then serves as a guide for further analysis and interpretation of the text data from which it was derived.

Once an MDS plot is created, a measure of "stress" (which ranges from 0 to 1) is used to evaluate the extent to which the original input distances match the resulting diagram. "Stress" therefore refers to the amount of distortion between the actual numerical values in a proximity matrix and the representation of those values in the MDS plot (Clark et al. 1998). Zero stress indicates a perfect fit of the data, so the closer the "stress" is to zero, the better the fit of the MDS diagram. A traditional rule of thumb is that stress below 0.1 indicates a good fit between the actual proximities and their representation in the plot (Kruskal 1964). Note, though, that guidelines in this regard are evolving (see Sturrock and Rocha 2000).

As with hierarchical clustering, data designed to be analyzed using MDS can be entered into ANTHROPAC software (Borgatti 1996a) or other statistical software packages such as SPSS. These data can originate from words or thematic codes created in the process of qualitative analysis of text data, or from less traditional qualitative methods like pile sorting or triadic comparisons (e.g., Weller and Romney 1988). Data are first converted to proximity matrices, in a procedure similar to that outlined in the example from Guest and McLellan above, and are then analyzed using MDS. To keep things relatively simple, the following example is based on a rather small sample of pile sort data, collected in one location; however, the same methods of data preparation and analysis are applicable to, and even more useful for, larger sets of data collected in multiple sites.

Thairu (2005) asked a purposive sample of women from the Pemba Island of Tanzania to sort thirty-four cards, each containing a short description of a common caregiving practice for newborns in the community. To ensure that responses across participants were comparable, she restricted the number of piles that respondents could make to four. If an informant put any two items in the same pile, the items were considered to be similar; conversely, if the informant put any two items in different piles, the items were judged to be different (Weller and Romney 1988). In preparing the data obtained for analysis, each informant's similarity judgments were represented as an item-by-item matrix in which each cell contained either 1 for items that appeared in the same pile or 0 for items that appeared in different piles (Borgatti 1996b). One matrix represented each informant.

Thairu calculated the aggregate similarity for any two items, Item A and Item B, by adding the values in Cell AB across all N informants and dividing by N. The resulting number was the percentage of informants in the sample who placed Item A and Item B in the same pile. The aggregate similarity matrix served as the input for multidimensional scaling. Using ANTHROPAC (Borgatti 1996a), she compared similarities among the items and found a set of points in space such that the distances among these points corresponded as closely as possible to the input proximities.

Table 7.2 shows the level of stress (or fit) of the model created with the data, using an increasing number of dimensions. As shown in the table, increasing the number of dimensions reduced the level of stress. However,

Table 7.2.   Stresses Obtained from the Multidimensional Scaling Algorithm

Dimensions	Stress Obtained
1	0.425
2	0.243
3	0.143
4	0.098
5	0.068

increasing the number of dimensions above two makes it difficult to display on paper, and even more difficult to comprehend. As Borgatti (1996b) argues, beyond four or more dimensions, MDS does not make complex data accessible to the human mind. For this reason, while recognizing that adding more dimensions would provide a more accurate geometric representation, Thairu chose to stop at three dimensions with a stress of 0.143. The MDS plot in figure 7.2 shows the spatial clustering of items from the pile sort activity, in two dimensions.

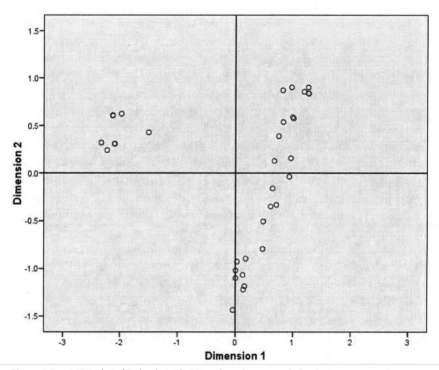

Figure 7.2.   MDS plot of judged similarities of newborn care behaviors among rural women.

In the analysis, one grouping of behaviors was observed to be located at the upper left extremity of the two dimensions, while other behaviors formed an ellipse spanning the right extremity of the two dimensions. The clusters were loosely grouped and interpreted as shown below in figure 7.3, with specific items detailed in table 7.3.

According to Thairu, in the diagram, the first dimension allowed a separation between the infant feeding cluster and the other cluster of behaviors. The second dimension represented a continuum of "time" indicating the behaviors respondents undertook following birth and as the infant grew older.

Thairu noted that there was considerable ambiguity and looseness in the groupings she found with respect to the rationale for some of the behaviors. For example, for many of the women interviewed, the practices of *calling the baby to prayer* and *applying soot on the baby's feet, palms, and face* were classified together because they were perceived to be "traditional" behaviors. In discussing their grouping decisions for these behaviors, women commented on their traditionality. On the other hand, some of the women

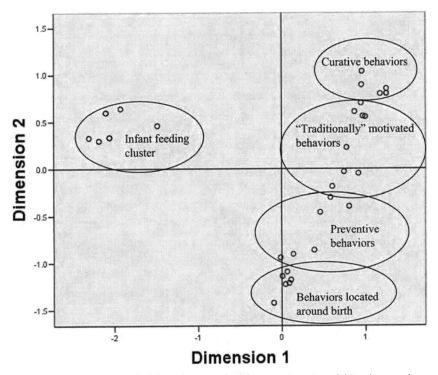

Figure 7.3. Clusters identified through MDS of rural women's sorting of thirty-four newborn care behaviors.

Table 7.3.   Specific Behaviors Contained in Each of the Clusters

Cluster Label	Specific Items Grouped within the Cluster	
Feeding behaviors	Baby given liquids using a spoon Baby given liquids using a bottle Baby given biscuits	Baby given powdered milk Baby given water Baby given cow's milk Baby given porridge Baby breast-fed

Preventive behaviors	Baby wrapped
	Baby wrapped with a khanga
	Baby washed with water
	Baby washed with soap
	Oil applied on baby's skin
	Olive oil applied on baby's skin
	Oil applied on fontanelle
	Baby massaged with warm hands
		Baby massaged with coconut oil
		Oil used to massage baby does
		  not have a strong smell
		Soap used to wash baby does
		  not have a strong smell
		Baby washed with Swahili
		  medicine

Curative behaviors	Part of baby's hair shaved and
	  medicine applied on shaved
	  part
	Baby not washed
		Baby made to inhale smoke from
		  burned Swahili medicine

"Traditionally"
  motivated
  behaviors
	Baby called to prayer
	Soot applied on baby's feet,
	  palms, and face
	Kohl applied on baby's forehead
	  or eyes
		Oil mixed with Swahili
		  medicine applied on baby's
		  skin
		Baby passed the doorway seven
		  days after birth

Birth-related behaviors	Giving birth at home Giving birth in the hospital Baby vaccinated	Razor used to cut the cord boiled Cord tied using a string or thread Placenta buried

chose to group the same behaviors as preventive care practices that are undertaken to avert unfavorable outcomes for the infant.

Not surprisingly, most women in Thairu's sample could not provide clear labels or concepts for their sorting, so she had to create labels that reflected her understanding of the emic picture. This inability to articulate cultural knowledge illustrates the utility of cognitive mapping exercises, and also highlights the care that must be taken in interpreting them. Prior familiarity with the data, context, and research problem is a prerequisite to accurate interpretation, since this knowledge enables the researcher to distinguish between "good" and "bad" groupings when confronted with them.

Comparing Qualitative Data

Many large qualitative research projects are designed to explore similarities and differences between two or more sites, groups of people, or other dimensions of interest. Such an objective often requires direct comparisons of data, yet comparing qualitative data in a meaningful way can be challenging, given the unstructured nature of responses. Certainly, a semistructured instrument—in which similar or identical questions are asked of all respondents, preferably in the same order—facilitates comparison, but certain issues remain. Even if, for example, a semistructured instrument is used, is it meaningful to say that theme x was identified in text from 75 percent of the participants in one group and only 25 percent in a comparison group? Or, what if a particular theme (or specific word, in the case of classic content analysis) is present in 20 percent of the transcripts from one site and in none of the transcripts from the other site? At what point do we say there is a meaningful difference between the two groups?

One possibility is to construct cross-tabs and carry out nonparametric procedures on frequencies, such as chi-square or Fisher's Exact Test (see chapter 11, this volume). Because these are nonparametric approaches, sampling requirements are not as rigid as for those associated with other statistical tests, and are suitable to the types of studies that employ qualitative methods. However, their use comes with some caveats, as some issues arise that are unique to comparing open-ended responses.

The response possibilities for an open-ended question are infinite, as opposed to finite categories in a fixed-response question. And, in the case of fixed-response questions, a particular answer is mutually exclusive of other response categories. The same cannot be said for responses to open-ended questions. We therefore have to assume that the same conditions are acting upon the responses across all of the groups being statistically compared. This is often not the case in team research, where interviews are sometimes conducted by different team members. Despite the best training efforts and the use of relatively structured interview guides, different interview styles and probing techniques will emerge between team members, thereby producing different responses and biasing the pattern of responses.

That said, if an analysis plan calls for the use of nonparametric statistics and multiple interviewers are to be employed, we recommend that the interviewees are distributed randomly (or at least evenly with respect to interview group) among interviewers. If random or even allocation of interviews is not feasible, all interviewers should at least have a chance to interview a few participants from each group to be compared; the subsequent chi-square analysis can then be stratified to control for interviewer effect.

The presence of a theme in one group of respondents and its absence in a different group of respondents is likely meaningful, and should be reported and interpreted accordingly. Graphical displays of frequencies relative to each other can also help in interpreting comparative data. Using a technique derived from MacQueen et al. (2001), Guest et al. (2005) created

a simple line graph showing the relative percentage of participants expressing key themes for respondents of two different age groups (figure 7.4).
While a greater percentage of the younger group expressed the key themes,
for the two age groups the relative frequency among themes was virtually
identical. The graphs indicate that the themes held the same relative importance for each group, but that the younger group was more vocal about
the subject matter overall.

Co-occurrence of data elements can also be compared in graphical
form. Separate cluster analyses or MDS outputs can be created for particular groups of interest and compared and interpreted qualitatively.[1] In the
Pemba island example, Thairu subsequently compared the results of the
newborn care pile sorting by rural women to the results of a sample of
peri-urban women (compare figures 7.3 and 7.5). She found striking similarities in both samples: the infant feeding grouping remained separate
from other clusters of behaviors, and the other clusters were not distinctly
separated. However, for the peri-urban women, the feeding cluster was located at the bottom left of the two-dimensional graphical representation in
contrast to the top left for the rural women. This indicated subtle differences between the two samples' conceptualizations of infant feeding,
which were confirmed in the thematic analysis of interview transcripts.

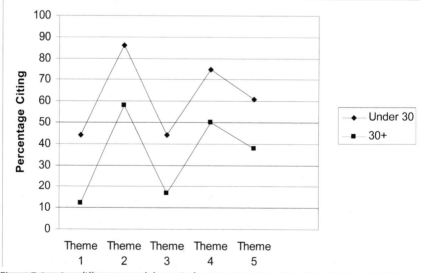

Figure 7.4.   Age differences and thematic frequency.

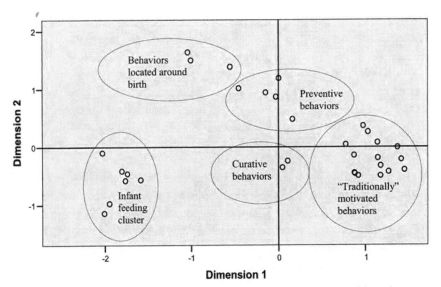

Figure 7.5.   Clusters identified through MDS of peri-urban women's sorting of thirty-four newborn care behaviors.

Qualitative Data Analysis (QDA) Software

For many (but not all) of the analytical techniques we have described above, QDA software technology is essential. Choosing an appropriate software package for a particular analysis task depends on the researchers' analysis objectives, as well as the size and complexity of both the data set and the analysis team (see MacQueen 2005). Lewins and Silver (2007) present a helpful list of questions to ask before choosing a qualitative data analysis software package, and provide reviews of several commonly used software systems, including ATLAS.ti 5, HyperRESEARCH 2.6, MAXqda2 (MAXdictio & MAXmaps), N6, NVivo2, NVivo7, QDA Miner, Qualrus, and Transana. For up-to-date reviews of the capabilities and limitations of different software packages, we suggest that the reader visit the CAQDAS (pronounced "cactus") Networking Project website, at caqdas.soc.surrey.ac.uk.

Conclusions

There is no single "right" way to approach analysis of a large qualitative data set, and often an assortment of complementary approaches, building one upon another and triangulating findings, is preferable. As discussed in this chapter, researchers may use content analysis of words or phrases as an initial method to filter the data and reduce the data set, or they can undertake structural coding of an entire data set before proceeding with further thematic analyses. Once data have been coded for themes, we have proposed checking codes for co-occurrences and code frequencies, or using the codes in similarity matrices to produce graphical data displays. A combination of these techniques may be particularly useful for researchers working on team-based and/or multisite projects, to help simplify large amounts of textual data. Simplification allows researchers to focus their attention on the rich, descriptive, and expressive details of qualitative data, without getting lost among those details.

As sociobehavioral research designs become larger and more complex, qualitative researchers have a greater opportunity to test and expand the range of methods in their repertoire to make the best use of resources and data generated by multisite, team-based research. We hope that the examples presented in this chapter serve as a starting point for wider exploration of innovations in qualitative data analysis.

Note

1. For additional ideas for visually displaying data, we recommend looking through Edward Tufte's colorful trilogy: *Envisioning Information* (1990), *The Visual Display of Quantitative Information* (1992), and *Visual Explanations: Images and Quantities, Evidence and Narrative* (1997). All three books provide numerous and unique examples of how data can be brought to life and made intuitive through graphical representation.

References

Aldenderfer, M. S., and R. K. Blashfield
1984   *Cluster Analysis.* Thousand Oaks, Calif.: Sage.

Anderberg, Michael R.
1973   *Cluster Analysis for Applications.* New York: Academic.

Barnett, G., and J. Danowski
1992   The structure of communication: A network analysis of the International Communication Association. *Human Communication Resources* 19:164–285.

Bernard, H. R., and G. Ryan
1998   Text analysis: Qualitative and quantitative methods. In H. R. Bernard, ed. *Handbook of Methods in Cultural Anthropology.* Pp. 595–645. Walnut Creek, Calif.: Altamira.

Borgatti, S.
1996a ANTHROPAC 4.0. Natick, Mass.: Analytic Technologies.

1996b 4.0 Methods Guide. Natick, Mass.: Analytic Technologies.

Centers for Disease Control and Prevention
2004 *AnSWR: Analysis Software for Word-based Records, Version 6.4.* Altanta, Ga.: Centers for Disease Control and Prevention.

Clark, L., C. Vojir, N. O. Hester, R. Foster, and K. L. Miller
1998 MDS and QAP: How do children rate painful experiences? In V. C. de Munck and E. J. Sobo, eds. *Using Methods in the Field: A Practical Introduction and Casebook.* Walnut Creek, Calif.: AltaMira Press.

Danowski, J.
1993 Network analysis of message content. In D. Richards and G. Barnett, eds. *Progress in Communication Science, XII.* Pp. 197–221. Norwood, N.J.: Ablex.

Dey, I.
1993 *Qualitative Data Analysis: A User-friendly Guide for Social Scientists.* New York: Routledge.

Doerfel, M., and G. Barnett
1996 The use of Catpac for text analysis. *Cultural Anthropology Methods Journal* 8(2):4–7.

Glaser, B., and A. Strauss
1967 *The Discovery of Grounded Theory: Strategies for Qualitative Research.* New York: Aldine.

Guest, G., and E. McLellan
2003 Distinguishing the trees from the forest: Applying cluster analysis to thematic qualitative data. *Field Methods* 15(2):186–201.

Guest, G., E. McLellan-Lemal, D. M. Matia, R. Pickard, J. Fuchs, D. McKirnan, and J. L. Neidig
2005 HIV vaccine efficacy trial participation: Men who have sex with men's experiences of risk reduction counseling and perceptions of risk behavior change. *AIDS Care* 17(1):46–57.

Johnson, R. A., and D. W. Wichern
2002 *Applied Multivariate Statistical Analysis.* Upper Saddle River, N.J.: Prentice Hall.

Kearney, M., S. Murphy, and M. Rosenbaum
1994 Mothering on crack cocaine: A grounded theory analysis. *Social Science and Medicine* 38:351–361.

Krippendorf, K.
1980 *Content Analysis: An Introduction to Its Methodology.* Beverly Hills, Calif.: Sage.

Kruskal, J. B.
1964 Multidimensional scaling by optimizing goodness of fit to a nonmetric hypothesis. *Psychometrika* 29:1-27.

LeCompte, M. D., and J. J. Schensul
1999 *Analyzing and Interpreting Ethnographic Data.* Walnut Creek, Calif.: Altamira.

Lewins, A., and C. Silver
2007 Choosing a CAQDAS package. In A. Lewins and C. Silver, eds. *Using Software in Qualitative Research: A Step-by-Step Guide.* London: Sage.

MacQueen, K. M.
2005 What to look for in software for qualitative data analysis. In Priscilla R. Ulin, Elizabeth T. Robinson, and Elizabeth Tolley, eds. *Qualitative Methods in Public Health: A Field Guide for Applied Research.* Pp. 172–174. San Francisco: Jossey-Bass.

MacQueen, K. M., E. McLellan, D. Metzger, S. Kegeles, R. Strauss, R. Scotti, L. Blanchard, and R. Trotter
2001 What is community? An evidence-based definition for participatory public health. *American Journal of Public Health* 91:1929–1937.

MacQueen, K. M., and B. Milstein
1999 A systems approach to qualitative data management and analysis. *Field Methods* 11: 27–39.

MacQueen, K. M., E. Namey, D. Chilongozi, S. Mtweve, M. Mlingo, N. Morar, C. Reid, A. Ristow, S. Sahay, and the HPTN 035 Standard of Care Assessment Team
2007 Community perspectives on care options for HIV prevention trial participants. *AIDS Care Journal* 19(4): 554–560.

Miles, M. B., and M. A. Huberman
1994 *Qualitative Data Analysis: An Expanded Sourcebook* (2nd ed.). Thousand Oaks, Calif.: Sage.

Osgood, C.
1959 The representational model and relevant research methods. In I. de Sola Pool, ed. *Trends in Content Analysis.* Pp. 33–88. Urbana: University of Illinois Press.

Pacific Northwest National Laboratory
2004 *IN-SPIRE, 2.3.* Seattle, Wash.: Pacific Northwest National Laboratory.

Patton, M. Q.
1990 *Qualitative Evaluation and Research Methods* (2nd ed.). Newbury Park, Calif.: Sage.

Ryan, G., and R. Bernard
2000 Data management and analysis methods. In Norman Denzin and Yvonna Lincoln, eds. *Handbook of Qualitative Research.* Pp. 769–802. Thousand Oaks, Calif.: Sage.

Ryan, G., and T. Weisner
1996   Analyzing words in brief descriptions: Fathers and mothers describe their children. *Cultural Anthropology Methods Journal* 8:13–16.

Schiffman, S. S., L. M. Reynolds, and F. W. Young
1981   *Introduction to Multidimensional Scaling: Theory, Methods, and Applications.* New York: Academic.

Schnegg, M., and H. R. Bernard
1996   Words as actors: A method for doing semantic network analysis. *Cultural Anthropology Methods Journal* 8(2):7–10.

Sturrock, K., and J. Rocha
2000   A Multidimensional Scaling Stress Evaluation Table. *Field Methods* 12(1):49–60.

Thairu, L.
2005   Ethnographic case studies of infant feeding in the context of HIV/AIDS and newborn care in sub-Saharan Africa. Ph.D. dissertation, Division of Nutritional Sciences, Cornell University, Ithaca, N.Y.

Tufte, E.
1990   *Envisioning Information.* Cheshire, Conn.: Graphics Press.
1992   *The Visual Display of Quantitative Information.* Cheshire, Conn.: Graphics Press.
1997   *Visual Explanations: Images and Quantities, Evidence and Narrative.* Cheshire, Conn.: Graphics Press.

Weber, R. P.
1990   *Basic Content Analysis.* Newbury Park, Calif.: Sage.

Weitzman, E. A., and M. B. Miles
1995   *Computer Programs for Qualitative Data Analysis.* Thousand Oaks, Calif.: Sage.

Weller, S., and A. Romney
1988   *Systematic Data Collection.* Newbury Park, Calif.: Sage.

Wright, K. B.
1997   Shared ideology in Alcoholics Anonymous: A grounded theory approach. *Journal of Health Communication* 2(2):83–99.

QUALITY CONTROL
AND ASSURANCE

III

*A real understanding of Quality doesn't just serve the System,
or even beat it or even escape it. A real understanding of
Quality captures the System, tames it, and puts it to work for
one's own personal use, while leaving one completely free to
fulfill his inner destiny.*

ROBERT M. PIRSIG, *ZEN AND THE ART OF MOTORCYCLE MAINTENANCE*

Qualitative Data Management $\qquad$ 8

ELEANOR MCLELLAN-LEMAL

R EGARDLESS OF THE SCOPE OF A STUDY and the number of interviews, focus groups, observations, or document reviews undertaken, qualitative research tends to produce an exorbitant amount
of information. Organizing and inspecting this information in an attempt
to make sense of it is by no means an easy task. In team-based qualitative
research even more data gets produced, so a system for effectively, efficiently, and methodically storing, accessing, and managing this volume of
information is imperative. Without such a system, the quality of the data
analysis may be hampered. Lyn Richards's (2005) experience suggests that
"the majority of people doing qualitative research have no training in qualitative research" and that those who have had training "learned of the philosophy of method and/or ways of making data, but not what to do with
data if they ever had any." While her comment is more than likely directed
toward data analysis and interpretation, data management may also be of
concern.

When we talk about a lack of understanding of what to do with qualitative data, it is necessary to consider who is using the methodology and
how they are using it. Qualitative data collection techniques, independent
of theoretical and methodological principles, are used for nonresearch purposes and by nonresearchers. In the nonresearch context, a research design,
sampling approach, and analysis plan are more than likely lacking even if
the person leading the project has some level of qualitative research training. Moreover, it is unlikely that the qualitative project is reviewed by an
institutional review board (IRB) or a similar body to ensure that ethical
conduct and protection of human subjects are established and maintained.

In some instances, references to ad hoc or internal discussions may be the only clues we get that these activities are not based on a systematic scientific inquiry. Other times, it becomes clear that the activities to understand where a group, organization, community, individual, or some other entity stands on a particular issue or topic are entirely self-serving. An organization may hold several focus group discussions with staff or consumers to get their input on how to improve its public image. Or a journalist can interview a few selected persons regarding their thoughts on a particular topic in an attempt to obtain confirmatory views. In the nonresearcher scenario, indigenous community members may be brought in to conduct interviews, lead group discussions, or confirm the veracity of conclusions or statements being made by the project sponsors about the information collected. Incidentally, formal data analysis is not likely in either of these scenarios. The attitude is usually that analysis is not needed because they have a sufficient understanding of what is important given that they participated in or were present during the data collection, listened to the audio recordings, or watched the video clips.

If we remove these two types of qualitative-methods consumers and focus on scientific researchers engaged in team-based qualitative research, what certainty do we have that they know how to properly work with data possibly collected from multiple methods, data sources, researchers, and sites? Qualitative researchers come in many shapes and forms. Novice researchers are not necessarily untrained researchers. They may just be entirely new to qualitative methods or have limited experience applying qualitative methods, including data management and analysis. Similarly, the seasoned qualitative researcher may not be trained or experienced in all qualitative approaches. Moreover, the seasoned qualitative researcher, who is accustomed to undertaking research alone, may not be suitable for team-based projects. How can we ensure that persons involved in team-based qualitative research are prepared to both gather and work with qualitative data? Cutcliffe and McKenna (2004) introduce the concept of the expert qualitative researcher as possessing six traits: he or she is someone who

1. is experienced;
2. uses a different data analysis process [i.e., not formulaic or prescribed] because he or she has a big-picture understanding of the phenomenon under study;
3. does not rely on analytical principles to connect his understanding or explanation of the phenomenon to findings that are authentic as well as credible;

4. develops through his extensive and cumulative research experience an intuitive grasp on qualitative data analysis that permits him to zero in on the key themes and core features of the findings;
5. undertakes a fluid, flexible, and highly proficient analysis because he is no longer conscious of [i.e., constrained by] qualitative data analysis rules; and
6. is able to go "beyond the words" to reach a particular finding because analytical decisions are rooted in a preconscious processing.

Because creativity and intuition are the hallmarks of qualitative data analysis for the expert qualitative researcher, he is often reluctant, unable, or uninterested in explaining the steps taken for working with the data or strategies to reach interpretations and conclusions (Cutcliffe and McKenna 2004). The emphasis on increased methodological rigor in team-based research as well as the possible absence or limited role of the expert qualitative researcher in this context may downplay creativity and intuition. Moreover, an approach that favors creativity and intuition over methods usually does not work well in team-based research. Even if all the data collection and analysis is handled by one team member, the rest of the team needs to be able to understand the process. Huberman and Miles (1994:429) observe that "qualitative studies, especially those done by inexperienced or lone-wolf researchers, are vulnerable when it comes to data management." My experience with a variety of large team-based projects has taught me that every data analyst attempts to do something slightly different in handling the qualitative data even when detailed oral and written guidance are provided. Procedures have to be established to ensure that consistency is maintained. All exceptions to the guidelines require documentation and every piece of data must be inspected to ensure that it complies with the revised guidelines. Fernald and Duclos (2005) similarly stress that "in a team setting, little should be left to chance." Without clear guidelines and practices for analyzing and handling qualitative data, a team will not be successful in moving the analysis forward. Notably, a team-based research situation requires the availability of training materials and resources to support the less-than-expert qualitative researcher in dealing with the challenges and rewards of gathering and working with qualitative data (see chapter 4, this volume).

If we take a step back and think about how qualitative research is usually presented, we find that there is a tendency to describe it in terms of stages or phases. And, while repeated emphasis is made that a linear process does not occur in qualitative research, these stages are usually presented as the design phase, the data collection phase, the transcription phase, and the analysis phase. Missing is reference to what connects these phases together. The missing component, of course, is data management. Thus, in this chapter, I will provide a working definition of qualitative data management and propose eight basic principles for managing qualitative data: (1) data labeling and tracking; (2) data inspection and monitoring; (3) data storage, archiving, and disposal; (4) data structure and layout; (5) data quality; (6) data linking; (7) data synchronization; and (8) data enrichment. Observational case studies derived from various public health research projects I have been involved in over the past decade are presented to help illustrate the importance of good data management practices. Calling for standardization of qualitative data management is not the goal of this chapter. Instead, emphasis is on familiarizing teams undertaking qualitative research with these principles so that they make informed decisions about how to best manage their data so that it complements their data collection, theoretical, analytical, and resource needs.

Defining Qualitative Data Management

The *Infoserve Technologies Corporation* (2004) defines data management as including "all the disciplines related to managing data as a valuable resource, including acquisition, database administration, storage, backup, security and quality assurance." While this definition is consistent with the one provided by Huberman and Miles (1994), they further clarify that qualitative data management operations focus on ensuring "(a) high quality, accessible data; (b) documentation of just what analyses have been carried out; and (c) retention of data and associated analyses after the study is completed" (p. 428). These two definitions will be adapted here to include all the processes necessary for systematically and consistently collecting, tracking, preparing, processing, organizing, storing, securing, retrieving, verifying, and sharing qualitative data so that it can be used to (a) inform subsequent data collection and (b) perform data analysis, including triangulation and interpretation.

Whatever is done with or to the data has an influence on how it can be analyzed, interpreted, and presented. The "seemingly practical task of sorting and ordering of data" involves decisions and assumptions that ultimately "open up some analytical possibilities and . . . close off others" (Mason 2002). Mismanagement of qualitative data can confound, delay, or instill doubts about the authenticity and trustworthiness of findings, and even raise questions about whether the use of qualitative methods is appropriate. Moreover, the increasing popularity of team-based qualitative research, mixed-methods research designs,[1] and the call to make qualitative methods more accessible and transparent requires that we go beyond deconstructing the qualitative data analysis process and address qualitative data management. Huberman and Miles (1994) point out that the absence of a "coherent system" eventually lends itself to "data management limbo" where data can be disregarded or lost. To escape this limbo, whereby data has been collected but analysis does not really move forward or encounters a number of setbacks, a research team must have a common understanding of what is meant by data management and basic procedures for undertaking that process.

Research teams using qualitative methods regardless of training and experience may be incapable of recognizing and resolving bad data situations because they can only see a two-step process ahead of them: collect the data and analyze the data. Such an approach tends to focus on turning out products (e.g., conduct fifty interviews, moderate eight focus groups, identify three reasons for communication failure between parents and teens, generate a report, develop measures for a quantitative questionnaire). Even if analysis is deliberately cursory or succinct because the aim of the study is to arrive at a quick snapshot of a particular situation or issue so as to immediately inform the development or evaluation of other studies, programs, services, or policies, the data has to be appropriately managed to allow this to happen.

Persons who are not involved in collecting or analyzing the data may be assigned the task of managing it. Ideally, a qualitative data manager[2] should be familiar with the research methodology, aware of what is taking place in the field at all times, and understand the basics of qualitative data analysis. A review of current job postings on the Internet, however, suggests that a new generation of technologically savvy data managers experienced in handling both qualitative and quantitative data are favored. The possibility that such a data manager's qualitative research skills and knowledge are comparable to or exceed his or her quantitative research skills is unlikely. In part this is due to the contrasting paradigms between quantitative and qualitative approaches, especially when it comes to data analysis. Putting aside the objective versus subjective issue, quantitative researchers are taught to focus on predication and inference, whereas qualitative researchers are taught to focus on understanding how a phenomenon comes to be as well as the possibility that multiple explanations account for the phenomenon. Hence, there is a possibility that a researcher, who is trained predominately in quantitative methods, may be unable to manage and make sense of a large volume of qualitative data and resort to handling it as a quantitative data set. Those concerned with the denigration of qualitative research (Morse 2001) may argue that by providing principles for managing qualitative data there is the danger of allowing persons with little qualitative experience to adopt what Barbour (2003) calls "technical essentialism" (i.e., overemphasis on completing perfunctory checklists). Given Richards's (2005) observation, however, it is clear that the challenge of what to do with data will not go away. Working with qualitative data involves much more than coding it, generating a list of concepts or themes, and extracting interesting or salacious quotes.

Technology and Data Management

From the early use of recording equipment to punch cards for categorizing and sorting text, technology has provided tools that have influenced how we acquire and work with qualitative data.[3] Given the complexity involved in even the most basic team-based qualitative project, technological tools, including electronic data management systems, are optimal for team-based research. An electronic qualitative data management system (EQDMS) does not abandon the concept of creating a "good paper trail" and, in many instances, requires the application of paper-and-pencil techniques. Presumably, such a system can be quickly accessed and shared. An EQDMS does not require use of computer-assisted qualitative data analysis software (CAQDAS), but should complement the selected software if it is used. A list of the minimal components that a CAQDAS system should include to support effective data management is provided at the end of this chapter.

At this time, most CAQDAS does not support the importing of spreadsheets or other types of databases. This, however, should not be used as a disincentive for striving to bring together information that better informs research design, theoretical orientation, and analytical objectives. The task of organizing and sorting qualitative data requires careful planning and execution (Mason 2002). It can be time-consuming, but the payoff is well worth the effort. Teams will find that components of one data management system can easily be transferred, replicated, or adapted to other projects.

Data Management Challenges

There are three challenges associated with qualitative data management. First, there is limited access to information on how to do it. Detailed information on qualitative data management is usually found in a research proposal or a procedural manual that is rarely accessible to researchers outside of a study. Methods courses, books, and journal articles frequently refer to strategies or tools for managing qualitative data, but then focus exclusively on describing data reduction and analysis approaches, namely code-and-retrieval methods. An exception to these trends is a qualitative training manual that includes examples of data management procedures and forms (Mack et al. 2005).

Second, there appears to be a common misconception that qualitative data management is synonymous with CAQDAS. The code-and-retrieval method may be one of the reasons that an association with CAQDAS has been established, especially given that this is the foundation for inductive-based content or thematic analyses. Most CAQDAS support the assembling of electronic audit trails that can help the researcher keep track of the "evolving analysis" as well as provide documentation to funding sources or research auditors that will help facilitate review or further assessment of the qualitative study (Rodgers and Cowles 1993). They also help provide "the textual and interpretive evidence" for building theory (MacQueen and Milstein 1999). It is, however, becoming increasingly common to find that researchers learn to use CAQDAS programs without having a complete understanding of either the various data that need to be managed or the range of data management tools the software has to offer. Those who have never undertaken qualitative data analysis are likely to believe that CAQDAS operate very similar to a statistical package: data gets imported or entered, is followed by some data cleanup or verification routine, and is then ready for analysis. Such persons also tend to assume that, rather than supporting number crunching, qualitative data analysis software will support concept crunching. Salient themes and relationships or patterns between themes will be automatically recognized by the software system and appropriate output reports generated.

Third, qualitative data management is neither a linear nor sequential process, nor does it occur independently of data collection and analysis (Huberman and Miles 1994, Rodgers and Cowles 1993). Coding is viewed by some researchers as a data management activity, while others approach it as an analysis procedure. It is both. It generally starts out as a data management task, moves toward analysis and interpretation, and returns to managing data at numerous times throughout the process. The analysis codebook, for example, starts out very much as a data management activity, but needs to be continually evaluated against the data to ensure that the codes appropriately correspond with the text. One of the dangers of forgetting this is the reification of codes (Drisko 1998). Wolcott (1994) makes the distinction between the mechanical and conceptual aspects of working with qualitative data. The mechanical tasks of coding, indexing, sorting, retrieving, and manipulating are how the data are managed or processed. Conversely, the conceptual aspect encompasses three concurrent strategies for transforming data: description, analysis, and interpretation. Wolcott (1994) explains,

> *Description* addresses the question, "What is going on here?" Data consists of observations made by the researcher and/or reported to the researcher by others.

> *Analysis* addresses the identification of essential features and the systematic description of interrelationships among them—in short, how things work. In terms of stated objectives, analysis also may be employed evaluatively to address questions of why a system is not working or how it might be made to work "better."

> *Interpretation* addresses processual questions of meanings and contexts: "What does it all mean?" "What is to be made of it all?"

If we use this distinction to think about what needs to be done with the qualitative data, it becomes easier to develop data management plans and procedures appropriate for team-based research. Notably, as qualitative data collection and analysis must balance rigor with flexibility, so too must the techniques for managing the data be flexible. When detailed yet flexible guidelines for managing data are not prepared in advance, data management decisions are likely to be made as the research study unfolds. In such a scenario, instructions for how to handle or process data are usually communicated post facto and create the potential that data may be lost or may become unusable. Moreover, questions about its authenticity or integrity may result. Miles and Huberman (1994) advise us to question what we think our data management needs might be as well as how much thoroughness is required. They provide us with examples of *what* we need to store, retrieve from, and retain, but ultimately leave us wishing that they had shared more of their knowledge on *how* to initiate and structure the data management process.

Data Management Approaches

Two decades ago, Levine (1985) borrowed from the information and library sciences to identify five basic principles of qualitative data storage and retrieval: formatting, cross-referral, indexing, abstracting, and pagination. While these principles provide exceptional tools for developing a retrieval system that facilitates data reduction,[4] the mechanics for how to manage qualitative data are incomplete. MacQueen and Milstein (1999) offer more comprehensive guidance, both conceptually and architecturally, on designing a data management system that supports systematic handling of qualitative data and that is conducive to team-based research. They emphasize that a system should be able to capture distinctions between the types of data generated during qualitative research and identify the relationships between such data.[5] In addition, the system should support coordination of data collection, management, and analysis tasks. Lastly, it should provide a framework to assess strengths, weaknesses, and biases within a database by making the content explicit. The field of business intelligence (BI) offers a third model that focuses on data quality in terms of information technology and financial cost-effectiveness. The BI model centers on five principles:

- *Data profiling* refers to the procedures for checking the data for errors, inconsistencies, redundancies, and incomplete or missing information
- *Data quality*, which includes the steps for correcting, standardizing, and verifying the data, is defined as "data is accurate, consistent, valid, unique, complete, and timely" (Hunley 2004)
- *Data integration* is the matching, merging, or linking of data from different data sources
- *Data enrichment or augmentation* uses information from internal and external data sources
- *Data monitoring* is the process of checking and controlling data integrity over time

By merging elements derived from these three approaches, it becomes possible to illuminate the "black box of data management" referred to by MacQueen and Milstein (1999). This conceptual merger results in practical strategies for working with and working on all qualitative data in both a systematic and simplified manner, and helps develop a centralized, coherent data management system. Moreover, it heightens the importance of data management and makes it unacceptable to approach qualitative research without a plan for ensuring the quality and integrity of the data and the ability to share those data with other members of the research team.

Tales of Data Mismanagement

I have selected three case studies to help illustrate why establishing good data management guidelines and procedures is imperative in qualitative team-based research.

Case Study 1

Research Team 1 uses qualitative interviewing methods to examine perceptions toward incorporating a diagnostic testing procedure into routine adult primary care. The multisite team collects data from more than 180 individual interviews and twenty-four focus groups. Persons interested in taking part in the study are screened to make sure they meet age and race/ethnic eligibility criteria. All persons presenting for screening are assigned a unique study participant identification (Source ID) label composed of alphanumeric characters that correspond with data collection site and type of interview (individual vs. group). If enrolled, this same Source ID is assigned to their demographic information and interview data. If ineligible or not enrolled, the Source ID is assigned only to the screening information. At one site, the research team deviates from this participant tracking system. Instead, they assign an initial screening Source ID; a second Source ID if the person is eligible, agrees to participate, and completes a brief demographic questionnaire; and a third Source ID if the person participates in an individual or group interview. Linkage between three Source IDs is not consistently maintained, thus making it difficult to connect demographic data with interview data as well as to document the number of people screened, the number eligible, and number successfully enrolled in the study. Analytic comparisons are limited to data collection site and type of interview completed.

Case Study 2

Research Team 2 administers a survey to 450 health service representatives that includes a qualitative component (three open-ended questions). They rely on a contractor who provides qualitative research design and data analysis assistance among its wide range of research services to code the open-ended responses. Each coded text response is associated with a unique participant ID number, hence presenting the possibility of merging the qualitative and quantitative databases. After coding is completed, it is discovered that it is not possible to merge the two databases because of discrepancies in IDs in the qualitative database. When the coded responses are examined more closely, it is discovered that in addition to assigning the wrong ID to 30 percent of the responses, new IDs have been created. In correcting the ID discrepancies, it is then noted that text containing similar concepts are coded entirely differently. Examination of the codebook reveals that several pairs of codes have overlapping definitions, that definitions for some codes are not consistent with their usage, and that there are codes that had never been used. Modifications to the codebook and re-coding of the open-ended responses necessitate going back to look at the interview questions. At this point, it is discovered that two of the questions are problematic. One question is presented as close-ended and produces predominately yes/no responses. The other is a double-barreled question, which makes it difficult or impossible to discern to which part of the question participants responded.

Case Study 3

Research Team 3 includes a trained qualitative researcher with no prior experience in team-based research to oversee the data management and analysis of interview data collected at six research sites by multiple interviewers. Audiotapes are transcribed verbatim by a transcription service. It is, therefore, the responsibility of the data manager/analyst to document audiotapes submitted for transcription, record when transcripts and audiotapes are returned by the transcription service, verify the accuracy of transcripts against the audiotapes and note any problems with sound quality, remove names and other potentially sensitive information, add the transcripts to a CAQDAS database, and destroy the audiotapes. The data manager/analyst is provided oral and written instruction about data management and analysis procedures. After some preliminary coding is completed, it is noted that the CAQDAS database contains duplicate versions of several transcripts. To identify and resolve the problem, the data manager/analyst is asked to provide the data management documentation. The documentation is found to be incomplete; however, it is possible to partially reconstruct it by using billing records and e-mails from the transcription service. Completion of the remainder of the documentation requires inventorying the audiotapes, which are still in storage. The data manager/analyst has separated the audiotapes into two boxes. The box labeled "Verified and Ready to Be Destroyed" is found to contain a number of the audiotapes that were never sent to the transcription service and transcripts that have not been verified for accuracy but have already been included in the CAQDAS database. Data analysis activities are consequently suspended until the data management issues are resolved.

Eight Principles of Good Data Management

With these case examples in mind, the remainder of this chapter will focus on describing the eight principles of data management. In setting up or developing a data management system, consideration should be given to the resources needed (materials, supplies, equipment, personnel, software, facilities, etc.) and their availability as well as the type of expertise that is required to work with the data. In addition, the team also needs to take into account the different types of data that will need to be managed, the amount of data to be collected and analyzed, and the number of persons who will require access to the data. The data management systems should also cover the logistics for sharing data, the theory and method for analyzing the data, and the level of analysis required (rapid vs. in-depth), including the level of granularity that will best support analysis. Granularity refers to the level of specificity or detail applied in reducing the data, segmenting or splicing the text, and developing the codes and other analytical constructs, including themes and patterns. A coarse granularity represents abstract ideas and meanings, while a fine granularity focuses on more concrete ones.

Principle 1: Data Labeling and Tracking

Data labeling refers to the procedures for tagging or identifying information, while data tracking is the physical documentation (audit trail) of every process and procedure the data have undergone from acquisition to analysis. Ideally, the research design or procedures manual includes a naming protocol that instructs the research team on what labels must be assigned to every key component that characterizes the data collected. For example, the study ID starts with initials that identify the data collection site. This information is followed by an interview number. Focus groups are assigned one series of ID numbers while individual interviews are given another series. Huberman and Miles (1994) suggest that information on how data will be tracked accompany the sampling plan. The type of data to be collected, information about the study sample, and the proposed timeline help identify what needs to be tracked, and may inform the key data labels needed to facilitate data retrieval. Also, conventions for how materials are to be date-stamped should be determined in advance. Questions that may inform the data labeling and tracking process include the following:

1. Will identification labels (IDs) be assigned or will some other identifier be used to catalog data collected?
2. In addition to recording the date the data were collected, are there other dates that require documentation (e.g., date of transcription, date transferred from handwritten notes to an electronic file)?

3. How will different forms of data collection be identified, including pilot-test data (e.g., in-depth interviews, focus group discussions, observations, social network data, quantitative questionnaire, diary)?

4. How will different classifications of interview participants (e.g., patients, healthcare providers, traditional healers) or observation sites (e.g., clinic, village plaza, market place) be noted?

5. How will the mode of data collection (community map, handwritten notes, audiorecorded, videotaped, diary entry) or any deviations from the preferred mode be documented?

6. If data collection is done in a language other than English, how will this be documented? And if translation is performed, is it necessary to include who translated it?

7. How are modifications to memos tracked (e.g., original entry vs. subsequent expansions to an existing entry)?

8. What are the conventions for naming codes? What are essential components of the analysis codebook? (Chapter 6 in this volume describes principles for codebook development.)

Principle 2: Data Inspection and Monitoring

Data inspection requires checking the data for both completeness and comparability. Inspection takes place as you collect, manage, and analyze the data. While data are being collected, it is important to inspect audio recordings, handwritten notes, transcripts, and other records to ensure that sufficient data have been collected to address your research question and that data are audible and legible and that no part of it had been inadvertently omitted. Where data may not be complete, documentation should identify and explain missing information.

Constant data inspection (monitoring) also helps guarantee that comparable data are collected. In team-based research the use of semistructured interview guides is common. If one member of the data collection team decides to consistently omit a particular question or fails to probe on specific information that is relevant to the research objectives, the ability to perform comparisons across the data before you get into the in-depth analysis may be affected. Below are examples of data inspection considerations:

1. Identify which questions were asked and then determine if they were asked in a comparable manner. For example, if an interview guide item focuses on how a person can become infected with

HIV (risk factors), an interviewer asking "How does a person not get HIV?" (protective factors) raises data comparability issues. Other times, it may be more challenging to figure out if rewording or paraphrasing of a question alters its intent.

2. Determine if a relevant response is given for each interview guide item presented. Emphasis may shift from examining data for meaningful information to determining if saturation has been achieved.

3. If it is determined that a particular question or set of questions is not working (e.g., not relevant to the study population or usually elicits "no comment" or "I don't know anything about that"), reassess the need to continue asking this question (if saturation has been reached) or including it in the analysis.

4. Are distinctions between a pair of questions artificial (e.g., respondents repeatedly state "I think I already answered that")? If so, determine if it is possible to identify which one of the questions makes most sense to respondents and elicits the more detailed responses, and omit the duplicate item. Alternatively, decide if responses to these pairs or sets of questions need to be extracted and analyzed together.

5. Where appropriate, reconcile any data inconsistencies or gaps with respondents (e.g., probe or ask comparison questions) and with other members of the qualitative research team.

6. When data are being prepared (i.e., undergoing the transcription phase), inspection is the necessary step for ensuring that data are cleaned or scrubbed before analysis is undertaken. This can involve checking for typos, correct labeling, completeness, and consistent formatting. It can also involve transforming verbatim transcripts that include only what was captured in the original audio, video, or written record into edited transcripts that contain supplemental contextual or environmental information. In inspecting prepared data, it is useful to have written guidelines that detail the "raw to cooked" transcription process and checklists that can be used to verify that conventions have been followed.

Keep in mind that data inspection does not end with the preparation phase. During analysis it is important to continually inspect the data to make sure that the categorizing and sorting process produces no inconsistencies or incompatibilities with what is actually contained in information provided by the study respondents. Moreover, the data analysis phase results in the creation of new data (codes, themes, relationship patterns). The development of analytical constructs and codes also requires inspection for completeness and comparability. In terms of data analysis, data inspection may require generating reports or preparing comparison tables to verify that all relevant data have been coded, that codes have been applied correctly, and code application is consistent for the entire project. In addition, data inspection can be used to document information not provided when it should have been or document insufficient description or elaboration of key areas of inquiry.

Principle 3: Data Storage, Archival, and Disposal

Where and how data will be stored to facilitate retrieval needs to be planned in advance. The physical and electronic locations for data storage should be identified prior to data collection and procedures put in place to ensure that access is limited and secured. Moreover, procedures for backing up or archiving data should be clearly delineated, including the intervals at which these two tasks should be undertaken. Backups of analog or digital audio or video data may need to be made. Analog data requires appropriate physical storage safe from environmental and climatic elements. Digital files require sufficient space on a network server, hard drive, or compact disk.

It is generally a good idea to store raw qualitative data separately from processed/prepared data. In situations where it is necessary to use archived data, a new copy should be made instead of altering the archived document. It is not uncommon for servers to crash, electronic files to become corrupted, or documents ruined; hence, it is recommended that multiple archival mediums be used to store records. Participants' personal data, especially any information that could make their identity known (consent forms, telephone logs, interview schedule, etc.), should be stored in a separate location and secured. When appropriate, names and other personal identifiers should be substituted (encrypted) or removed from transcripts. Unlike quantitative data sets, breaking the link between a participant study ID and the person's name may be more complex, especially if a limited social role or position must be maintained (e.g., medicine man, midwife, village chief, CEO).

Decisions about how and when to dispose of data also need to be specified. Disposal of raw data and removal of links to personal data needs to be appropriately timed. When a project reaches completion, the team may disband. Archived and stored data cannot remain in its location indefinitely. Moreover, there is an ethical responsibility to ensure proper disposal of data after they are no longer being used. Considerations may include the following:

1. How many people will require access to the data?
2. How often should data be backed up? Will data backups be stored in multiple locations, servers, or digital mediums?
3. How much storage space will be required? What modifications will need to be made to the storage area to ensure that it can accommodate the data and that the data are secured (e.g., locked cabinets, computer firewalls)?
4. When will the data be disposed? Can some parts be disposed sooner than others? What should be retained?
5. In storing electronic data long-term, what software considerations must be made to ensure that changes in technology do not negatively impact data access and usability?

Principle 4: Data Structure and Layout

Presumably, in collecting and preparing your data for analysis, the team has given careful thought to how specific units of information (data elements/objects) must always remain connected to one another (e.g., text is linked to the source that provided it) as well as to connections that need to be established (e.g., relationships between codes). Data elements/objects are then subject to particular rules or logic that help ensure that the structure supports the analytic availability and function of these connections. Hence, the structure must contain both fixed and flexible attributes. If a form, data table, or spreadsheet includes a demographic field for documenting a respondent's occupation, all entries in that field should be related to the type of work that provides livelihood. While the team may determine that livelihood need not be limited to a source of monetary income, the field is nevertheless fixed. On the other hand, if the team is studying a polygamous society and men are reporting that marrying wealthy widows is their livelihood, the existing structure should accommodate the creation of a new field for documenting information that may not be captured otherwise.

Because text is typically the crux of qualitative data analysis, how information is organized within a document (i.e., layout) is of importance. The document layout includes the ordering of items, document header, page margins, font size, paragraph breaks, speaker labels, and so on. The goal is to have similar items use the same layout guidelines to make it easier to inspect the data and ensure their quality. Because a qualitative team shares numerous documents, it is quite easy to become overwhelmed by the amount of text that needs to be reviewed. By developing a consistent layout, researchers are able to efficiently handle all the study data, rather than only their own data contributions.

If qualitative software will be used to analyze the data, it is important to plan the data layout so that it is consistent with the software requirements. What may work for one program may not be appropriate for another. Chapter 5 in this volume provides more details regarding data transcription and layout.

Principle 5: Data Quality

After inspecting the data, it is necessary to determine if they are ready to be analyzed and shared. Data quality is about improving the data, that is, its "fitness of use" (Tayi and Ballou 1998). With quantitative data, four dimensions provide the foundation for assessing the data's fitness of use: accuracy, completeness, consistency, and timeliness. Accuracy refers to the exactness or correctness of the data records, completeness to the availability of all relevant information recorded, adherence to a standardized format for recording relevant records, and timeliness to the appropriateness (in terms of generalizability and in addressing research gaps) of the information (Tayi and Ballou 1998).

With qualitative data, the dimensions of accuracy, completeness, consistency, and timeliness need to be approached differently. The labels themselves are not problematic; it is the rigidness affixed to them that complicates their utility. While it is possible to check the accuracy of transcripts against the audio recordings, there may be times that technical failure, environmental factors (air conditioners, thunderstorms), interruptions (ringing telephones, baby crying), or speaker attributes (mumbles, whispers, speaks rapidly) create audio difficulties that make whatever an interviewer or respondent has said inaudible or undecipherable. Does this make the transcript unfit for use because it is incomplete by "hard data" standards? Data quality in qualitative research involves reflexivity, triangulation, auditability, constant comparison, respondent validation, transferability, and mindfulness to incorporating a wide range of perspectives, including attention to divergent or negatives cases, settings, and events (Mays and Pope 1996, 2000, Taylor et al. 2005). Chapter 10 in this volume presents a more complete discussion of these items.

Principle 6: Data Linking

Frequently, standardized information (although not necessary demographic data) is collected from study participants. To ensure that this information can be used to describe the study population and associate characteristics of respondents with particular perspectives and experiences, it is necessary to link the source with what the source had to say. Other times, nonstandardized information that is consistently documented by the research (e.g., observation or network data) can be linked with groups or communities of whom each participant is a member. It is therefore important to establish a system for linking data that is both efficient and that ensures the security of the data.

Principle 7: Data Synchronization

Because qualitative research is frequently iterative, it is important to ensure that any new procedural or analytical decisions have been consistently applied to all the data and that all related data elements can be properly connected (i.e., data linking is feasible). It is also important that all changes be documented. To bring together all relevant data for analysis, procedures for sorting and organizing it, including the system for cataloging it, needs to be coordinated. This is particularly true when developing, applying, and revising the analysis codebook.

Principle 8: Data Enrichment

Sometimes it is necessary to supplement data collected with other internal or external information that will help describe or contextualize the data that were collected. In terms of an internal data sources example, medical chart abstraction completed for prison inmates taking part in a qualitative study could provide information on a participant's medical and mental health status as well as other pertinent information (e.g., tattoos and body piercings acquired prior to and during their incarceration period). Other times, it may be necessary to rely on external data sources to help provide context for characteristics of the study population. For example, in examining utilization of health services, it may be worthwhile to compile data for each respondent regarding the number of service providers within the postal zip code of his or her area. Again, it is important to ensure that any linkages between the data sources are kept secure to protect participant confidentiality.

Data Management and Qualitative Data Analysis Software

Personally, I cannot begin to imagine how team-based qualitative data management and analysis could be accomplished entirely without the aid of qualitative data analysis software. Having said so, I must clarify that hard copies of transcripts, codebooks, and other documents are necessary in working with the data. Because data management and analysis are intricately interwoven, a single system for handling both is optimal. In the absence of such a system, finding tools to merge the two is critical.[6] Not all CAQDAS programs have the same data management capabilities. Data sharing is at times a challenge. Hence, there are many factors to consider when choosing a CAQDAS program. For a multisite project, it is important to keep in mind the needs and abilities of users at every site. The list in table 8.1, which was inspired in large part by MacQueen and Milstein (1999), may assist you in selecting CAQDAS that meets your data management as well as theoretical and analytic objectives.

Table 8.1.   Components of QDA Software

Component	Examples
Easy to set up and modify structures (e.g., text files, code books, and data tables)	▪ Requires minimal formatting of text files, including the need for special headers and footers ▪ Supports user-defined demographic data fields ▪ Sets no limits in terms of the number of textual files that can be added or the size of those files ▪ Allows file description comments; provides information about file name and directory paths if it is located outside of the system ▪ Alerts user to or prevents user from creating duplicate entries for text files, codes, and participant IDs ▪ Includes tools for quality control and assurance ▪ Permits multiple users to access the system, but prevents them from overwriting one another's work ▪ Creates user-defined and data-driven networks, coding trees, relationship maps, and data matrices (e.g., code, respondents/data source, demographic, coder) ▪ Creates a date stamp when something is added to or updated in the system
Easy to create audit trails	▪ Supports documentation of the procedures used to transform "raw" data into analysis-ready files ▪ Permits multiple users to create and track their own memos ▪ Includes tools for omitting, substituting or encrypting sensitive/confidential information

(continued)

Table 8.1.   *(continued)*

Component	Examples
Easy to modify data	■ Lets you add, remove, or clean raw text files ■ Provides an ability to rename files, participant IDs, and code labels
Easy to link data elements/objects (e.g., text segments, codes, and specific observations in data tables)	■ Supports user-defined links, but is capable of using this information to automatically create new links ■ Creates links to audio or visual files
Easy to retrieve information	■ Provides quick summaries about how many text files are stored, the number of participant IDs, number of codes in codebook, etc. ■ Lets you view, print, or export qualitative and quantitative codebooks with or without data ■ Includes a variety of reports that let you look at your data visually, numerically, or textually ■ Displays or prints information using specific selection criteria
Protects data integrity	■ Locks text files when coding has been initiated ■ Prevents accidental deletion of codes applied to the text ■ Includes tools for ensuring that all analysts use the same code label definition to guide their application of a code
Graphical user interface is not intimidating	■ Lets users customize views of windows and toolbars
Cost is within your budget	■ Does not require an annual site license renewal to run ■ Permits you to purchase multiple site licenses at a discount rate
Accessible technical support	■ Includes a user-friendly manual ■ Provides access to technical support ■ Enables interested users to interact via e-mail, Web, or telephone to provide hands-on support for one another

Lessons Learned

Working with qualitative data is not an easy task. To date, data handling has focused predominately on analysis strategies and tools. In general, greater attention needs to be given to how data is managed. Team-based research, in particular, demands greater systemization and centralization to ensure data quality, integrity, and comparability. A "black box" approach to qualitative data management serves only to increase the possibility of information mismanagement and misuse of qualitative data. Only by defining what is meant by qualitative data management and identifying principles for working with qualitative data can we minimize the errors that compromise accuracy, time, resources, and usability of qualitative data. Moreover, by incorporating the principles identified in this chapter, qualitative research teams can create coherent systems that avoid "data management limbo." Lastly, persons engaged in team-based qualitative research, regardless of their training, require both an in-depth orientation and a hands-on practicum to ensure that they completely understand the procedures for collecting, managing, analyzing, and theorizing qualitative data specific to their project. If a team does not include a seasoned qualitative researcher that has taken part in at least two team-based projects, the study would benefit greatly by identifying an outside researcher with such a background to provide this type of mentoring and guidance.

Each team must determine what data management approach works best for the project. Once identified and implemented, the approach must be centralized. Ideally, one person should be responsible for coordinating and monitoring the data management activities. Where this is not feasible, project timelines should incorporate multiple opportunities for ensuring that comparable data management is in place and for synchronizing both the procedures and products of data management.

Finally, a data management system once identified requires ongoing evaluation. Modifications should be made whenever problems are found in accessing, storing, retrieving, and sharing data. Care must be taken to ensure that all data has been reprocessed to meet the new specifications. The more time and effort that goes into the initial data management plan and procedures, the less time will be needed to overcome mistakes like those presented in the three case studies.

Notes

1. See R. Burke Johnson and Anthony J. Onwuegbuzie, "Mixed Methods Research: A Research Paradigm Whose Time Has Come," *Educational Researcher* 2004;33(7):14–26. The authors define mixed methods as "the class of research where the researcher mixes or combines quantitative and qualitative research techniques, methods, approaches, concepts or language into a single study."

2. References to a data manager in this chapter are to persons rather than software applications.

3. For a more comprehensive discussion on technology and qualitative research see Graham R. Gibbs, Susanne Friese, and Wilma C. Mangabeira, "The Use of New Technology in Qualitative Research," Introduction FQS 2002;3(2). Retrieved from www.qualitative-research.net/fgs/

4. Data reduction is the first of the three elements of data analysis that are introduced by Miles and Huberman (1994). The other two elements are data displays and conclusion drawing and verification. They define data reduction as the "process of selecting, focusing, simplifying, abstracting, and transforming the data that appear in written up field notes or transcriptions" (pp. 10–11).

5. An excellent resource for learning about relational databases is Michael J. Hernandez, *Database Design for Mere Mortals: A Hands-on Guide to Relational Database Design* (Massachusetts: Addison-Wesley, 1997).

6. Crystal Reports is a business intelligence application used to design and generate reports from a wide range of data sources, including Excel spreadsheets and Access tables or queries.

References

Barbour, R. S.
2003   The newfound credibility of qualitative research? Tales of technical essentialism and co-option. *Qualitative Health Research* 13(7):1019–1027.

Cutcliffe, J. R., and H. P. McKenna.
2004   Expert qualitative researchers and the use of audit trails. *Journal of Advances in Nursing* 45(2):126–133.

Drisko, James W.
1998   Using qualitative data analysis software. *Computers in Human Services* 15(1): 1–19.

Fernald, D. H., and C. W. Duclos
2005   Enhance your team-based qualitative research. *Annals of Family Medicine* 3(4):360–364.

Huberman, A. M., and M. B. Miles
1994   Data management and analysis methods. In N. K. Denzin and Y. S. Lincoln, eds. *Handbook of Qualitative Research*. Thousand Oaks, Calif.: Sage.

Hunley, E.
2004   SAS data quality: A technical overview (paper 099-29). 12 2204, at Cary, N.C. SAS Users Group International Group 29 Conference Proceedings. Montréal, Canada, May 9-12, 2004. Available at: sas.com/proceedings/sugi29/099-29.pdf. Accessed on September 22, 2006.

Infoserve Technologies Corporation
2004   "Data risk management." Available at: infoserveusa.com/2asp.net/DRisk Mgnt.html. Accessed February 22, 2007.

Levine, H. G.
1985   Principles of data storage and retrieval for use in qualitative evaluations. *Educational Evaluation and Policy Analysis* 7(2):169–186.

Mack, Natasha, Cynthia Woodsong, Kathleen McQueen, Greg Guest, and Emily Namey
2005   *Qualitative Research Methods: A Data Collector's Field Guide.* Research Triangle Park, N.C.: Family Health International.

MacQueen, Kathleen M. and Bobby Milstein
1999   A systems approach to qualitative data management. *Field Methods* 11(1): 27–39.

Mason, J.
2002   *Qualitative Researching.* Thousand Oaks, Calif.: Sage.

Mays, N., and C. Pope
2000   Qualitative research in health care. Assessing quality in qualitative research. *BMJ* 320(7226):50–52.
1996   Rigour and qualitative research. In P. Mays and C. Pope, eds. *Qualitative Research in Health Care.* London: BMJ Books.

Miles, M. B., and A. M. Huberman
1994   *Qualitative Data Analysis: An Expanded Sourcebook* (2nd ed.). Thousand Oaks, Calif.: Sage.

Morse, J. M.
2001   The awfulness of simplification. *Qualitative Health Research* 11(4):435.

Richards, Lyn
2005   Handling qualitative data: The challenge for teachers and researchers. Available at: wcer.wisc.edu/tqm/HandlingQualitativeDataIntro.html. Accessed August 25, 2006.

Rodgers, B. L., and K. V. Cowles
1993   The qualitative research audit trail: A complex collection of documentation. *Research in Nursing and Health* 16(3):219–226.

Tayi, Giri Kumar, and Donald P. Ballou
1998   Examining data quality. *Communications of the ACM* 41(2):54–57.

Taylor, Celia, Graham R. Gibbs, and Ann Lewins
2005   Quality of qualitative research. Available at: onlineqda.hud.ac.uk/Intro_QDA/qualitative_analysis.php. Accessed September 22, 2006.

Wolcott, Harry F.
1994   *Transforming Qualitative Data: Description, Analysis, and Interpretation.* Thousand Oaks, Calif.: Sage.

A Framework for Monitoring Sociobehavioral Research

9

GREG GUEST, EMILY NAMEY, AND KATHLEEN M. MACQUEEN

T HE LONE ETHNOGRAPHER HAS LITTLE NEED for formal monitoring procedures. With one person playing the multifaceted role of principal investigator, data collector, research analyst, and disseminator of results, all of the information about a research project resides with that one individual. Team-based research presents an entirely different picture. With the dispersal of project roles and activities across multiple individuals, the list of logistical and methodological challenges grows. If a project is housed in multiple locations, the challenge of monitoring study documents and ensuring protocol adherence becomes even more difficult.

One way to deal with the challenges that the dispersal of roles in team research presents is to set up study procedures to document activities and facilitate adherence to study protocols. Other chapters in this book address this need, either directly or indirectly, and provide suggestions and tools for improving rigor, transparency, and documentation of procedures in team-based studies. Yet procedures must be followed correctly in order to be effective, and monitoring a study helps ensure proper implementation of procedures. In this chapter, we present a framework for monitoring sociobehavioral research. In the first part of the chapter we present a rationale for the need to formally monitor sociobehavioral studies. In the second half, we describe a monitoring process we developed and field-tested in multiple countries. Our description is complemented with step-by-step monitoring instructions and a model checklist in the appendix. Although the process described in this chapter will be most helpful to research managers and principal investigators, it is equally relevant to anyone who is tasked with project oversight and responsibility for study conduct, as well as research team members.

For purposes of clarity, we first need to set the context and provide a few definitions regarding collaborative research. This chapter is written from the perspective of a study **sponsor**, which we define as the organization providing scientific direction and oversight for a research project, and which may or may not carry out data collection activities on the ground. A study sponsor is usually a person or organization that takes responsibility for the initiation, management, and/or financing of a study. In most cases, the principal investigator from the sponsoring institution is in the position of most accountability.

A sponsor is often accountable to a study's **funder**, whose main role is to provide financial resources upon review and approval of a research proposal and/or protocol. Sometimes the role of sponsor and funder is held by the same institution. In cases where the sponsor is not carrying out data collection, resources from the funder will likely be channeled through the sponsor and to one or more local **contracting agencies**. Contracting agencies are the organizations or individuals that are subcontracted to carry out the research activities according to an agreed-upon scope of work and corresponding budget. Contracted agencies can be nonprofit or for-profit institutions. In situations where the sponsoring organization is doing the data collection, a contracting agency is typically not necessary.

The key message in the above paragraph is that accountability for how a study is conducted rests primarily in the hands of the study's sponsor. Monitoring research is an integral part of a sponsor's role, and helps ensure compliance with ethical, scientific, and methodological guidelines and standards set out by international organizations, ethics committees, and funding agencies. Despite this responsibility, explicit guidelines or templates for monitoring sociobehavioral research are virtually nonexistent.

Detailed guidelines do exist, though, in other fields. They have been developed, for example, to aid in quality control and assurance in clinical research (International Conference on Harmonisation [ICH] 1996). These guidelines involve rigorous documentation of study communications, procedures, and events. Examples include documentation of adverse events, breaches in confidentiality, and results of study tests performed on participants. The basic premise behind clinical monitoring is that rigorous oversight and documentation of a study protects the participants' well-being and provides public and regulatory assurance that findings from a study are scientifically sound. Such explicit guidelines for social and behavioral research are wanting, and are generally limited to reporting and presenting data (see chapter 10, this volume; Des Jarlais et al. 2004) or listings of ethical principles prescribed by professional organizations. We hope to rectify this absence, at least partially, with the contents of this chapter.

Why Monitor Sociobehavioral Research?

Sociobehavioral research is as accountable to national and international ethical guidelines as clinical research, and is as susceptible to methodological pitfalls as clinical trials or any other type of research. This is especially true for collaborative research, which tends to be more complex in structure. In addition, sociobehavioral research is becoming increasingly international, often encompassing multiple sites and countries. Proof of rigorous and ethical conduct of such studies is becoming more and more important to a variety of international audiences that impose scrutiny on the international research arena (see chapter 2, this volume). In short, a study that provides good documentation of adherence to approved protocols benefits funding agencies, sponsors, the research team, participants, and civil society stakeholders in the research.

Monitoring is essential for ensuring compliance with the study protocol and scientific and ethical requirements. Documentation of ethics committee approvals and informed consent, for example, are requirements outlined in various domestic and international research ethics regulations and guidelines (e.g., Belmont Report, United States Code of Federal Regulations, Helsinki Declaration), and apply equally to clinical and sociobehavioral research (although the procedures may differ across study types). Increased recognition of the importance of sociobehavioral considerations for the planning, conduct, interpretation, and translation of clinical research has also led to increased scrutiny of sociobehavioral research standards (Des Jarlais et al. 2004). There is a need in the social and behavioral sciences for mechanisms that ensure quality, accountability, and transparency in research.

One model for such a mechanism exists in the field of clinical research. In the 1980s the International Conference on Harmonisation was created to facilitate public assurance of proper conduct of clinical trials. A detailed set of guidelines was developed, the most internationally known and accepted one being the *Guideline for Good Clinical Practice (GCP) (ICH-E6)*.[1] Good clinical practice is defined as

> an international ethical and scientific quality standard for designing, conducting, recording and reporting trials that involve the participation of human subjects. Compliance with this standard provides public assurance that the rights, safety and well-being of trial subjects are protected, consistent with the principles that have their origin in the Declaration of Helsinki, and that the clinical trial data are credible. (ICH 1996:1)

Protection of study participants is encompassed by the fundamental principles of research ethics—respect for persons, beneficence, and justice—and

these principles apply to all research. Protection of human research participants is equally vital to sociobehavioral research, which can involve social,
economic, and psychological harms (Labott and Johnson 2004). Social stigma
surrounding HIV/AIDS, for example, can have a devastating effect on research participants in studies associated with the virus, whether they are infected with the virus or not (Sheon et al. 1998). Individuals can lose their jobs,
be denied health insurance, or become victims of persecution (Ellis 1999).

All research can benefit from monitoring, but it is especially important
for team-based studies where research designs tend to be complex and mul-
tisited. Monitoring helps ensure that participants are protected. We know
of one international study, for example, in which the approved protocol
was not followed by a contracting agency, resulting in protocol violations
such as inadequate informed consent and breaches of participant confidentiality that came to light only after the study had been completed. Had
it been employed, the monitoring process we present below may have prevented these violations or identified them early enough to limit the damage and salvage the study.

In another example, based on a routine monitoring trip for one of our
own studies, a potential breach of confidentiality was observed. Local accounting practices at two of our research sites required inclusion of names
on receipts for reimbursements given to participants. These practices were
followed despite a week-long training of local investigators and field staff
that emphasized the importance of not collecting identifying information
from study participants. We subsequently addressed this breach by having
the accountants discontinue the practice, blacking out names on all receipts, and filing reports with both the in-country and the sponsor's ethics
committee. The site then developed alternative documentation strategies
for dispersing participant reimbursements.

Methodological problems and issues of data credibility are also not exclusive to clinical trials, and can be equally troublesome for sociobehavioral
research. Misunderstandings between the study designer(s) and fieldworkers can arise regarding any aspect of research design, and render serious
problems for consistency of data collection and management, thus compromising data integrity. Potential for error is amplified when protocols are
complex, involve multiple methods, and require large field teams (perhaps
spread across multiple study sites). In one international research project, for
example, inconsistent monitoring (owing to staffing changes at the sponsoring institution), combined with an overly ambitious local investigator,
led to a number of serious data collection and management issues, such as
the hiring of unqualified staff, use of inappropriate research methods,

poor-quality data collection instruments and techniques, transcription in-accuracies, and sampling errors (e.g., not sampling a particular subgroup of individuals as per the protocol). The result was poor-quality data that was virtually unusable.

Regular monitoring would likely have prevented the aforementioned problem. During a monitoring trip for one of our multisite studies, we discovered that the local research team in one site had used the wrong data collection instrument for a particular focus group, despite training and regular e-mail communication. We caught the mistake in time to correct it and the site was able to collect the data as intended. In another case, we observed errors in transcription of qualitative data and were able to correct the problems in situ. For example, text headers were not typed according to the transcription protocol, an oversight that had slowed down the transcription process and would have prevented the analysis software from performing correctly. An added benefit of being physically present in this latter case was the ability of the monitors to demonstrate, in person, additional software functions useful for transcription. We trained transcribers on the "Replace" function in MS Word and saved hours of effort in fixing the mistakes and in the subsequent typing of transcripts.

Comprehensive training, as discussed in other chapters of this book, can reduce the likelihood of the aforementioned problems occurring, but regular monitoring is also essential. It helps ensure that field teams maintain ethical standards, methodological rigor, and a solid understanding of the research objectives. Researchers have an obligation to inform all of the ethics committees that approve a given study about social or physical harm to participants, changes to the study design, or protocol violations such as breaches in confidentiality. Likewise, funding agencies have the right to audit a research study, and proper documentation is critical to being able to demonstrate methodological rigor and ethical conduct of the study. A rigorous monitoring process facilitates all of these things.

The Monitoring Process

In this section we begin with a general overview of a monitoring process that we developed and field-tested. The process includes logistics, instructions on how to use the checklist in the appendix, and general recommendations regarding documentation of procedures. The second part of this section provides the rationale for each component of the process we delineate. We have divided the process into seven different components; however, we recognize that conceptual overlap exists between some of the sections and stress that it is not necessary to follow the exact order of process presented here. A monitoring checklist and detailed instructions are provided in tables 9.1 and 9.2, respectively, and are intended as tools to be used in the field. Note also that in table 9.1 we have included real examples of notes taken during various monitoring visits, to give the reader a sense of how the form might be used.

We field-tested the monitoring process outlined below in three West African countries—Ghana, Nigeria, and Cameroon—among contracted agencies conducting formative, qualitative research for a clinical trial of an oral HIV chemo-prophylactic (see chapter 1, this volume, for a description of that study). On the basis of the test results, we revised the process and checklist. The revised monitoring process and companion checklist have since proven useful in identifying potential issues related to confidentiality, methodological rigor, and data integrity in numerous research contexts and international study settings. We have attempted to make the procedures as generic and widely useful as possible, although they may require modification for some research endeavors.

Basic Steps

The first part of the monitoring process begins at the monitor's office, a few weeks before the monitoring visit. The monitor should make copies of all of the documents necessary for the trip (see table 9.2 in the appendix) and prepare the local contact (usually the local lead investigator) for the trip, via a cover e-mail or letter. The letter should explain the purpose of the trip, and be accompanied by the checklist in table 9.1. Sending the checklist ahead of time provides the local contact(s) with an understanding of what the visit will cover and gives them enough time to gather and organize the required documents, thus making the monitor's visit more efficient. Make sure in the letter to inform the contact that the monitor will be expecting them, and/or an appropriate representative, to be able to quickly produce the documentation outlined in the checklist. A tentative agenda can also be sent ahead of time, if the complexity of a particular study warrants.

The size of any study will partly determine the amount of time needed to conduct a monitoring visit. One of our studies, for example, involved qualitative methodology and about 150 participants per site, per phase of research. We found that with two monitors we needed at least one full day to review each location where data were collected, processed, and stored. If studies are exceptionally large or data are located in different locations (e.g., data may initially be stored in a particular city or office and then transferred to another location for analysis), we suggest scheduling an additional day or bringing along an additional qualified person to divide the workload.[2]

Once on site, the monitor should document any emergent problems and make the appropriate corrections on site, if possible, according to study-specific correction procedures. Steps taken to correct a problem should also be documented, and any breaches in protocol or harm to participants should be reported by the local lead investigator, or responsible party, to the local ethics committee, with a copy to the study monitor. In turn, the monitor should report the event to any additional ethics committees that have approved the study, applicable oversight or regulatory agencies, and the study sponsor if different from the monitor's organization.

During the monitoring process, review the documents listed in the checklist and note their physical location(s). Review the adequacy of documents. Record the absence of, or difficulties in locating, any of the documents. Enquire as to reasons for any absent documents, record the response, and make appropriate corrections or recommendations.

Monitoring Objectives and Rationale

The overall objectives of any monitoring visit are to ensure and document (1) the scientific integrity of the research process, (2) the ethical conduct of the study, and (3) proper management of study funds.[3] The specific reasoning behind each of the review components in table 9.1 are briefly explained below, within the context of these objectives.

The facility review is related to all three of the above objectives: on-site observations of the local facilities ensure that the data and other documentation are securely stored, and that the appropriate equipment has been purchased and is functioning properly. While at the facility, it is extremely important to review all ethics committee documentation and to make sure that it is accessible, up-to-date, and properly stored. Additional local collaborating agencies (if any) should also have copies of the protocol and all ethics committee approval letters on hand and easily accessible. The same is true if the study has multiple sites that are managed by one organization. Having documentation readily available may not intuitively seem important, but if the research being conducted attracts any sort of public or regulatory attention, it is instrumental for the researchers to be able to provide quick documentation of adherence to the approved study procedures.

Protocol compliance is important for the scientific and ethical integrity of a study. Compliance not only entails adherence to procedures outlined in the protocol, but also requires that field staff maintain adequate knowledge of the research objectives and that this knowledge is translated into action throughout the study. The procedures we outline regarding compliance are intended to assess the degree to which prescribed protocol procedures are being followed on the ground. As illustrated in the example above of an incorrect focus group guide, distance and time have a way of degenerating or morphing complex processes and systems.

It is the responsibility of a research study's monitor to ensure that qualified individuals are carrying out the work on behalf of a sponsor and/or funding agency (refer to chapter 11, this volume). Part of this task is covered in the hiring process and subsequent training of staff. However, it is often the case that local exigencies force new staffing arrangements midway through a project. If new staff are hired, they will require proper training. In fact, some research organizations and funding agencies have specific requirements concerning training, particularly with respect to research ethics. Recognition of the fluidity of local conditions and the need for continuity of quality work is the rationale behind carrying out a staffing review.

A second component of the staffing review involves assessing local collaborative relationships, if the study involves, either directly or indirectly, more than one contracting agency. We have found from experience that local researchers may not always be candid about their working relationships with other institutions or groups, so we suggest inquiring about collaboration explicitly and setting up meetings with all researchers and organizations involved with a study.

Given the ultimate goals of ensuring high-quality data and maintaining data security, monitoring the flow and storage of data is of utmost importance. A rule of thumb is that a good data management system, if followed properly, will allow the easy location of any given piece of data or report upon request. The instructions we provide are designed to assess the degree of rigor and control being exerted over data at a local site. The more care given to collecting, managing, and storing data, the less chance there will be of losing them. Moreover, participant confidentiality is a key concern with any study, so it is important to ensure that data management procedures are being properly followed and that data are securely stored.

The primary reason for the financial assessment is to make sure that a funder's money is being used appropriately and that reported expenses have proper documentation. The level of detail to which a monitor will delve into an organization's financial records will depend on the nature of the project, the time available for monitoring, and the degree to which questionable activity is suspected.

The final component in the process we outline regards feedback for the monitor. Recognizing that projects are collaborative and that improvements can be made on both sides of a subagreement or contract, we suggest asking members of the local contracting agency, including fieldworkers, to provide feedback on all of the processes outlined above. This not only helps sponsors identify issues in their own systems, but it also helps build trust between institutions.

Conclusion

In this chapter we provide researchers and monitors with practical tools for quality assurance of social and behavioral research endeavors. We view this contribution as an initial step in the development of guidance for the conduct of team-based and multisite sociobehavioral research. The need for adequate monitoring to ensure protection of human research participants and scientific integrity of such research will grow with the continued expansion of sociobehavioral research into multi-institutional research projects, such as health sciences research (Bachrach and Abeles 2004), and with the implementation of larger and more complex sociobehavioral research protocols.

The framework presented here is not intended as a substitute for evaluating interventions, or as a way to ensure useful interventions are developed and funded; other processes and mechanism have been developed for these purposes (Peersman and Rugg 2004, Sharma 2003). Our monitoring process is intended to help ensure that studies, once designed and funded, are conducted according to protocol specifications, and that scientific and ethical integrity are maintained.

Notes

1. While GCP is commonly used, it has been criticized on various grounds. For a summary of these, see Grimes et al. (2005).

2. Monitoring clinical trials requires specific qualifications. For sociobehavioral research such formal requirements do not exist. However, individuals monitoring a sociobehavioral study should, at the very least, have a solid understanding of the study protocol and research ethics in general.

3. While study finances are not part of the monitoring process outlined by GCP (section 5.18), we believe it to be a good idea to review large financial transactions if this responsibility is not already assumed by another individual or group.

References

Bachrach, C., and R. Abeles
2004   Social science and health research: Growth at the National Institutes of Health. American Journal of Public Health 9:22–28.

Des Jarlais, D., C. Lyles, N. Crepaz, and the TREND Group
2004   Improving the reporting quality of nonrandomized evaluations of behavioral and public health interventions: The TREND statement. *American Journal of Public Health* 94:361–366.

Ellis, G.
1999   Testimony on medical record privacy before the Senate Committee on Health, Education, Labor, and Pension. February 24, 1999. Electronic document. Available at: http://www.hhs.gov/asl/testify/t990224a.html. Accessed August 2, 2004.

Grimes, D., D. Hubacher, K. Nanda, K. Schulz, D. Moher, and D. Altman
2005   The good clinical practice guideline: A bronze standard for clinical research. *The Lancet* 366:172–174.

International Conference on Harmonisation
1996   Guideline for good clinical practice: ICH harmonised tripartite guideline. Electronic document. Available at: http://www.ich.org/UrlGrpServer .jser?@_ID=276&@_TEMPLATE=254.

Labott, S., and T. Johnson
2004   Psychological and social risks of behavioral research. *IRB Ethics and Human Research* 26(3):11–14.

Peersman, G., and D. Rugg
2004   Intervention research and program evaluation: The need to move beyond monitoring. *New Directions for Evaluation* 103:141–158.

Sharma, R.
2003   Putting the community back in community health assessment: A process and outcome approach with a review of some major issues for public health professionals. *Journal of Health and Social Policy* 16(3):19–33.

Sheon, A., L. Wagner, M. J. McElrath, M. Keefer, E. Zimmerman, H. Israel, D. Berger, and P. Fast
1998   Preventing discrimination against volunteers in prophylactic HIV vaccine trials: Lessons from a phase II trial. *Journal of Acquired Immune Deficiency Syndrome and Human Retrovirology* 19:519–526.

Appendix

Table 9.1.   Monitoring Checklist with Examples

Task	Status	Comments
Review of facilities		
Security of Data Storage		
Adequacy of Equipment	Good	Tape recorders and headsets functioning well. Computers include two new Dell desktops and one older PC that needs to be evaluated by the data manager to determine what is needed to upgrade it for effective use by the team. This should be a priority task as the additional computer is needed for efficient functioning of the team.
Ethics committee documentation		
Protocol as submitted		
Cover letter to ethics committee		
Official ethics committee forms		
Letter of ethics committee approval	Excellent	Documentation is up-to-date.
Ethics committee composition		
Ethics committee composition changes		
Informed consent documentation	Very good	▪ Ethics committee approvals for waiving signed informed consent on file. Consent forms with signatures of team member obtaining consent included in data envelopes. ▪ One envelope lacked this documentation as a result of an administrative error. Local team member responsible was instructed to write a memo for the file, explaining the error and verifying that consent was obtained as otherwise specified in the protocol. ▪ Audiotapes include confirmation of consent, and this is transcribed.
CV of Investigators		
Interim/annual reports to ethics committee	N/A	Not required from local ethics committee.

(continued)

Table 9.1.   *(continued)*

Task	Status	Comments
Social/physical harms		
Confidentiality breaches		
Protocol amendments		
Additional information given to participants		
Additional ethics committee–related correspondence		
Protocol compliance		
Data collection procedures and instruments		
Recruiting/sampling procedures	Good	Reviewed verbally. No problems identified. Local investigator will send a detailed written description of recruiting procedures to sponsor in the upcoming week.
Field staff project knowledge		
Deviations from protocol		
Written reports		
Staffing review		
List of staff and assignments		
Staffing changes	Yes	Team secretary/typist, Ms. Jones, was replaced by Mr. Smith in May 2004. Mr. Smith has not completed the required research ethics training course, but will do so within two weeks. Sponsor will follow up to ensure completion.
Signed staff confidentiality agreements		
Staff training documentation		
Collaborative relationships		

Table 9.1. *(continued)*

Task	Status	Comments
Data management		
Data log	Poor	The data log was limited to the list of assigned archival numbers. No overall data tracking system had been implemented. A tracking log was drafted by the end of the monitoring visit and the team will finalize the log document and tracking procedures, and implement them as quickly as possible.
Completeness/Accuracy: source documents		
Completeness/Accuracy: processed data		
Data storage files (hard and electronic)		
Back up copies of source documents		
Communications regarding data		
Financial assessment		
Signed subagreement		
Financial status of project		
Receipts for expenses claimed		
Participant incentive receipts		
Feedback for monitor		

Implementing agency accountant requested a $5000 advance to cover monthly salaries. Also requested e-mail notification when funds are wired.

Table 9.2.   Monitoring Instructions

Preparation

- Send letter and checklist to local contact (at least two weeks in advance)

Documents to Bring
- Study protocol
- Subagreement/Contract
- List of local staff
- Recent financial report(s)

Review of facilities

- Ask to see all of the locations where data are stored, including electronic files.
- Turn on and test computer equipment, tape recorders, and any other electronic equipment to make sure they are working properly.
- Check the storage and configuration of files/folders on computers, as well as paper files in filing cabinets.
- Determine who has access to the study computer(s) and whether computers and/or electronic files are, or need to be, password protected.

Ethics committee documentation

- Note the location(s) of all ethics committee–related documentation listed below, as well as any documents that are missing.
- Ask the local lead investigator about local ethics committee reporting procedures, and enquire of all field staff about the presence of any social or physical harms associated with the study.
- Review documentation of informed consent. Make sure that informed consent documents exist and that they contain the appropriate signature. For example, if the study is anonymous and requires only oral consent, make sure that no personal identifiers are collected and that the *interviewer's* signature is recorded on the consent form as documentation.

Documents to Review
- Protocol and cover letter as submitted to the local ethics committee
- Local ethics committee letter of approval and a list of the ethics committee members
- Documentation of local ethics committee composition changes since protocol approval (if applicable)
- Letter(s) to local ethics committee notifying of social harms or breaches in protocol (if applicable)
- Interim or annual reports sent to local ethics committee (if required)
- Protocol amendments (if any)
- Any additional information given to study participants (e.g., informational brochures)
- Investigator CVs
- Any additional local ethics committee–related correspondence or official ethics committee forms (e.g., protocol amendments, ethics committee–related letters to the monitoring organization)
- Informed consent documentation

Protocol compliance

- Review data collection instruments being used (including translated versions) and any raw data or interim reports as a measure of quality control and to gauge interim progress, respectively.

Table 9.2.   *(continued)*

- Ask the field staff questions to assess their degree of knowledge about the project.
- Discuss recruiting and sampling procedures with senior research staff to ensure compliance with the protocol, and enquire as to deviations from the protocol.
- Review a few audiotapes if oral consent is expected to be recorded. If the monitor does not speak the language recorded on the tape, hire a translator (nonstudy staff) to help.
- Discuss the study with the field team and ascertain overall progress.
- Trouble-shoot any problems and ask the field team for input regarding how processes could be improved.

Documents to Review
  - ☐ Data collection instruments
  - ☐ Written reports or data analysis notes (if applicable)
  - ☐ Documentation of deviation from procedure as specified in the protocol (if any)
  - ☐ Documentation of details surrounding recruiting and sampling procedures (if any)

Staffing review

- Ask to see a list of all staff currently working on the project and their roles; compare this to the original staffing list, and note any changes.
- Ensure that arrangements are made for any new staff to receive the proper training and that they have signed all of the required study documentation such as confidentiality agreements.
- Ask senior staff about the overall performance of the fieldworkers.
- Meet with representatives from all local collaborating agencies to assess working relationship.

Documents to Review
  - ☐ Original list of site staff and assigned roles
  - ☐ List of site staff and assigned roles at the time of monitoring
  - ☐ Documentation of staff training
  - ☐ Signed field staff confidentiality agreements

Data management

- Ask the local investigator to conduct a physical walk-through of the entire data management process, from the point data are received, through data entry and storage, to transfer of data to external sources.
- Ask staff for a demonstration of data entry and cleaning procedures; for qualitative data this will include translation/transcription procedures.
- Look for both hard and electronic copies of data, assess the security of each, and note if and where backup copies of source documents exist.
- If study participation is anonymous, make sure that no personal identifiers exist in any form or location.
- Ensure that the master data log is up-to-date and completed correctly, and that all data are labeled with correct archival numbers.
- Check to see if data storage files are complete and can be accounted for.
- Review the data themselves for accuracy and quality; include samples of source documents, such as original data collection forms, audiotapes, or field notes, as well as cleaned and processed data. Make sure to review a sample of data collected from each fieldworker.
- Compare the source data with processed data (including any interim reports) to check for consistency and accuracy of processing.

(continued)

Table 9.2.   (continued)

Documents to Review
- ☐ Data archival log
- ☐ All source documents (original data collection forms, audiotapes, field notes, etc.)
- ☐ Cleaned, processed, and stored data (hard and electronic)
- ☐ Backup copies of source documents (hard and electronic)
- ☐ Any external communications regarding data (e.g., e-mails to the monitor or funder)

Financial assessment

- At the minimum, receipts for large expenses and staff salaries should be reviewed.
- Look also for "petty cash" flows that are not documented.
- Ask for receipts for less expensive items if there is an indication of being overcharged.
- If study participation is designed to be anonymous, review participant incentive receipts to make sure that they do not contain identifiers.
- Discuss with senior staff the overall financial status of the project and any emergent or anticipated monetary problems.

Documents to Review
- ☐ Signed subagreement or contract
- ☐ Budget in subagreement or contract
- ☐ Recent monthly financial report sent to monitoring agency
- ☐ Receipts for large items
- ☐ Participant incentive receipts

Feedback for monitor

- Ask the local investigator, accountant, and field staff for general feedback on the project and their perceptions of the overall relationship with the monitoring and/or funding agency.
- Inquire as to how processes on the monitor's or funder's end could be improved and discuss ways in which the collaboration could be made more efficient and productive.

10

Reevaluating Guidelines in Qualitative Research

GREG GUEST AND KATHLEEN M. MACQUEEN

T HE QUESTION OF HOW TO PRESENT QUALITATIVE RESEARCH findings came to the foreground in the mid-1980s (Flick 1998). Despite the attention paid to data presentation in subsequent decades, many researchers still perceive a lack of guidelines in reporting qualitative research (Caan 2001, Roberts et al. 2002) and advocate increased standardization (Dingwall et al. 1998, Hoddintott and Pill 1997, Popay et al. 1998). Lists of criteria have been created to aid in this endeavor (Boulton et al. 1996, Seale and Silverman 1997).[1] The objectives of this chapter are threefold. First, we address the fundamental question of whether or not qualitative research should be subject to guidelines, and present our case for the affirmative. We then discuss the range of qualitative research and how the definition one uses affects the guidelines proposed. We provide an expanded definition of qualitative research that reflects the full range of its application in the social, behavioral, and health sciences and discuss the implications for the presentation and evaluation of qualitative research reports. During our review of the literature, we also observed that the guidelines outlined tend to lack the detail necessary to help reviewers adequately assess report quality. Our third objective, therefore, is to summarize previously recommended guidelines and provide enhanced explanations to aid in their use.

Why Bother with Guidelines?

Undoubtedly, one's response to this question will depend on the epistemological perspective taken with respect to social and behavioral research (and science in general). We know, for example, qualitative researchers who proclaim that they don't believe in research methods, or in the practice of providing supporting evidence for research findings reported. For researchers in this camp, it is enough to tell an interesting story and give voice to an otherwise oppressed group of people. We don't have the mandate in this chapter to review the extensive philosophy of science literature around which this complicated debate is centered. Nor do we attempt to persuade researchers engaged with a more postmodern perspective to follow the path of positivism. Rather, we address the specific critiques aimed directly at the proposition of establishing guidelines for reporting qualitative research.

We should note here that we have purposely chosen to use the word *guidelines* rather than *standards*. Standards refer to edicts that confer an imperative of adherence. Guidelines are more flexible than standards—recommendations rather than absolute rules. This chapter is, therefore, about providing suggestions for how to present qualitative research in a way that conveys rigor; it is not about advocating the *only* way to go about writing up qualitative findings.

The first argument against having guidelines we wish to address pertains to scholarly agreement. Guideline critics argue that we should not, or cannot, establish guidelines because practitioners of qualitative research do not agree on what these guidelines should be, or if in fact we should have guidelines at all (Chapple and Rogers 1998, Sandelowski and Barroso 2002). We take a different perspective. In our view, disagreement is part of the research and reporting process; scholars seldom agree on anything. Not everyone may agree, for example, with all aspects of the various international guidelines for research ethics, but such disagreement does not mean that the existing guidelines are not necessary or useful. We should also point out that guidelines are not immutable and serve as an important point of discussion for the evolution of a discipline or practice (Werner 1998).

Another criticism posited is that there is no guarantee that reviewers will apply guidelines consistently (Sandelowski and Barroso 2002). We agree that this is a possibility, but this critique applies to any guidelines or standards. All guidelines—including laws, ethical codes of conduct, or religious proscriptions—are open to interpretation. They can, and often are, applied differently depending on the context and the view of those in charge of review. Ironically, however, this criticism is an argument for, rather than against, using guidelines. Surely, evaluation of research findings (or of anything, for that matter) would be even less consistent in the absence of guidelines.

A third criticism is that checklists are overly prescriptive and, in and of themselves, do not confer rigor (Barbour 2001, Eakin and Mykhalovskiy 2003). Critics warn that guidelines are focused too much on procedure and methods, and that uncritical application would "legitimize substandard research" (Lambert and McKevitt 2002). We partially agree with this position. Guidelines are intended to provide direction for writers and reviewers, and help make the reporting and review process more systematic and exhaustive. They are not designed to be substitutes for good judgment and critical thinking. Uncritical application of anything will likely result in a substandard product, and we would not recommend blindly assessing anything as complex as research with only a checklist. It should be regarded as a tool and nothing more.

Related to the above criticism is the fear that checklists will permit laypersons to carry out (presumably poor) qualitative research. According to Lambert and McKevitt (2002), "qualitative research is in danger of being reduced to a limited set of methods that requires little theoretical perspective, no discipline-based qualifications, and little training." We agree that this is possible, but the same possibility exists for almost any subject matter. There are textbooks, for example, instructing its readers on how to conduct neurosurgery. The existence of this publicly available information, however, does not entitle laypersons, or give them the skills necessary, to perform brain surgery. The same could be said of quantitative sociobehavioral research and the use of, say, statistical regression. A regression checklist wouldn't be of much use for someone who is unfamiliar with the method. Here, we agree with Eakin and Mykhalovskiy (2003) that a researcher needs the underlying knowledge to properly use and apply checklists, but disagree that by developing guidelines substandard research will ensue. Peer review for research funding and publication of findings is designed to mitigate this very problem. It should also be noted that a lack of guidelines and tools such as checklists is hardly a guarantee of quality.

The last criticism we wish to address is the belief that guidelines will constrain the direction and content of qualitative research, and that any form of imposed structure contradicts the very inductive essence that characterizes qualitative inquiry (Lambert and McKevitt 2002). We respectfully disagree. Guidelines, properly applied, do not necessarily impose constraints. Recommending, for example, that qualitative studies employ purposive samples over convenience samples does not imply that convenience samples should never be used. Such a guideline recognizes that purposive sampling is more rigorous than convenience sampling. However, a convenience sample may be the only type possible in a particular situation, and shouldn't be precluded in such a case. The sampling guideline above would direct the researcher to outline the rationale for not sampling purposively, justify his or her decision to use a convenience sample, and explicitly consider the types of biases likely to result. The guideline itself doesn't constrain the method but makes the researcher accountable for using a less rigorous approach. Once again, this brings us back to selection of terminology: guidelines provide direction, not absolute rules. They need to be applied intelligently and with good judgment.

As Miles and Huberman (1994) observe, a well-told story can still be wrong. The guidelines we discuss below not only help improve methodological rigor, they more importantly increase transparency of the data collection and analysis process. Transparency is what makes evaluation of a research study possible. This is perhaps the best reason of all to support the development and use of reporting guidelines.

The Range of Qualitative Research

Guest (2005) points out that most of the guidelines proposed for qualitative research assume a narrow definition of qualitative inquiry, and focus almost exclusively on analytic methods that can be generally described as interpretive. But so much more can be done with data generated from qualitative research than thematic analysis or thick description. As Bernard (1996) astutely notes, most definitions of qualitative research fail to distinguish between the data themselves and the analyses performed on them. This is an important distinction, and one that is especially pertinent to the following discussion.

Qualitative research generates or uses raw data with no numeric value (Nkwi et al. 2001) and typically takes the form of text. Given this definition, note that qualitative research involves two distinct analytical approaches, each with corresponding limits and assumptions. In figure 10.1, quadrant A encompasses typical conceptualizations of qualitative research, depicted as interpretation of meaning in text from small samples, and exploratory in nature. Grounded theory, for example, is a common approach to qualitative data analysis within this quadrant. Grounded theory involves identification of categories and concepts or themes that emerge from the data. Relationships among the emergent categories and themes are used to build theoretical models that are constantly compared against the data (Glaser and Strauss 1967).

The cultural models approach is another analytic method within quadrant A. The method entails systematic analysis of semantic structure in large

Type of Data

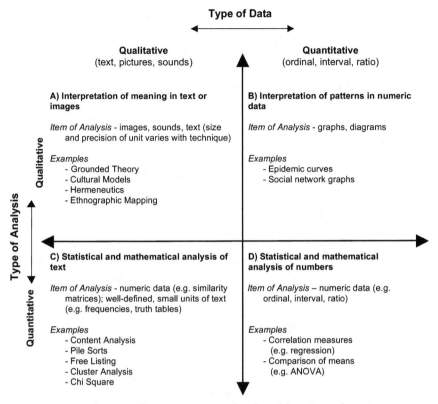

Figure 10.1.   Qualitative and quantitative research (adapted from Bernard, 1996).

bodies of text along a given dimension of inquiry and across a given group of people. The resulting product is a conceptual model that ostensibly represents the cognitive structure shared among a particular group of people for a given conceptual domain, such as the American model of marriage (Holland and Quinn 1987). Other forms of analysis in this quadrant include hermeneutics—the interpretation of underlying meaning in free-flowing text or observed behavior (Biesele and Tyler 1986, Geertz 1973)—and ethnographic mapping—the creation of annotated geographical maps depicting sites and activities relevant to the research objectives, from multiple data sources (Oliver-Velez et al. 2002).

Often overlooked is quadrant C, which encompasses the transformation of qualitative data into numeric values and application of mathematical analyses, permitting hypothesis testing and examination of variation across respondents. One example is content analysis, a technique that applies preestablished numeric codes, representing conceptual categories of interest, to qualitative data. Content analysis is typically quantitative in nature (e.g., word frequencies/co-occurrences) and employed on large data sets (Krippendorf 1980). Also included in this quadrant are pile sorts, a data collection technique that requires participants to arrange items (usually cards with names or pictures of objects or concepts on them) into piles that make the most sense to the participant. Pile sorts are useful for understanding how people cognitively structure items within a domain of inquiry (Weller and Romney 1988).

Free listing is a simple, yet powerful, technique that falls within this quadrant. In a free-list task, respondents are asked to generate a (usually exhaustive) list of items within a specific domain of inquiry, such as types of animals or diseases. Free lists are typically used to determine the breadth of a conceptual domain, but can also indicate saliency of a particular item or concept within a domain (Weller and Romney 1988). Data reduction techniques, such as cluster analysis, also fall into quadrant C, since they reduce observations in a data set to numbers and produce an output based on the relationship between observations (Aldenderfer and Blashfield 1984). Cluster analysis can be applied to numerically coded raw text or thematic codes (Guest and McLellan 2003; see also chapter 7 in this volume).

Quadrant D refers to commonly used quantitative analyses, such as regression and ANOVA. Assumptions and rules for using these methods are fairly well developed, as are guidelines for assessing this type of research (Begg et al. 1996, Grimes and Schulz 2002). Quadrant B contains the qualitative representation and analysis of numerical data. In this quadrant, mathematical modeling, such as social network analysis (Rothenberg and Narramore 1996) and computer models for disease transmission (Anderson and Garnett 2000, Halloran et al. 2002), make use of quantitative data to reach a qualitative understanding of complex processes that are summarized in graphic form.

Below we review the criteria proposed for evaluating qualitative research. We do so using the framework presented in figure 10.1 as our basis for defining qualitative research. Owing to the scope of this book, we limit our remarks to quadrants A and C, which, in our view, comprise a comprehensive range of qualitative research.

Summary of Criteria for Assessing Quality

We conducted a literature search in various social science and health science databases and qualitative research books. Our search strategy was broad, encompassing publications that discuss guidelines, standards, or recommendations for reporting and/or evaluating qualitative research. We also reviewed references within the articles and chapters identified in the initial literature search. Below, we briefly summarize and evaluate the recommended criteria, and add explanations where appropriate. In addition to the narrative below, we provide a list of our recommendations for enhancing rigor and transparency in table 10.1, at the end of this chapter.

In our discussion, we do not include criteria that we believe apply universally to all types of research (and which in fact comprised a large part of the discussion in the literature reviewed)—good research design and appropriate choice of methods, clear description of procedures, logic of argument, clear writing at a level suitable for the intended audience, and relevance to current theory or practice. These are important whether one is writing about an ethnographic study or a highly controlled laboratory experiment. We therefore limit the scope of our discussion to issues that are especially important for qualitative inquiry.

Scope and Purpose of Research

Some authors suggest that qualitative research is limited to documenting the subjective understanding of, or context surrounding, a phenomenon (Elliott et al. 1999, Fossey et al. 2002, Horsburgh 2003, Popay et al. 1998). Others restrict the purpose of qualitative research to explanation and generation of hypotheses (Barbour and Barbour 2003, Russell and Gregory 2003). While qualitative research is uniquely equipped for such objectives, a more comprehensive definition encompasses the ability to reveal variability in a population and to test hypotheses (e.g., figure 10.1, quadrant C). First, hypotheses can be qualitatively oriented and thereby tested in a qualitative manner. An example of this would be a hypothesis such as: event x has had an effect on group y. By simply expressing effects of event x in an interview, participants in group y support the hypothesis. Note that no mention is made of frequency or quantification. Another point to remember is that outcomes or behaviors can be quantified, translated into frequencies, and input into nonparametric statistical models, such as a chi square, to test for differences and assess hypotheses (as long as the assumptions associated with the method chosen are met).

We should also point out that qualitative research is not the only way to understand subjective understandings or context. The purpose of psychometric scales, for example, is to measure subjective feelings, understandings, and traits of an individual. Likewise, context surrounding a given event or structure can be measured and documented numerically. Both qualitative and quantitative approaches can investigate such topics; they just do so in different ways and with different analytical goals in mind.

Sampling

Most authors agree that presentation of qualitative research should include a clear description of the sampling rationale and recruitment process (Bluff 1997, Elder and Miller 1995, Fossey et al. 2002, Greenhalgh and Taylor 1997, Hoddintott and Pill 1997, Malterud 2001, Russell and Gregory 2003). Likewise, a description of the sample itself is recommended (Miles and Huberman 1994).

In terms of sampling strategy, a purposive sample is generally recommended (Giacomini and Cook 2000, Popay et al. 1998). Purposive sampling groups individuals according to preselected criteria (e.g., HIV-positive women in city x). Most guidelines suggest that purposive sample sizes be determined on the basis of theoretical saturation—that is, the point in data analysis when new incoming data produces little or no change to the existing code network (Glaser and Strauss 1967). The number of participants should be stated, as well as evidence that theoretical saturation or data redundancy was achieved (Bluff 1997, Giacomini and Cook 2000).

We agree with the above sampling guidelines, but add two caveats. First, nonpurposive samples may be possible, and desirable, to obtain (see Carey and Gelaude, this volume). Opportunities might exist to study an entire population of interest, such as all twelve decision makers in a Ministry of Health. Moreover, as qualitative methodology is increasingly folded into large research projects and population-based surveys, so too the opportunity and need grows to select random and quota samples. In our work, we have, for example, randomly sampled participants for qualitative interviews from the sampling universe of four hundred clinical trial enrollees. Quota samples can also be used. Quota sampling is similar in some ways to a purposive sampling strategy. The approach identifies participants based on selected criteria, but is more specific with respect to sizes and proportions of subsamples. Subgroups are sampled to correspond with their relative proportions in the larger population (Last 1988), such as the ratio of male to females.

Second, clearer explanations of, and empirical evidence for, theoretical saturation are needed. Guest et al. (2006) provide a review of nonprobabilistic sample sizes that includes evidence-based sampling recommendations for qualitative research. In their analysis, they found that after twelve in–depth interviews on a narrowly defined topic among a relatively homogeneous

sample (West African sex workers in large cities), data had reached a significant degree of saturation with respect to thematic content. There is other
empirical research suggesting that saturation may occur after interviews with
only six or seven participants (Nielsen and Landauer 1993, Romney et al.
1986). Work by Handwerker and Wozniak (1997) further shows that if participants in a sample are knowledgeable about a cultural domain, and there is
a high level of agreement among them, small convenience samples are sufficient. Focus groups require similar considerations (population homogeneity,
topical focus) but are adjusted for the group-process setting. The bottom line
is that sampling parameters need to consider the level of cultural expertise
and homogeneity within the sample and the nature of the domain of inquiry. Generally speaking, sample sizes will need to be increased (a) as the focus of inquiry broadens, (b) as the level of expertise and homogeneity among
participants diverges, (c) as the domain of inquiry becomes more esoteric
(i.e., not constructed through social interaction), and (d) the greater the need
to document variability (or its absence) among responses.

Systematic investigations to generate evidence-based guidance for theoretical saturation and nonprobabilistic sample sizes in qualitative research
are needed. In the meantime, we advise that reports describe how theoretical saturation was determined and qualitative studies would do well using
sample sizes of at least twelve to fifteen in-depth interviews (Guest et al.
2006) and/or two focus groups (Krueger 1994) per group of interest.

Data Collection

Bluff (1997) notes that authors should provide a description of "when,
where and how data was collected," but the author fails to say what should
be included in this description. We offer the following specifications.

At minimum, the year(s) data were collected should be reported. If temporal factors such as seasonality, day of the week, or time of day potentially
impact the research process, these also need to be described. The region of
the country where research took place should be reported, unless there is
reason to believe it will stigmatize a community or violate participant confidentiality. The specific context from which participants were recruited, as
well as where data were collected (e.g., local bar, clinic), should be specified. The type of research instrument used to guide data collection should
also be described and specific questions provided where appropriate.

RECORDING AND TRANSCRIPTION. To compensate for limitations of
human memory and note-taking abilities, we advocate, along with others

(Fitzpatrick and Boulton 1996), audiotaping in-depth interviews and focus groups. Notwithstanding, we recognize with Carey and Gelaude (this volume) that audiotaping is not always possible, or that there may be ethical considerations that mitigate against this level of documentation (see chapter 2, this volume). Exceptions can also be made for less verbose qualitative data, such as free lists and pile sorts; notes can typically capture these data accurately. If audiotaping is not employed, for whatever reason, justification should be provided for its absence.

Transcription of recordings is not necessary; it does not guarantee rigor and in some cases can detract from it if transcription quality is poor (McLellan et al. 2003). Transcription is also expensive and time-consuming. However, when done properly, transcription makes analysis easier and provides more analytic opportunities: transcripts can be scrutinized more quickly than tapes and content can be analyzed using computers. Transcripts are especially invaluable in team-based and multisite research, because both require a significant amount of data sharing and subsequent discussion of content (MacQueen et al. 2001). If transcripts are created, the translation/transcript process should be made explicit (Pitchforth et al. 2005).

REFLEXIVITY. Because qualitative data collection often uses open-ended instruments that require a more informal type of interaction between researcher and participant, it is often argued that the potential for a researcher to bias responses is greater than for close-ended surveys. Qualitative researchers are therefore advised to be reflexive (Dey 1993, Mays and Pope 2000, Pitchforth et al. 2005), and describe how their presence may have affected the data collection process (Byrne 2001, Horsburgh 2003, Malterud 2001). We disagree with the notion that this issue is uniquely problematic for qualitative research; the research process and context can affect all types of data collection (see, e.g., Macalino et al. 2002, McCombie and Anarfi 2002, Parsons 1974, Paulhus 1991, Rosenthal 1966, Weeks and Moore 1981). Even quantum physics is subject to observer bias! Given the pervasiveness of this methodological issue, it seems neither productive nor fair to ask practitioners of qualitative research to discuss reflexivity or response bias to a greater degree than is expected of other researchers. In line with good scientific practice generally, we recommend that qualitative researchers report the known potential for, and measures taken to minimize, relevant biases.

Data Analysis

RELIABILITY. Reliability, in a general sense, refers to the ability to achieve the same results when repeatedly applying a particular technique to the same object. In quantitative behavioral research, the "technique" would typically be a survey and the "object" a group of people. Although qualitative researchers rarely repeat the same study within the same population, the issue of reliability is still relevant. Unlike, for example, quantitative surveys that have structured response categories, qualitative data collection instruments are usually open-ended and the resulting raw data unstructured in nature. In team qualitative research, data collection and analysis are generally done by more than one person and inductive probing and data interpretation can vary from one team member to the next. So, while qualitative researchers may not need to concern themselves with reliability *between* studies, they should be concerned about ensuring reliability *within* a single study. In multisite research, team members may be continents apart, further exacerbating the potential for poor reliability. Retaining a similar question format across participants increases the ability to assess reliability, as does documenting code definitions used to construct data categories subsequent to data collection. Carey and Gelaude (this volume) provide a thorough set of procedures for enhancing reliability in qualitative research carried out in teams.

The appropriate method of data analysis depends on the research objectives and nature of the data collected. However, a description of decision rules for arriving at judgments (Cesario et al. 2002), or an "audit trail" of the analysis process, should be provided (Hills 2000, Miles and Huberman 1994, Sharts-Hopko 2002). Generally, this requires a description of how codes were developed and applied, and the method used to address coding reliability (see chapters 6 and 11, this volume).

Engaging multiple coders can also increase reliability in qualitative research as it reduces subjective biases when creating and applying codes (Carey and Gelaude, this volume). While Morse (1997) argues that multiple coders are not required if analysis is done by the person who collected the data—on the grounds that much information from an interview is captured in the interview process itself—this argument does not address the reasoning behind multiple coding, which is to minimize the effect of subjective biases one person may bring to an analysis. Our position is, along with others (Ambert et al. 1995, Miles and Huberman 1994), that coding checks are essential and that the use of multiple coders imparts additional reliability to an analysis. This is particularly true for content-driven analysis, such as grounded theory, because codes and themes are not predetermined but are generated from reviewing the data.

When multiple coders are engaged, the method for assessing intercoder agreement should be described. Percent agreement and Cohen's kappa statistic are two commonly used techniques. Cohen's kappa is preferable because it accounts for chance agreement, but it may not be appropriate for small samples (Carey et al. 1996, Lombard et al. 2002).

DATA RANGE AND SALIENCE. One potential problem in qualitative analysis, particularly when dealing with large data sets, is the loss of perspective. Sometimes what appears to be salient in the mind of an analyst turns out to be less important than originally thought when the data are systematically summarized (or vice-versa), so it is always good practice to double-check initial interpretations of data salience or prevalence. A report should indicate how pervasive findings are within the sample (Dey 1993, Mays and Pope 2000, Miles and Huberman 1994, Patton 2002, Pitchforth et al. 2005, Seale and Silverman 1997, Secker et al. 1995). Researchers can indicate the prevalence of identified themes by using simple frequencies, general descriptors (e.g., a few, the majority, all), or percentages if the sample size is large enough. Conflicting data should be reported, as should the absence of such data (Dey 1993, Elder and Miller 1995, Mays and Pope 2000, Seale and Silverman 1997). Analysis of deviant cases can add value to an analysis (Fossey et al. 2002, Pope and Mays 2000), but, in our view, is not necessary if reexamination of the data indicates that such cases are true outliers and not indicative of an important underlying social process.

DATA ANALYSIS SOFTWARE. Qualitative data analysis software is not required for sound analysis, particularly if the data set is small (e.g., less than twenty interviews). Systematic coding can be, and has often been, done by hand, but this is a time-consuming task for large data sets. Software facilitates coding, as well as the analytic process, and fosters a systematic approach to analysis, thereby minimizing reporting bias (Namey et al., this volume, Seale and Silverman 1997). If software is used, the name and version of the program should be provided as well as the reporting functions used in the analysis.

Data Interpretation

VALIDITY. The concept of "validity" in qualitative research has a long and complex history, and has been described by a wide range of terms (Golafshani 2003). To complicate matters, some qualitative researchers suggest that the term itself, because it is derived from a positivist tradition, is not applicable to qualitative inquiry. The result has been a growing list of substitute terminology (Seale 1999), the most well known of which was developed by Lincoln and Guba in the 1980s—*trustworthiness* and *credibility* (Lincoln and Guba 1985). Delving into the details of this debate exceeds the scope of this chapter. We do argue, however, along with Morse et al. (2002), that the term *validity* can indeed be appropriately applied to qualitative research, and that doing so mitigates the further marginalization of the methodological approach from mainstream science (and funding sources). For the purposes of this chapter we will use Bernard's (2000) definition of *validity* as "the accuracy and trustworthiness of instruments, data, and findings in research" (46).

In qualitative research a lot happens between the point of data collection and the presentation of findings. It thus behooves a researcher to give evidence of some sort to support interpretation of the raw data, and to show the reader that the findings presented are accurate and trustworthy representations of what is happening on the ground (Cesario et al. 2002, Drisko 1997, Fitzpatrick and Boulton 1996, Patton 2002). We agree with Patton that one can use numerous criteria for judging a qualitative study, and that the criteria employed will vary between philosophical frameworks (Patton 2002:551). But we also believe that there is at least one common denominator that connects all types of qualitative research—raw qualitative data. As Chenail (1995) stresses, raw data should be the "star" of a qualitative report. Quotes are essential in defining key concepts, domains, or themes—which are often complex and multidimensional—and they help the reader assess face and content validity.[2] Quotes give the reader the opportunity to assess an author's interpretation. We recommend, therefore, that verbatim quotes be presented (especially for research in quadrant A), since they reflect the raw data behind an interpretation. Quotes presented in a report should be selected according to their ability to exemplify an intended concept (Bluff 1997, Secker et al. 1995). Pitchforth et al. (2005) further recommend that quotes be accompanied by labels that identify key demographics of the participant being quoted.

As a further indication of validity we recommend, along with others (Bluff 1997, Drisko 1997, Giacomini and Cook 2000, Mays and Pope 2000), that researchers seek and document feedback on their interpretation of data from the study population whenever possible. This process is sometimes referred to as "member checking" (Byrne 2001), and can be a good gauge as to whether or not the research team "got the story right."

If space permits, authors can also provide code definitions (perhaps in an appendix) as an additional means for reviewers to assess validity. Access to code definitions allows other researchers to replicate the study (assuming interview questions are also available) and assess reliability.

TRIANGULATION. The term *triangulation* comes from the field of trigonometry and is used to describe the process of using two known co-ordinates to determine the unknown location of a third. Researchers in the social and behavioral sciences have adopted the term and generally use it to refer to a research design strategy that explicitly combines data collection methods (Williamson et al. 1982)—namely, a mixed-methods approach (e.g., Creswell 2003, Tashakkori and Teddlie 1998, 2003). While this connotation is the one most commonly used in social and behavioral research, triangulation also refers to the process of combining multiple observers, theories, and data sources. The rationale is that by combining multiple points of reference, researchers can minimize the intrinsic bias that comes from single-method, single-observer, and single-theory studies (Denzin 1989:307). Various authors recommend using triangulation as a method to enhance validity and rigor in qualitative research (Ambert et al. 1995, Byrne 2001, Fossey et al. 2002, Malterud 2001, Miles and Huberman 1994, Russell and Gregory 2003, Sharts-Hopko 2002). We agree that triangulation is desirable for qualitative research (or any type of research endeavor, for that matter), but also recognize that a triangulated design is not always possible within certain budgetary or logistical constraints, nor may it be warranted if the research question and context are very precise and straightforward. In sum, we view it as an important and desirable component of research design, but acknowledge that it is not always necessary or possible.

Conclusion

A checklist can never replace sound research. A study that meets all of the criteria outlined in table 10.1 but is poorly conceived, or not adequately described, should not be given a passing grade. The criteria we outline are suggestions for enhancing rigor and transparency but, in and of themselves, are not sufficient to guarantee excellence in qualitative research. Moreover, as mentioned in this chapter's introduction, qualitative research should exemplify general standards applicable to all forms of research—a well-thought-out research design, proper choice of methods, effective writing and logical presentation of data, and an explicit connection to current theory or practice.

Table 10.1.   Required and Recommended Criteria

Required Criteria

Connection between research objectives, research design, and methods logical and clearly articulated

At least one of: ___ Purposive sample (includes chain referral)
                                ___ Random sample
                                ___ Entire population

Number of participants/observational events stated

Rationale for sample selection discussed and commensurate with objectives

Evidence for theoretical saturation (for purposive samples only)

Year(s) data collected stated

Temporal factors associated with data collection described (if time-sensitive)

Region of country/city specified

Specific location of recruitment and data collection (e.g., bar, street) described

Type of research instruments specified

Sample questions provided where appropriate

Interviews/focus groups audiotaped (unless explicit justification provided)

Code development/application process specified

Reliability of coding addressed

Range of findings presented

Prevalence of findings presented

Conflicting data addressed (if applicable)

Name of software and reporting functions used provided (if used)

Verbatim quotes provided to support interpretation of data

Claims to generalizability of findings (if any) compatible with sampling strategy

Recommended Criteria (Rigor Enhancing Elements)

Verbatim transcripts or audiotape used as data source

Multiple coders used and percent agreement or Kappa scores provided

Deviant case analysis presented (if applicable)

Software used in data management and analysis

Participant feedback provided on researcher's interpretation of data

Code definitions provided

Reflexive analysis presented

Triangulation of data sources

Notes

1. Not surprisingly, most of the discourse surrounding guidelines is found in the health sciences literature, where there exists a history of establishing procedural

standards and evidence-based practice. And, many journals in the medical and public health fields now have guidelines for reviewing manuscripts based on qualitative research. As a result, most of our examples in this chapter are derived from health sciences research. Notwithstanding, the issues we discuss are germane to all disciplines that engage in qualitative research.

2. Face validity refers to the extent to which an empirical measure, at face value, adequately reflects the meaning of a concept. For example, most researchers would agree that an increase in condom use is a valid measure of HIV sexual risk reduction. Content validity refers to the range of meanings that comprise a particular concept. The concept of HIV risk reduction, for instance, would be composed of multiple behavioral and epidemiological measures.

References

Aldenderfer, M., and R. Blashfield
1984   *Cluster Analysis.* Thousand Oaks, Calif.: Sage.

Ambert, A., P. Adler, P. Adler, and D. Detzner
1995   Understanding and evaluating qualitative research. *Journal of Marriage and the Family* 57:879–893.

Anderson, R., and G. Garnett
2000   Mathematical models of the transmission and control of sexually transmitted diseases. *Sexually Transmitted Diseases* 10:636–643.

Barbour, R. S.
2001   Checklists for improving rigour in qualitative research: A case of the tail wagging the dog? *BMJ* 322:1115–1117.

Barbour, R. S., and M. Barbour
2003   Evaluating and synthesizing qualitative research: The need to develop a distinctive approach. *Journal of Evaluation and Clinical Practice* 9(2):179–186.

Begg, C., M. Cho, S. Eastwood, R. Horton, D. Moher, I. Olkin, R. Pitkin, D. Rennie, K. Schulz, D. Simel, and D. Stroup
1996   Improving the quality of reporting randomized control trials. *JAMA* 276(8): 637–639.

Bernard, H. R.
1996   Qualitative data, quantitative analysis. *Cultural Anthropology Methods Journal* 8(1):9–11.
2000   *Social Research Methods: Qualitative and Quantitative Approaches.* Thousand Oaks, Calif.: Sage.

Biesele, M., and S. Tyler
1986   The dialectic of oral and literary hermeneutics. *Cultural Anthropology* 1(2), Special issue.

Bluff, R.
1997 Evaluating qualitative research. *British Journal of Midwifery* 5(4):232–235.

Boulton, M., R. Fitzpatrick, and C. Swinburn
1996 Qualitative research in health care: II. A structured review and evaluation of studies. *Journal of Evaluation in Clinical Practice* 2(3):171–179.

Byrne, M.
2001 Evaluating the findings of qualitative research. *Association of Operating Room Nurses Journal* 73(3):703–706.

Caan, W.
2001 Call to action. *BMJ* 322:7294.

Carey, J., M. Morgan, and M. Oxtoby
1996 Intercoder agreement in analysis of responses to open-ended interview questions: Examples from tuberculosis research. *Cultural Anthropology Methods Journal* 8:1–5.

Cesario, S., K. Morin, and A. Santa-Donato
2002 Evaluating the level of evidence of qualitative research. *Journal of Obstetric, Gynecologic and Neonatal Nursing* 31(6):531–537.

Chapple, A., and A. Rogers
1998 Explicit guidelines for qualitative research: A step in the right direction, a defence of the 'soft' option, or a form of sociological imperialism? *Family Practice* 15(6):556–561.

Chenail, R.
1995 Presenting qualitative data. *The Qualitative Report* 2(3). Available at: www .nova.edu/ssss/QR/QR2-3/presenting.html. Accessed September 2006.

Creswell, J.
2003 *Research Design: Qualitative, Quantitative, and Mixed Methods Approaches* (2nd ed.). Thousand Oaks, Calif.: Sage.

Denzin, N.
1989 *The Research Act: A Theoretical Introduction to Sociological Methods* (3rd ed.). Englewood Cliffs, N.J.: Prentice Hall.

Dey, I.
1993 *Qualitative Data Analysis: A User-friendly Guide for Social Scientists.* New York: Routledge.

Dingwall, R., E. Murphy, P. Watson, D. Greatbatch, and S. Parker
1998 Catching goldfish: Quality in qualitative research. *Journal of Health Service Research Policy* 3:167–172.

Drisko, J. W.
1997   Strengthening qualitative studies and reports: Standards to promote academic integrity. *Journal of Social Work Education* 33(1):12.

Eakin, J., and E. Mykhalovskiy
2003   Reframing the evaluation of qualitative health research: reflections on a review of appraisal guidelines in the health sciences. *Journal of Evaluation in Clinical Practice* 9(2):187–194.

Elder, N. C., and W. L. Miller
1995   Reading and evaluating qualitative research studies. *Journal of Family Practice* 41(3):279–285.

Elliott, R., C. T. Fischer, and D. L. Rennie
1999   Evolving guidelines for publication of qualitative research studies in psychology and related fields. *British Journal of Clinical Psychology* 38:215–229.

Fitzpatrick, R., and M. Boulton
1996   Qualitative research in health care: I. The scope and validity of methods. *Journal of Evaluations in Clinical Practice* 2(2):123–130.

Flick, U.
1998   An introduction to qualitative research. Thousand Oaks, Calif.: Sage.

Fossey, E., C. Harvey, F. McDermott, and L. Davidson
2002   Understanding and evaluating qualitative research. *Australian and New Zealand Journal of Psychiatry* 36:717–732.

Geertz, C.
1973   *The Interpretation of Culture.* New York: Basic Books.

Giacomini, M., and D. Cook
2000   Users' guide to the medical literature XXII: Qualitative research in health care. Are the results of the study valid? *JAMA* 284:357–362.

Glaser, B., and A. Strauss
1967   The discovery of grounded theory: Strategies for qualitative research. New York: Aldine.

Golafshani, N.
2003   Understanding reliability and validity in qualitative research. *The Qualitative Report* 8(4):597–607.

Greenhalgh, T., and R. Taylor
1997   How to read a paper: Papers that go beyond numbers (qualitative research). *BMJ* 315:740–743.

Grimes, D., and K. Schulz
2002   An overview of clinical research: The lay of the land. *The Lancet* 359: 57–61.

Guest, G.
2005   The range of qualitative research. *Journal of Family Planning and Reproductive Health Care* 31(2):165.

Guest, G., A. Bunce, and L. Johnson
2006   How many interviews are enough? An experiment with data saturation and variability. *Field Methods* 18(1):59–82.

Guest, G., and E. McLellan
2003   Distinguishing the trees from the forest: Applying cluster analysis to thematic qualitative data. *Field Methods* 15(2):186–201.

Halloran, M., I. J. Longini, A. Nizam, and Y. Yang
2002   Containing bioterrorist smallpox. *Science* 5597:1428–1432.

Handwerker, P., and D. Wozniak
1997   Sampling strategies for the collection of cultural data: An extension of Boas's answer to Galton's problem. *Current Anthropology* 38(5):869–875.

Hills, M.
2000   Human science research in public health: The contribution and assessment of a qualitative approach. *Canadian Journal of Public Health* 91(6):4–7.

Hoddintott, P., and R. Pill
1997   A review of recently published qualitative research in general practice. More methodological questions than answers? *Family Practice* 14:313–319.

Holland, D., and N. Quinn
1987   *Cultural Models in Language and Thought*. Cambridge: Cambridge University Press.

Horsburgh, D.
2003   Evaluation of qualitative research. *Journal of Clinical Nursing* 12:307–312.

Krippendorf, K.
1980   *Content Analysis: An Introduction to Its Methodology*. Beverly Hills, Calif.: Sage.

Krueger, R.
1994   *Focus Groups: A Practical Guide for Applied Research*. Thousand Oaks, Calif.: Sage.

Lambert, H., and C. McKevitt
2002   Anthropology in health research: From qualitative methods to multidisciplinary. *BMJ* 325: 210–213.

Last, J.
1988   *A Dictionary of Epidemiology* (2nd ed.). Oxford: Oxford University Press.

Lincoln, Y., and E. Guba
1985   *Naturalistic Inquiry*. Beverly Hills, Calif.: Sage.

Lombard, M., J. Snyder-Duch, and C. Campanella Bracken
2002   Content analysis in mass communication: Assessment and reporting of intercoder reliability. *Human Communication Research* 28:587–604.

Macalino, G., D. Celentano, C. Latkin, S. Strathdee, and D. Vlahov
2002   Risk behaviors by audio-computer-assisted self-interviews among HIV-seropositive and HIV-seronegative injection drug users. *AIDS Education and Prevention* 14:367–378.

MacQueen, K. M., E. McLellan, D. S. Metzger, S. Kegeles, R. P. Strauss, R. Scotti, L. Blanchard, and R. T. Trotter, 2nd.
2001   What is community? An evidence-based definition for participatory public health. *American Journal of Public Health* 91(12):1929–1938.

Malterud, K.
2001   Qualitative research: Standards, challenges, and guidelines. *The Lancet* 358:483–488.

Mays, N., and C. Pope
2000   Assessing quality in qualitative research. *BMJ* 320:50–52.

McCombie, S., and J. Anarfi
2002   The influence of sex of interviewer on the results of an AIDS survey in Ghana. *Human Organization* 61:51–57.

McLellan, E., K. M. MacQueen, and J. Niedig
2003   Beyond the qualitative interview: Data preparation and transcription. *Field Methods* 15(1):63–84.

Miles, M., and A. Huberman
1994   *Qualitative Data Analysis* (2nd ed.). Thousand Oaks, Calif.: Sage.

Morse, J.
1997   "Perfectly healthy, but dead": The myth of inter-rater reliability. *Qualitative Health Research* 7:445–447.

Morse, J., M. Barrett, M. Mayan, K. Olson, and J. Spiers
2002   Verification strategies for establishing reliability and validity in qualitative research. *International Journal of Qualitative Methods* 1(2). Available at: www.ualberta.ca/~iiqm/backissues/1_2Final/html/morse.html. Accessed November 2006.

Nielsen, J., and T. Landauer
1993   A mathematical model of the findings of usability problems. Proceedings of ACM INTERCHI Conference. Pp. 206–213. New York: ACM Press.

Nkwi, P., I. Nyamongo, and G. Ryan
2001   *Field Research into Social Issues: Methodological Guidelines.* Washington, D.C.: UNESCO.

Oliver-Velez, D., H. Finlinson, S. Deren, R. Robles, M. Shedlin, J. Andía, and H. Colón
2002   Mapping the air-bridge locations: The application of ethnographic mapping techniques to a study of HIV risk behavior determinant in East Harlem, New York, and Bayamón, Puerto Rico. *Human Organization* 61:262–276.

Parsons, H.
1974   What happened at Hawthorne? *Science* 183:922–932.

Patton, M.
2002   *Qualitative Research and Evaluation Methods* (3rd ed.). Thousand Oaks, Calif.: Sage.

Paulhus, D.
1991   Measurement and control of response bias. In J. Robinson et al., eds. *Measures of Personality and Social Psychological Attitudes*. Vol. 1, pp. 17–59. New York: Academic.

Pitchforth, E., M. Porter, E. van Teijlingen, and K. Forrest Keenan
2005   Writing up and presenting qualitative research in family planning and reproductive health care. *Journal of Family Planning and Reproductive Health Care* 31(2):132–135.

Popay, J., A. Rogers, and G. Williams
1998   Rationale and standards for the systematic review of qualitative literature in health services research. *Qualitative Health Research* 8(3):341–351.

Pope, C., and N. Mays
2000   *Qualitative Research in Health Care*. London: BMJ Books.

Roberts, K. A., M. Dixon-Woods, R. Fitzpatrick, K. R. Abrams, and D. R. Jones
2002   Factors affecting uptake of childhood immunisation: A Bayesian synthesis of qualitative and quantitative evidence. *The Lancet* 360:1596–1599.

Romney, A., W. Batchelder, and S. Weller
1986   Culture as consensus: A theory of culture and informant accuracy. *American Anthropologist* 88:313–338.

Rosenthal, R.
1966   *Experimenter Effects in Behavioral Research*. New York: Appleton-Century-Crofts.

Rothenberg, R., and J. Narramore
1996   The relevance of social network concepts to sexually transmitted disease control. *Sexually Transmitted Diseases* 1:24–29.

Russell, C. K., and D. M. Gregory
2003   Evaluation of qualitative research studies. *Evidence Based Nursing* 6:36–40.

Sandelowski, M., and J. Barroso
2002   Reading qualitative studies. *International Journal of Qualitative Methods* 1(1):article 5.

Seale, C.
1999   Quality in qualitative research. *Qualitative Inquiry* 5(4):465–478.

Seale, C., and D. Silverman
1997   Ensuring rigour in qualitative research. *European Journal of Public Health* 7:379–384.

Secker, J., E. Wimbush, J. Watson, and K. Milburn
1995   Qualitative methods in health promotion research: Some criteria for quality. *Health Education Journal* 54:74–87.

Sharts-Hopko, N. C.
2002   Assessing rigor in qualitative research. *Journal of the Association of Nurses in AIDS Care* 13:84–86.

Tashakkori, A., and C. Teddlie
1998   *Mixed Methodology: Combining Qualitative and Quantitative Approaches.* Applied Social Research Methods Series, 46. Thousand Oaks, Calif.: Sage.

Tashakkori, A., and C. Teddlie (eds.)
2003   *Handbook on Mixed Methods in the Behavioral and Social Sciences.* Thousand Oaks, Calif.: Sage.

Weeks, M., and R. Moore
1981   Ethnicity-of-interviewer effects on ethnic respondents. *Public Opinion Quarterly* 45:245–249.

Weller, S., and A. Romney
1988   *Systematic Data Collection.* London: Sage.

Werner, O.
1998   Short take 24: Do we need standards for ethnography? *Cultural Anthropology Methods* 10(1):1–3.

Williamson, J. B., D. A. Karp, J. R. Dalphin, and P. S. Gray
1982   *The Research Craft: An Introduction to Social Science Methods* (2nd ed.). Glenview, Ill.: Scott, Foresman.

Systematic Methods for Collecting and Analyzing Multidisciplinary Team-based Qualitative Data

11

JAMES W. CAREY AND DEBORAH GELAUDE

I N THE SOCIAL AND BEHAVIORAL SCIENCES, qualitative studies traditionally have been relatively modest in size and scope, and often have employed nonprobability sampling techniques (Bernard 2002, 2006, Creswell 1998, Denzin and Lincoln 1998, Marshall and Rossman 1989, Miles and Huberman 1994, Patton 2002, Tesch 1990). Qualitative methods historically were developed to help researchers better understand the intricacies of cultural, social, and psychological processes, relying on limited amounts of data collected from small- or medium-sized samples. Such studies often employ cross-sectional research designs. And, prior to the development and widespread adoption of sophisticated qualitative data analysis software programs in the early 1990s, most qualitative researchers analyzed their data by hand (an approach that still may be the simplest and fastest option if the researcher only has limited amount of data from a small sample). In the past, when qualitative research teams were formed (if at all), they typically included practitioners from a single discipline (e.g., one or a very small number of university-based researchers, perhaps with the help of their graduate students conducting research in a single community). Findings from traditional small-scale qualitative studies in the social and behavioral sciences typically are disseminated via discipline-specific conferences, scholarly journals, and academic books.

Over the past two decades, however, researchers have been increasingly using qualitative research methods in fields such as business, social work, nursing, consumer research, and public health (Appleton 1995, Daly 1997, Drisko 1997, Kolbe and Burnett 1991, Lambert et al. 1995, Mantell et al. 1997, Sykes 1991, Ulin et al. 2002, 2005), in both applied and academic settings. In addition, as MacQueen and Guest (chapter 1, this volume) observe, qualitative studies over the past three decades have tended to become more complex and involve more disciplines. In the course of this expansion, researchers have found new ways to use qualitative methods that differ in several ways from their historical roots. The field of public health is a prime example. In public health, qualitative data are gathered for a broad array of scientific purposes, including formative research phases of larger community studies, evaluation of programmatic interventions and services, and as part of the primary data collection methods in large studies and intervention trials (Hahn 1999, Lambert et al. 1995, Mantell et al. 1997, Scrimshaw and Gleason 1992). Good public health policy needs to be grounded in rigorous scientific evidence (Holtgrave et al. 1997, Holtgrave and Curran 2005, Snider and Satcher 1997). Research findings generated with faulty scientific methods can lead to erroneous conclusions, as well as ineffective or harmful policies that waste resources in applied programmatic settings. Because of this enhanced need for scientific rigor, many qualitative researchers in public health (and other applied fields) expend considerable effort to ensure that systematic and rigorous methods and procedures are used throughout a study (e.g., Hruschka et al. 2004).

Public health also is highly multidisciplinary, and now includes behavioral and social scientists from a broad array of disciplines playing diverse roles (Galavotti et al. 1997, Rugg et al. 1997, Snider and Satcher 1997). Research teams often are quite large, and may include psychologists, physicians, epidemiologists, anthropologists, health educators, biostatisticians, sociologists, economists, microbiologists, and many others, depending upon the study objectives. The broader use of qualitative methods by multidisciplinary study teams has encouraged the development of training materials to assist team members that may be unfamiliar with qualitative research techniques (e.g., Mack et al. 2005, Ulin et al. 2002, 2005). Methods and findings in applied fields such as public health must be communicated in ways that are understandable and credible to an audience that not only includes scientists and policy makers from different backgrounds, but also community members and practitioners in health departments or community-based organizations. In contrast with most traditional qualitative research, contemporary public health studies may entail data collection from large samples obtained from more than one population or geographic location. And, qualitative data collection techniques may be woven into a broad array of research designs, including those used in epidemiology. Information generated using qualitative methods may be linked to data assessed with structured survey approaches, as well as laboratory-based or clinical methods. Findings from public health research not only are disseminated via multidisciplinary scientific journals, but also are used directly to shape public health programs and policies (Holtgrave et al. 1997). In sum, the ways qualitative methods are used in public health can differ substantively from their original historical applications in the social and behavioral sciences.

The qualitative methods literature does not sufficiently address these differences, leaving a significant gap. The purpose of this chapter (as well as this book) is to compile best practices and lessons learned from using qualitative methods in multidisciplinary, team-based public health studies. We use a case study approach to discuss and synthesize many of the issues covered in previous chapters. Specifically, we address issues related to qualitative research design, sampling, data collection instrument design, staffing and training, data management, and data analysis. We conclude with a discussion of how findings from team-based qualitative studies might be used for multidisciplinary scientific reports and programmatic applications. The ideas presented in this chapter are based upon qualitative research studies sponsored by the Centers for Disease Control and Prevention (CDC) in Atlanta, GA. Our hope is that other researchers from many disciplines using qualitative methods may benefit from our experiences as they design their own team-based studies. Although many of our examples are based in public health, our experiences and recommendations are applicable to multidisciplinary team-based qualitative studies in other fields outside public health.

Four CDC Case Studies

Although the ideas we present are based on a larger number of studies, we have selected four CDC qualitative research projects to use as illustrative case studies in this chapter. The first, smallest, and least complex of these case studies is an evaluation of the national HIV/AIDS control program in the country of Nicaragua (Carey 1994, Mobley et al. 1993). This evaluation most closely resembles traditional qualitative research in the social and behavioral sciences, because the Nicaragua project was conducted by a small team of three investigators, and relied upon a limited data set collected from a modest-sized nonprobability sample.

The second case example is a study of tuberculosis-related cultural beliefs among recent Vietnamese refugees to two counties in New York State (Carey et al. 1996, 1997). This information was collected to inform the design of a culturally appropriate tuberculosis preventive treatment program that was subsequently implemented in the same two counties. The project was conducted by a multidisciplinary team of investigators from the New

York State health department, local health departments, and community-based refugee service agencies in the two counties, as well as CDC staff.

The third case study involves collection of qualitative data from staff and patrons of two bathhouses in Los Angeles (Mutchler et al. 2003). These establishments are locations where some patrons (men who have sex with men, or MSM) engage in sexual practices that place them at high risk of HIV infection. The data in the bathhouse study were collected to help tailor on-site HIV prevention services to the needs of the bathhouse patrons, and also to serve as a formative research phase prior to the design and implementation of a larger quantitative survey of MSM patrons of other Los Angeles bathhouses. The interdisciplinary team involved with this project included staff from the Los Angeles county health department and CDC.

Finally, the Context of HIV Infection Project (CHIP) is our fourth, most complex, and largest case study. The project is ongoing, and its aims are to identify behavioral factors associated with elevated risk of recent HIV infection, and to identify missed program opportunities that could be used to avert future HIV infections (Carey et al. 2005). The CHIP project presently is in its final stages, and is being implemented by the CDC in partnership with the local health departments in Chicago and Los Angeles. CHIP collects information from MSM, non-MSM injection drug users, and other heterosexuals at high HIV risk. Several dozen local health department, university, contractor, and CDC staff have played various roles in the CHIP research team.

We use these case studies to exemplify some of the unique characteristics of, and challenges associated with, team-based qualitative research. We divide the research process into seven components—research design, sampling, data collection instrument design, interviewer selection and training, data quality assurance and management, data coding, and data analysis.

Research Design

As noted earlier, qualitative data traditionally have been collected in studies that utilize variations of cross-sectional research designs. Cross-sectional studies gather and compare information on a set of topics as they exist in a defined population at some point in time. Patterns of variation and correlations within the data typically are analyzed, often with nonstatistical methods or basic descriptive statistics when sample sizes are small (LeCompte and Schensul 1999a, Miles and Huberman 1994). Some researchers employ methods to identify specific themes present in text, and others use statistical content analysis approaches (Namey et al., this volume,

Guest and McLellan 2003, Krippendorf 2004, Weber 1990). Because of the temporal cross-sectional nature of the data in many qualitative studies, cause-and-effect relationships often cannot be unambiguously determined.

While limited, cross-sectional designs have their use in public health. For example, in the New York State Vietnamese TB beliefs case study, the investigators needed to document the prevalent tuberculosis beliefs with the sample of fifty-two respondents (Carey et al. 1997). This information was intended to be used to subsequently train outreach workers on what beliefs were present in the population, as a way to prepare them for potential health education and cross-cultural communication needs that they would encounter as they attempted to enroll eligible Vietnamese adults into tuberculosis preventive therapy treatment services. This process worked very well. After using the findings from the first study to design culturally appropriate health education and outreach efforts in the two counties, the results of a second evaluation study showed that 100 percent of thirty-one tuberculosis-infected Vietnamese adults agreed to participate in a directly observed preventive therapy program, and more than 95 percent of the doses were successfully administered under observation by an outreach worker (Jeffery et al. 1996). Because of this success, the New York State health department later adopted the overall approach for use with other refugee and immigrant groups.

However, it is important to recognize that there is no inherent reason why qualitative data necessarily must be collected only in cross-sectional designs or that samples must be small-sized. Qualitative data collection methods can be used in conjunction with other research designs that are commonly used in epidemiology, such as case–control, cohort, experimental, or quasi-experimental studies. For example, the Context of HIV Infection Project (CHIP) uses a case–control design (Carey et al. 2005). Cases include a sample of 129 persons with evidence of recent HIV infection in Chicago and Los Angeles, and they are compared with 387 HIV-uninfected controls matched to the cases based on city and HIV behavioral risk group. A structured quantitative questionnaire and semistructured qualitative questionnaire were used by interviewers with all the cases and controls to gather detailed information on variables that may be associated with the odds of recent HIV seroconversion.

When selecting a qualitative research design, we recommend that research teams do not automatically rely on cross-sectional studies, but also consider other options, such as case–control, experimental, quasi-experimental, cohort, or other study designs. In making their choice, investigators may need to first consider practical time, staff, and financial resource constraints because these limits may rule out the use of more complex and expensive designs that take a long time to implement. For example, in the Nicaragua HIV program evaluation study, the research team consisted of three people. The project had a very low budget and all data collection needed to be completed in a ten-day period (Mobley et al. 1993). After arrival in Managua, an unanticipated general transportation strike occurred, and large popular protests in the streets made it impossible for the team to even leave the capital city and to visit other parts of the country. By necessity, the team quickly revised its initial plans, created a semistructured qualitative interview guide, and administered it to a cross-sectional sample of thirty-four key respondents. The team augmented these data with an extensive review of written documents and statistical reports. Large-scale surveys or more complex designs were out of the question. However, even if these constraints had not been in place, the use of semistructured interviews and document reviews were an excellent mix of methods for systematically obtaining data relevant for this type of rapid programmatic evaluation (Beebe 2001, Carey 1994, Scrimshaw and Gleason 1992).

In addition to practical considerations, qualitative investigators should also consider the substantive purpose of the study when choosing an appropriate design (Johnson 1998). For example, if one needs to learn more about a specific population's public health needs, a researcher might employ a community identification process to interview and compare samples of target population members (key participants), persons who have formal service provider roles and informal interactions with the group in the community (systems providers and interactors), as well as individuals who can facilitate researcher entrée into the community (Higgins et al. 1996, Tashima et al. 1996). A simplified version of this process was used in the Los Angeles bathhouse study design; the investigators interviewed two samples of patrons and bathhouse staff (i.e., key participants and systems providers). Alternatively, if a researcher wishes to collect qualitative data as part of the evaluation of an intervention, an experimental or quasi-experimental design might be a better choice.

Sampling

A common stereotype is that qualitative data are always collected from small convenience samples. However, just as one can incorporate qualitative data collection into a variety of research designs, we recommend that investigators consider the strengths and weaknesses of various sampling methods when collecting qualitative data. There is no necessary rule that requires that small convenience samples be used when gathering qualitative data. As with selecting an appropriate research design, the choice of sampling methods depends upon a combination of practical constraints, as well as substantive research goals and objectives.

If an investigator chooses to use nonprobability sampling methods, a variety of options are available (Bernard 2002, 2006, Coyne 1997, Crabtree and Miller 1992, Johnson 1990, Morse 1991, Patton 2002). Some of these options may overlap, or can be used in combination with each other. One option has been called either the maximum variation or purposive method, and it entails selection of persons from as wide a range of situations or perspectives as possible. If used to gather interview data regarding health beliefs, for example, a maximum variation sample might help delineate the range of respondent cultural beliefs about a disease and its treatment in the larger population; but this type of sample will not yield information on the proportionate distribution of those beliefs in the populations from which the sample was drawn. In the Nicaragua case study, Mobley et al. (1993) used this technique to select key respondents from community-based HIV service organizations, various governmental ministries familiar with the HIV situation in the country, political advocacy groups, international donor agencies, condom distribution vendors, blood donor agencies, and members of populations at high HIV infection risk, such as female commercial sex workers or patrons of gay bars in Managua.

In contrast, a "homogenous" nonprobability sample might be constructed with the respondents being similar to each other in some way (e.g., shared socioeconomic or demographic background). This is a good choice to consider when inviting participants to be in a focus group, because having a shared common background may reduce respondent's inhibitions and allow them to speak frankly in front of their fellow focus group members (Kruger 1994, Schensul et al. 1999a).

The snowball, network, or chain-referral sampling method involves selecting an initial small number of persons to participate in a study. Following data collection with these persons, they are in turn invited to suggest names, introduce the researchers to other respondents, or otherwise facilitate sampling new individuals they think might also be willing to participate in the study. This approach can yield a small nonprobability sample, and is especially helpful in locating hard-to-identify populations (e.g., users of illegal injection drugs).

Heckathorn (1997) and his colleagues have shown how simple chain-referral sampling methods can be strengthened to yield a large sample that has the statistical characteristics of a true probability sample. These extended chain-referral techniques are termed respondent-driven sampling (RDS) methods in the literature. In a recent CDC study, Abdul-Quader et al. (2006) examined the utility of using RDS as a means to recruit a diverse sample ($N = 618$) of injecting and noninjecting drug users in New York City.

Another sampling method that can help researchers reach hard-to-identify populations has been called venue–day–time (VDT) sampling. The first step typically is to use traditional ethnographic interviews with key respondents to identify and map locations where the target population congregates. Next, efforts are made to physically observe and enumerate foot traffic of eligible target population members passing through these locations, taking special note of the variation between different days and times of the week. Finally, an attempt is made to design a systematic sampling strategy that allows the researchers to recruit a cross section of persons from these different locations, days, and times. Whenever possible, it is a good idea to compare the characteristics of a VDT sample with samples obtained in other studies as a means to better ascertain the degree to which it is representative of the larger population from which it was drawn. In public health applications, MacKellar et al. (1996), Mansergh et al. (2006), Muhib et al. (2001), and Stueve et al. (2001) have used VDT techniques to obtain samples of MSM in the United States and Thailand.

Finally, convenience samples are composed of respondents chosen in a haphazard manner; while they may be fast and inexpensive, they may reflect insufficient research planning, results can be difficult to interpret, and the study results may lack both generalizability and credibility. We recommend that convenience sampling should only be selected as a method of last resort when no better options are feasible.

As with all other aspects of a project's methods, when conducting a team-based qualitative study, it is essential that all members of the research team thoroughly understand and implement the agreed-upon sampling procedures. If different personnel are allowed to deviate from the project sampling protocol, the project runs the risk of having noncomparable data that will be difficult or impossible to analyze. Regardless of whether nonprobability or probability sampling methods are used, it is important for project administrators to ensure that staff have appropriate training and quality assurance supervision, and also to ensure that samples are obtained in a manner fully consistent with the study's intended protocol.

Probability sampling methods can also be used to select respondents for a qualitative study (Guest 2005, Guest and MacQueen, this volume). These methods have been well documented for many decades, along with the strengths and weaknesses of each approach (e.g., Ackoff 1953, Cochran 1977, General Accounting Office 1992, Levy and Lemeshow 1999). Compared with nonprobability methods, some advantages of probability samples are that they (1) can help reduce sampling biases and (2) may allow for better generalizability of the findings from the sample back to the larger population from which the sample was drawn. Many statistical procedures have underlying sampling assumptions. Under certain conditions and assumptions described in further detail later in this chapter (and chapters 7 and 10 in this volume), some forms of qualitative data may be evaluated using systematic thematic or content analysis methods, which may be analyzable with some multivariate statistics. The use of one type of research design often implies that the researcher adheres to a variety of sampling assumptions. For example, because the CHIP study uses a case–control design, the researchers were careful to ensure that the sampling plans for both the case and control arms corresponded with established sampling methods described in the literature (Schlesselman 1992).

However, for them to be statistically useful, many probability sample sizes need to be quite large compared with most nonprobability sample sizes, and they are often more expensive or time consuming to collect and analyze. Before embarking on a large-scale qualitative study, we strongly recommend that the investigators carefully consider if they have sufficient time, qualified staff, and financial resources needed to collect, code, and analyze the qualitative data. Qualitative data sets can quickly become very large. For example, the New York Vietnamese TB study used a semistructured interview guide with thirty-two open-ended questions, and a sample of fifty-two respondents. The final qualitative data set with the respondents' answers was approximately several hundred pages of double-spaced text. Much larger studies, such as the CHIP project, may generate considerably larger volumes of data. When designing and planning for resources needed for CHIP, we recognized at the beginning of the project that it would require a team including several dozen data collectors, data managers, data coders, as well as senior investigators in Los Angeles, Chicago, and at the CDC office in Atlanta.

Data Collection Instrument Design

Research teams conducting qualitative studies need to put significant effort into the development of data collection instruments, such as semistructured questionnaires, focus group guides, and other formats of qualitative data collection. In our experience on team-based studies it has been common for qualitative instruments to go through twenty to thirty major revisions; instruments require much careful thought, discussion among team members, and realistic pretests before they are ready to use (see also chapter 4, this volume, for discussion of some of the logistical challenges in this process).

The social and behavioral science literature contains many excellent discussions of the principles that go into the design of good questionnaires or other data collection instruments (e.g., Bernard 2002, 2006, General Accounting Office 1993, Lyberg et al. 1997). In this chapter, rather than attempting a comprehensive review of general questionnaire design considerations, we provide recommendations that are pertinent for team-based qualitative research:

1. *Instrument design in team-based qualitative research requires consistent and centralized coordination.* Whenever one assembles a team of talented researchers from different disciplines, it is very likely that each team member can independently draft a set of questions that addresses his or her individual interests. If this happens, one of the worst mistakes is to combine all the question sets in a draft questionnaire. The draft instrument would be far too long (e.g., perhaps as many as 100 to 150 open-ended questions could be generated from a large team of creative individual researchers). The draft is likely to lack conceptual coherence, and the logical flow would be problematic for both interviewers and respondents. Question-wording styles and level of abstraction would vary greatly. Question topics would be repetitive or overlap to varying degrees. From a project management perspective, team members will tend to become "wedded" to their own particular set of questions, hindering subsequent editing of the instrument. In contrast to this approach, we suggest that initial draft questionnaires be created by a small subset of team members highly familiar with the overall project research objectives. Multiple drafts can then be circulated, and constructively discussed by the entire team. Revisions are made based on full team member input (including senior scientific personnel, midlevel managers, interviewers, and data coding staff), as well as pretests with respondents drawn from the study population. Likewise, in multisite studies, it will be essential to include local perspectives, experiences, and needs in this process.

2. *Create an "intents list" for the data collection instrument.* We have found that one of the most helpful tools to use during team-based instrument development is to create an intents list to accompany the instrument. An "intents list" provides a succinct rationale for the purpose of asking each question on a questionnaire or interview guide. For example, the CHIP project uses a semistructured interview guide consisting of a series of open-ended questions consistently administered to each respondent in the sample. The corresponding CHIP intents list is an exact duplicate of the questionnaire, but includes a short statement written under each question describing why the question is being asked, what we hope to learn from asking it, and how the question feeds into the overall project research goals and objectives. If the group cannot articulate this type of clear explanation for any one specific item, consider dropping the question off the instrument. Written intents statements for different questions can be compared to eliminate redundant items, or to revise questions to reduce unwanted topical overlap. Elimination of unnecessary questions streamlines the instrument, and will save much time and money during data collection, data management, and data analysis phases. In other words, there is no need to collect information that serves no purpose. Intents lists help teams keep their instruments as simple and clear as possible.

The intents list also serves other important purposes. It can be compared with the goals and objectives of the project. This may highlight needed data collection topics that the team has neglected to include in earlier revisions of the questionnaire. In addition to the intents list, on the CHIP project we also developed an Excel spreadsheet that listed the project objectives, the specific question numbers that were intended to gather relevant data for meeting each objective, as well as background literature review citations for why specific items were included on the questionnaire. Finally, the intents list is also a very useful tool when training interviewers to administer the questionnaire (particularly how and when to probe), as well as for project managers to make sure that interview transcripts or interviewer field notes fully address all aspects of each question. This last feature is especially helpful for ensuring comparability of data collection efforts between a large team of different interviewers working in multiple research locations.

3. *Keep the instrument simple to use and easy to understand.* Even in the best circumstances, collecting good qualitative data is a complex task. Interviewers should be focused on eliciting thorough and clear qualitative information from respondents, and they do not need the added burden of a cumbersome or poorly worded questionnaire. Whenever possible, instrument developers should avoid complex question-skip patterns or other difficult-to-administer features. Input from interviewers or other data collection staff should be included as early as possible during instrument development. It also is important for instrument designers to seek advice from persons familiar with the local study population; this helps avoid inadvertently offensive or confusing question wording, and may facilitate development of plans to gain a respondent's trust. Another pitfall is that some multidisciplinary research team members may have a tendency to inadvertently use jargon or abstract theoretical constructs from their own fields when drafting question wording. This creates two problems. First, interviewers may not understand the intent of asking the question, and therefore administer it incorrectly during data collection. Second, respondents may be confused by academically worded questions, and may therefore provide vague, incomplete, or irrelevant responses that do not fully meet the purposes of the study. In general, it is much better to break apart complex topics into a series of specific and concrete subquestions.

Depending on the interviewers' skill levels, experiences, and preferences, it may help to provide them with checklists of follow-up probes after open-ended questions. A pitfall of this approach is that some novice qualitative interviewers may be overly reliant on such checklists, and may fail to actively listen to the respondent's comments and not follow up on other important issues. In our experience, we have found that interviewers vary in their idiosyncratic preferences for physical questionnaire format. To the extent possible, it is good practice to adapt the questionnaire format to meet the physical format and other usability preferences of the interviewer team working on a specific project.

Interviewer Selection and Training

When hiring interviewers or other data collection staff for a team-based qualitative study, initial considerations should include cultural and linguistic competence. For example, in the New York State Vietnamese project, two interviewers were employed. Both were from Vietnam, and were fully literate in both Vietnamese and English. In the Los Angeles bathhouse project, data were collected from MSM patrons at bathhouses. It would have been extremely awkward or impossible for women to enter these locations, so many of the interviewers employed were themselves MSM. In CHIP, we knew beforehand that some interviews would need to be conducted in Spanish, so we made certain that some of the interviewers in the Chicago and Los Angeles sites spoke Spanish.

In addition to having broad cultural and linguistic competence, interviewers should have several other skills. They should be highly motivated, and have an employment track record that demonstrated their ability to give meticulous attention to detail. Interviewers should have strong conversational, listening, and writing abilities. It is helpful if they also are computer literate with word processor software, but this may not always be possible (e.g., when working with low-literacy populations or in countries with little access or experience with information technologies). In addition, interviewers must be fully comfortable with the research subject matter and the targeted study population. For example, when conducting an HIV behavioral intervention study, interviewers may ask very detailed and personal questions about respondents' sex and illegal drug behaviors. It is essential that interviewers be able to do their job in a nonjudgmental and professional manner, regardless of what they might personally think about the respondent's past actions, opinions, or beliefs. When working with interviewers who find some question topics difficult or embarrassing to discuss, it is important to increase their comfort levels through formal training, role-play exercises, and practice interviews.

Good interviewers can be hired and trained from many different disciplines, educational levels, and personal backgrounds. Over the past decade, we have trained approximately five to six hundred interviewers, who have worked on a diverse array of team-based projects in various locations in two countries. We have worked with excellent interviewers who had varied formal education backgrounds, ranging from high school graduates to doctoral-level training in medical schools or PhD programs. One might expect that it is better to hire persons with previous interview or data collection experience. However, not all interviewing methods are equivalent, or prepare personnel to do a good job at collecting qualitative data on team-based projects. At times, having some types of prior interviewing experiences may hinder individuals' ability to conduct good qualitative interviews. For example, persons with experience doing structured interviews (e.g., perhaps doing sociological surveys or interviews that have gathered data as part of public health surveillance systems) may have an initial tendency to only read verbatim the exact wording of a question from the interview guide. When switching over to a qualitative study, they may have difficulty in learning how to ask appropriate follow-up probes to help a respondent provide a complete and relevant response to an open-ended question. Similarly, persons with social work, counseling, health education, or other intervention backgrounds may have a tendency to want to "correct" misperceptions or otherwise assist the respondent during an interview only intended to gather data that accurately describes existing beliefs. However, our experience suggests that regardless of their initial education or prior interview work experience, most interviewers can greatly improve their skills through training, diligence, practice, and constructively worded feedback and encouragement from supervisors and other interviewer peers working on the same team.

After interviewers are hired, rigorous and thorough interviewer training is extremely important to ensure data quality. Team-based projects generally require multiple interviewers, and it is essential that all share an accurate and comparable understanding about data collection procedures. Handing interviewers a written protocol to read is not sufficient. Yet time and financial constraints on most studies preclude lengthy training periods that extend over weeks or months. To illustrate how we approach this problem in our team-based qualitative research, we summarize below how we have trained interviewers to administer semistructured interview guides in at least eleven multisite and multidisciplinary studies in public health, including three of the case examples mentioned in this chapter. Researchers using focus groups, unstructured ethnographic techniques, or other qualitative data collection methods may need to modify this approach to better fit their needs. On most of these projects, we have focused on semistructured interview techniques. But in some projects, we have also included additional modules for focus groups or structured survey questionnaire administration. For a useful data collection and management training manual, readers can also refer to Mack et al. (2005).

Our CDC training workshop for interviewing is based roughly on Gorden's (1998) suggestions for a semester-long interviewer methods course at a university. We also have incorporated other advice from Bernard (2002, 2006), Spradley (1979, 1980), various other authors, and past CDC research experiences. The workshop is generally condensed to three to four days in length, depending on the complexity of the project. We encourage all project team members—including all senior and midlevel managers—to fully participate in the workshop, even if they are not personally involved with interviews. In multisite studies, this also may serve as an opportunity for different team members to meet each other face-to-face. Having all personnel participate in the training helps ensure that everyone fully understands both the "big picture" and the details of a complex project. We have observed that a common extra benefit is that it tends to promote social cohesion and it conveys a unified sense of purpose in projects with large teams or multiple research sites.

The workshop itself is a mixture of didactic presentations, group discussion, reading materials, and hands-on group exercises. We strive to build and improve interviewing skills in a step-by-step manner, in accord with Gorden's training suggestions. We also write and distribute to everyone a project-specific interviewer workshop manual that they can keep and later use as a reference. The manual length typically ranges from one hundred to two hundred pages. Manuals generally include copies of (1) an executive summary describing the rationale for the project and its goals and objectives, (2) a copy of the training PowerPoint slide handouts to facilitate note taking, (3) copies of the final or near-final drafts of the qualitative questionnaires and their corresponding intents lists, and (4) a variety of other project-specific appendices. Additional copies of the instrument are made for trainees to use during the workshop exercises. By the end of the training workshop, interviewers get a good sense of what will be expected of them, build or improve their interviewing skills, and understand how their work fits into the overall project goals.

Our workshop training begins with welcoming remarks, staff introductions, and an overview of the workshop goals, syllabus, and schedule. After this, we review in detail the purposes of the project. Next, we describe how the data collected by the interviews will fit into the larger picture, and go over the questionnaire intents lists in detail. While certainly not ideal, in practice we have discovered this may be the first time some of the interviewers have fully read or seriously thought about the project's interview instruments. After completing these initial steps, we typically subdivide the rest of the training into ten learnable skill sets:

- *Maintaining ethics and professionalism:* Respondent and interviewer safety and welfare; informed consent and other human subjects protection issues; how to avoid inappropriate situations (e.g., sexual advances, offers by the respondent to sell the interviewer illegal drugs); and how to handle unlikely adverse events or situations.

- *Motivating respondents:* Methods to establish initial rapport and trust with the respondent as a means to promote honest information disclosure; practical interview-scheduling issues and logistics; and maintenance of professional courtesy with respondents.
- *Methods for asking interview questions:* Review of differences between closed-ended versus open-ended questions; ways to keep an interview focused on the main topic; discussion of common interviewing pitfalls (e.g., how to avoid asking leading questions, rushing through interviews, not allowing respondents to speak, desire to correct respondent misperceptions or inaccurate health beliefs during the interview); importance of avoiding contamination of the data with the interviewer's preconceptions or assumptions; and a discussion of the interviewer's job to learn and record a complete and accurate understanding of the respondent's beliefs or experiences to the greatest extent possible.
- *Methods to listen to respondents:* Active listening skills; how to avoid listening obstacles (e.g., physical noise interference, bored-sounding interviewer); importance of thoroughly understanding the intents lists and other project-specific procedures; and importance of asking questions in a nonjudgmental and professional manner.
- *Understanding respondent communication:* Methods to fully understand what the respondent is communicating (e.g., nonverbal cues as well as their spoken statements), and being aware of how cultural or individual differences can affect the interview communication processes.
- *How to evaluate a response to an open-ended question:* Methods to assess the relevance and adequacy of a response, including whether the respondent has understood the question (relevant subject matter addressed in their response); does the response include information that falls into the correct recall time periods or physical setting; does the level of abstraction of the response fit the question wording; and finally how to compare the response adequacy with the intents list for that particular question.
- *How to probe responses:* Discussion of different types of follow-up probes (e.g., required follow-up questions that might be explicitly included on the instrument, versus discretionary probes used by the interviewer to assist a respondent to clarify or complete their thoughts and responses); and methods to avoid common probing errors (e.g., probing too much or too little, using leading probes to bias the respondent's answers).

- *Steps used in the project for data quality control:* Review of project-specific procedures for accurate data recording, including use of good note-taking methods and mechanical interview-recording devices; how to avoid interviewer biases and protocol drift; and how to ensure data security.
- *Generating postinterview writeups:* Procedures for creating accurate, thorough, and clear verbatim transcripts and interviewer-generated field note summaries.
- *Data entry issues:* Review how the data will be used to meet project objectives; roles of the interviewer in generating the text; roles of supervisors in data quality assurance; and how to use qualitative data analysis software programs for data entry.

It is extremely important to emphasize that interviewers cannot gain the necessary skills merely by reading the training manual or by only listening to a lecture on interviewing techniques. The best way we know of to help interviewers improve their skills is through hands-on practice using the project's instruments, coupled with provision of constructive encouragement and recommendations for further improvement. Throughout the workshop, we therefore include numerous practice sessions in which the workshop participants attempt to use the project questionnaire and their skills in progressively more difficult class exercises. However, participation in the workshop is not sufficient for most interviewers. After the workshop is completed, interviewers are required to complete full-scale practice interviews back in their home locations, including writing up of the practice data sets. As needed, retraining or refresher training is provided.

Some interviewers or other project staff may resist these postworkshop practice exercises, but we have discovered that it is essential not to skip or short-circuit these steps, even if some staff initially claim they do not need hands-on practice exercises. Intellectual understanding of the interview process does not necessarily mean interviewers can actually implement these skills in real-life practice. To avoid the generation of poor-quality data or the need to discard information from the initial respondents, it is critical to identify and improve training and protocol implementation deficits before real data collection starts. It also is a very good idea to conduct regular quality assurance reviews of interviews done by each interviewer throughout the data collection phase to avoid interviewer drift or inadvertent lapses into bad habits. Much of this training can take place while a project is waiting for the final approval of its research protocol by the human subjects institutional review board (IRB).

Data Quality Assurance and
Data Set Management

It is essential for team-based qualitative studies to have carefully designed data quality assurance and data management plans to avoid wasting resources or generating unusable data sets. These plans should be made well in advance of initial data collection. We recommend that teams take into account the following four areas of consideration when making their plans:

1. *Ensure sufficiency of time, staff, and financial resources:* Qualitative data sets can be very large and complex, especially on team-based multisite research projects, and senior project managers must understand the implications of this when they are planning their study. On the basis of our experiences, we estimate that a verbatim transcript from a typical one-hour ethnographic or semistructured interview with a single respondent typically will yield a word processor document of approximately thirty double-spaced pages. Even if data are collected from just ten key respondents, assuming that verbatim transcripts are written for each interview, the total volume of text would be as long as a PhD dissertation. Practical questions to consider are whether the project has sufficient time, qualified staff, and funds to collect, transcribe, manage, rigorously code, analyze, and write up the results from the anticipated amount of data to be collected from the projected number of respondents. If not, a redesign should be seriously considered prior to starting data collection.

2. *Choose a qualitative data analysis software program that matches project needs:* There are many qualitative data analysis software programs available (Fielding and Lee 1998, Weitzman and Miles 1995). Because of the rapid developments in qualitative data analysis (QDA) programs, another good source of up-to-date information for a researcher is to consult Internet discussion groups (e.g., Qual-Software 2006), or do Web searches for QDA software lists of programs. As with statistical analysis software, various QDA programs have their own strengths and weaknesses. Each QDA program usually has features that emphasize the research and data analysis preferences of the developers. There is no single "best" QDA software that is the optimum choice for all qualitative research projects. Some programs also have important prerequisites for how data are physically organized for use. For making a QDA software choice and appropriate data management plans,

researchers should be aware of these features and assumptions. Chapters 7 and 8 in this volume provide a comparative overview of data analysis and data management functions, respectively, of common QDA software.

In many of our studies at the CDC, we frequently use semistructured interview instruments administered to medium- to large-sized samples of individuals in multiple locations. In part to help meet data management needs in our projects, we developed our own QDA program, called CDC EZ-Text, because other existing QDA software did not satisfactorily meet the needs for collecting, managing, and analyzing the data on our team-based and multisite projects (Carey et al. 1998a, 1998b). In addition, we found that many other existing QDA programs had features that adversely constrained our ability to ensure high intercoder reliability and analyze large complex qualitative databases, and also to link qualitative results with quantitative data from other sources (e.g., variables abstracted from clinical records or laboratory tests, as well as from structured questionnaires administered to the study respondents). Although we did so to meet our particular set of research requirements, fortunately most other qualitative researchers will not need to develop their own QDA programs, and probably can choose between various existing software programs.

As one of its features, EZ-Text allows a user to create a data entry template that matches the organization of the semistructured interview guide. For each open-ended question, there is a corresponding box that allows the user to input a text passage that captures the respondent's answer to the question, regardless of the length or content of what the respondent told the interviewer. The database is organized by respondent ID number and the questionnaire itself; thus, if a small study has thirty respondents and twenty open-ended questions, the database will contain six hundred text passages. In our projects, we usually distribute a copy of the data entry template to each interviewer, who then enters his or her own data. A password lock prevents interviewers from modifying the template. After local quality assurance procedures, copies of the writeups for individual interviews are merged into a combined master database for subsequent coding and analysis.

3. *Decide if verbatim transcript or interviewer-generated summaries are to be used:* Many qualitative researchers prefer verbatim transcripts from

interviews or focus groups because they can provide an accurate and complete account of what respondents have said (see also chapter 10). However, verbatim transcripts have some disadvantages that should be considered, especially if one wishes to gather data from a large sample or faces resource and time constraints. First, creating transcripts is expensive and time consuming. In our experience, it may take anywhere from three to ten hours of transcription labor per hour of recorded interview. Many variables can affect transcript labor estimates: expertise of the transcriptionist; physical quality of the recording; accents or idiosyncratic phrases used by the respondents; ability of the respondent to express answers using clear and coherent statements; clarity and organization of the wording of items on the original data collection instruments; and the degree of precision needed in the transcript (e.g., Does a project need a highly accurate transcript of each word, linguistic nuance, and voice inflection, or is just the general idea sufficient for study purposes?). McLellan et al. (2003) and chapter 5 in this volume provide further detailed discussion of transcription issues. Recording devices, of course, also can have technical failures that may not be discovered until after an interview has been completed.

For some studies, it may be possible to not use transcripts, and instead interviewers can be trained to write good field notes that accurately summarize key points of a respondent's statements. Recordings can be made as backup for later verification when the interviewers are doing their writeups back at the office. In general, interviewer-generated notes can capture *what* respondents say, but not exactly *how* they express their ideas. By analogy, the process of an interviewer creating a summary of a respondent's statements is similar to a university student taking excellent notes during a classroom lecture, or someone writing up thorough minutes from a group staff meeting. The primary advantage is that notes are much less expensive to generate compared with full-scale verbatim transcripts. The computer files for notes usually are considerably smaller compared with transcripts, and this alone can significantly reduce labor costs. Field and Morse (1985) and others speak about the high "dross rate" in verbatim transcripts (*dross* refers to less useful verbal exchanges that will never be used for final analysis). Using interviewer notes reduces this problem. But if this approach is used, teams will need to spend time on interviewer note-taking and writeup training, and also on supervisor quality assurance to ensure that the note writeups are well done. When we have used this approach, we have found that taking good notes and using them to create good writeups, like other interview skills, is a trainable technique that can be improved through practice. Interviewers vary in the amount of time it takes for them to master these skills. It may be prudent to require less skilled interviewers to complete more practice and training before they are allowed to collect real data. In some extreme cases we had on our projects, a few interviewers have been reassigned to other duties because they could not master all the needed skills.

4. *Develop and consistently implement data quality assurance plans:* Regardless of whether verbatim transcripts, interviewer notes, or a hybrid combination of both are used, interview writeups should be reviewed by a local supervisor for clarity, accuracy, and completeness very soon after they are written. Supervisors can do this by comparing the writeups to the tape or digital recordings, if they are available. Supervisors should also make certain that writeups consistently and thoroughly address each question's intent. Some respondents tend to wander off-topic, and if the interviewer fails to steer the discussion back on topic, it is pointless to write up copious transcripts or notes containing irrelevant information. Writeups need to be succinct, clear, thorough, and accurate representations of the respondents' stated beliefs or reported behaviors, and they should thoroughly address the intents list purposes. If more than one interviewer is collecting data, the local supervisor also must make sure everyone is doing things in a comparable manner, and ensure that everyone is doing things in a way consistent with the overall project IRB protocol (e.g., exclusion of individual identifiers). If needed, local supervisors work with interviewers to make necessary edits and clarifications shortly after written first drafts from an interview are completed. Typically we have found that some interviewers initially have trouble writing good interview reports, but as they gain experience, fewer edits are needed. Feedback on writeups needs to be provided in a very constructive and diplomatic way to interviewers to avoid unnecessary hurt feelings about the quality of their work, especially when they are trying their best to do a good job. It is not helpful if interviewers become discouraged or demoralized. In multisite team-based studies, copies of the writeups are sent to a central

repository or senior data manager. After local supervisor review on multisite projects, central project managers complete an additional second layer of quality assurance review to help maintain consistency and comparability across research locations and different interviewer teams. If needed, edits or clarifications can be made to finalize the interview writeup for each respondent. Regardless of the specific steps used, at the end of these quality assurance processes, transcripts or summaries should be written so that a person unfamiliar with the interview can read them and get an accurate, clear, and thorough understanding of the respondent's reported beliefs, opinions, or behaviors related to each question topic addressed by the questionnaire. Finally, it is essential to complete all writeups and quality assurance steps within a few days after the interview. Otherwise interviewers may start to forget important details (i.e., as short-term memory fades over a few days, they may no longer be able to explain an unclear passage on a tape recording, or a cryptic entry that was scribbled too quickly in field notes written during the interview).

Data Coding

Qualitative researchers should develop plans for data analysis before data collection begins. We suggest that these plans be developed when finalizing research design, sampling, and instrument design plans. Analysis plans should be clearly explained and be included in the project's research protocol, including IRB document submissions. At that point, incompatibilities with overall project goals, available resources, or other methods and plans still can be rectified.

Numerous options for analysis of qualitative data are well covered in the literature (Bernard 2002, 2006, Boyatzis 1998, Creswell 1998, LeCompte and Schensul 1999a, 1999b, MacQueen et al. 1998, MacQueen and Milstein 1999, Miles and Huberman 1994, Namey et al., this volume, Weber 1990). In the broadest sense, most qualitative researchers use some type of approach to identify themes present in a segment of their text data (Ryan and Bernard 2003). A *theme* may be defined as a specific belief, opinion, reported behavior, or past experience stated by the respondent. *Segments* are specific portions of the text that a human coder can easily read and interpret for thematic content. Segments vary in length, depending on a researcher's purposes. To illustrate how this might work with a simple example, in some of our studies that use semistructured interviews, it has been possible to define segments as each respondent's answer to each open-ended question on the interview. If we imagine a short interview instrument with fifteen open-ended questions, and we talk with a sample of one hundred respondents, there would be fifteen hundred segments. Although they vary in the mechanics of accomplishing these two tasks, most QDA software (including EZ-Text) assist the user in dividing their data set into manageable segments, and assigning codes to each segment according to thematic content.

Regardless of how segments are determined in a study, some response text passages will be simple to understand, and contain only one or a few themes. Other responses will be long and highly complex, and may contain multiple or even contradictory themes. Themes and their corresponding codes should be very well defined in codebooks (Boyatzis 1998, MacQueen et al. 1998, see also chapter 6 in this volume). Codebooks will go through many revisions as the researchers come to understand the thematic content of their data, and researchers should anticipate this reality when developing project timetables (Hruschka et al. 2004, Miles and Huberman 1994). Ultimately the codes defined in a good codebook will clearly describe all the salient themes present in the qualitative data set. MacQueen et al. (chapter 6, this volume) provide suggestions for developing qualitative codebooks in a team setting.

In essence, identification of themes is a reading comprehension task; qualitative data coders assigned to do this job should have this essential skill. These project staff also should be capable of giving meticulous attention to detail. They should know or be trained in how to use the QDA software that will be used to code the data on the project.

For large, complex, multisite qualitative studies using semistructured interviews, we recommend approaching the data from a content-driven perspective; the data are coded in accordance with the goals of the research project. This approach focuses on the development of a rigorous and reliable codebook, allows the data to be analyzed at various levels, and prepares the data for future reporting needs (Bernard 2002, 2006, Boyatzis 1998, Carey et al. 1996, Hruschka et al. 2004, MacQueen at al. 1998). If desired, it also may permit the codes to be analyzed using data reduction techniques and/or advanced statistical software (e.g., Guest and McLellan 2003, Krippendorf 2004, Weber 1990). For team-based projects, we divide codebook development into the following steps (see also chapter 6 in this volume):

- *Assign one staff member for coordinating and managing the data analysis procedure:* This individual coordinates all aspects of codebook development and intercoder reliability testing. He or she will also meet with researchers on a regular basis to discuss codebook development, and to ensure that the coding format is consistent with the needs of the team and project goals.

- *Create a coding team:* This team will be trained in data analysis and will meet frequently to discuss codes and coding challenges.
- *Develop a basic structural codebook:* This first draft of the codebook likely will reflect the question intents and samples of early interviews.
- *Give each code a concise description and rules for usage* (Boyatzis 1998, Carey et al. 1996, Hruschka et al. 2004, MacQueen et al. 1998).
- *Make codebook revisions until it appropriately matches the themes in the text:* Researchers should accept the fact that codebooks will go through numerous revisions before the codes accurately define all the salient themes in the data (Carey et al. 1996, Hruschka et al. 2004, Miles and Huberman 1994). Coding qualitative data is an inductive process that may require considerable time, depending on the skill of the coders, the amount of data, and the complexity of the data topics.
- *Ensure intra- and intercoder reliability:* A common problem in identifying themes and coding is subjectivity in the identification of themes present in the responses. To control for this problem, two or more coders should work on a coding team. Ideally, when given the same set of text passages and the same well-constructed codebook, these coders should be able to independently identify the same themes nearly all of the time. Initial reliability tests of this kind almost always will be very poor (e.g., 30 or 40 percent agreement). Discrepancies are used to edit and create a new codebook draft that more effectively captures the themes, defines code usage rules, and also to address possible coder training deficits. It is possible to arrive at very high levels of reliability on team-based qualitative projects (Carey et al. 1996, Hruschka et al. 2004). We also suggest that researchers choose a QDA program that supports the computation of intra- and intercoder reliability statistics. Both of CDC's qualitative analysis programs AnSWR and CDC EZ-Text have these abilities (Carey et al. 1998a, 1998b, Centers for Disease Control and Prevention 2004, McLellan et al. 2004). If the selected QDA program does not offer these features, researchers may need to calculate reliability statistics by hand.
- *Decide upon an acceptable final reliability level:* Reviews of the methods to develop a codebook and assess reliability levels can be found elsewhere (Carey et al. 1996, Hruschka et al. 2004, MacQueen et al. 1998). Inter- and intracoder reliability testing should be systematically approached to provide rigor in the qualitative data

analysis process and to provide multidisciplinary research team members a rigorously and reliably coded data set for further analyses. After determining a reliability threshold (usually between 70 and 90 percent), coders take a subsample of the data set (around 10 or 20 percent) to test for reliability. The level of acceptable reliability for a study depends upon the needs of the study, as well as practical time and resources constraints. In most of our work, we aim to achieve a kappa statistic value greater than or equal to 0.90 for each code in our codebooks. Kappa is a measure of intercoder agreement that adjusts for chance; perfect agreement on using a code would yield a statistic value of 1.00 (see Carey et al. 1996 and Hruschka et al. 2004 for specific examples). If the sample is large enough, reliability testing can occur at the same time data are being collected. When the sample is small, analysis and testing for intercoder reliability will occur after all data have been collected. During each round of reliability testing, the codebook undergoes refinement until the reliability threshold is achieved. In smaller samples for which reliability testing occurs after data collection is complete, each round of reliability testing includes coding, kappa testing, and codebook revisions for all the respondents and questions in a subset. Once completed, a new round is begun with a new subset. If the sample is large, and data collection slow and not completed before reliability testing begins, each round may be focused on a specific question(s) or section(s) of the data collection instrument. After testing and codebook revisions, the coding team begins a second round with a new question(s) or section(s). Once the reliability threshold is achieved, coders code the entire data set. To ensure continued reliability, additional reliability tests can be performed to prevent coder drift or code favoritism (this is especially recommended for large data sets).

- *Plan sufficient time and resources for the coding process:* In addition to the level of final acceptable reliability, factors that influence the length of time needed to achieve the desired level of reliability include clarity of the questionnaire wording. Asking a respondent a murky, complex, or poorly worded question usually often means that they will provide a response that is equally difficult for coders to subsequently understand and code. Other factors include the clarity and organization of the interview writeups, the number of questions and sample size, the skill of the coders, and the experience and organization skills of the coding team manager.

Often, especially in large data sets that take some time to reliably code, coder turnover will be high. New coders will require some practice with the data set, even with a reliable codebook, before beginning coding (usually over the first month of their introduction to the project and the data). Practice coding should focus on understanding the question intents, the codebook rules of usage, and also provide an opportunity to refine the codebook further as new sets of eyes pick up small discrepancies in coding rules or code descriptions otherwise missed. Once up to speed, a new coder can successfully begin coding. Once a data set is fully and reliably coded, researchers can use it for additional analyses to address project goals and objectives.

Data Analysis and Dissemination

After completing the data collection, data entry, and coding, the research team is ready for subsequent analysis and dissemination. By itself, gathering data does nothing to advance public health or scientific knowledge if analyses are not completed and results are not disseminated to appropriate audiences in a timely manner. As with earlier components of team-based research, we recommend a systematic process for planning and implementing this phase. Listed below are a series of suggestions that may help teams approach analysis and dissemination of their data and findings.

First, by definition the majority of team members have professional research careers. Most will have a practical need to be authors or coauthors on written scientific products such as peer-reviewed journal articles. Both in university and in nonuniversity research settings, job tenure, promotion, professional recognition, and annual performance ratings are based in part upon having an ongoing publication track record, regardless of an investigator's seniority level or academic discipline. To minimize ill feelings and time-consuming battles over which team members will write up study findings and be authors on publications, we suggest that teams write an agreed-upon project publications policy statement. Development of these guidelines should not be postponed to the end of the project, but instead should occur at the start of the project. In creating these policies, multidisciplinary teams may wish to consult broader authorship guidelines created by various professional associations such as the American Medical Association, the American Psychological Association, and other groups (e.g., American Psychological Association 2001, Centers for Disease Control and Prevention 2005, International Committee of Medical Journal

Editors 2006, Iverson et al. 1998). New members joining a research team at later points should be familiarized with the project authorship document as part of their orientation, and have the opportunity to voice possible questions and concerns. If needed, agreed-upon edits can be made by the team at any time. Although they may be tailored to the needs of specific projects, many of the publications guidelines used on our past CDC projects share the following characteristics:

- *Project summary:* This section of the document describes the project's background, as well as key goals and objectives. It reminds team members what the project set out to accomplish.
- *Membership of a project publications committee:* Typically this group includes, at minimum, senior researchers from all sites on a multisite research project. Often membership is expanded to include all interested team members, which helps ensure that all concerned parties have a chance to help shape product dissemination policies that may affect their personal careers.
- *Shared principles guiding the publications committee actions:* These may include ensuring appropriate (1) professional recognition for all team members' contributions, (2) opportunity for team members to play an active role in analysis and dissemination, (3) equity and fairness to reduce the possibility of one person accumulating disproportionate "publication rights" to the exclusion of others on the team, and (4) timeliness in completing a specific product, such as having a target date on when a manuscript should be completed after gaining approval from the committee.
- *Scope of what is and is not covered by the publications guidelines and committee review process:* For example, the committee may decide that they are primarily concerned with journal publications, presentations or posters at professional conferences, theses or dissertations, and Internet products. They may be less concerned about internal unpublished progress reports or updates presented to coworkers or supervisors within a team member's employment organization.
- *Description of steps that team members should take to generate a dissemination product proposal:* Examples might be (1) a team member develops a product concept sheet; (2) submission procedures to the publications committee (e.g., via e-mail one full week before a regularly scheduled team meeting or conference call); (3) expectations and processes for keeping the committee informed of

progress and for getting appropriate team feedback on product drafts; (4) how to share copies of the final finished product with the committee, other interested team members, and outside partners; and (5) how to involve and inform key persons in the wider community (e.g., major stakeholders in the communities or populations where the research was conducted).

- *Product proposal cover sheet:* Items on this sheet commonly include (1) dates when the product was submitted, discussed, and approved by the publications committee; (2) draft title of the proposed product; (3) product type and anticipated outlet (e.g., a peer-reviewed journal manuscript, and the name of the intended journal where it will be submitted); (4) proposed author and coauthor list, along with the tentative author order; (5) proposed list of acknowledged persons and organizations; (6) specific hypotheses or objectives to be addressed in the product; (7) specific parts of the data to be used; (8) description of analysis methods; (9) draft table shells or other description of how the results will be presented in the product; (10) intended audience; and (11) estimated product completion date.
- *Steps to keep the committee informed:* After receiving the product proposal, the authors should discuss it with the committee during a meeting or conference call. If needed, revisions can be made, and work on the product can begin following receipt of committee approval. In many cases, initial plans may need to be revised during analysis and writeup; authors should keep the committee updated about these changes to avoid surprising the committee with a substantively different final product. Finally, a committee member should be assigned the responsibility to maintain a database of submitted and approved proposals, along with completed products, as part of a project's permanent records.

In addition to having a process to guide authorship, a second area to consider when planning data analyses and dissemination entails a return to the original goals and objectives of the project. Assuming sufficient written plans were made at the beginning of the project, these goals and objectives should have been clearly stated in the research IRB protocol. (Presumably all data have been collected, computer entered, cleaned, and coded and are ready for analysis by this point.) In developing dissemination products, teams should review the original project goals and objectives to make certain that someone is responsible for completing the corresponding data analyses and for writing up the results into a journal article manuscripts or other products. Moreover, because multidisciplinary qualitative research often leads to unexpected findings or insights, researchers should also think about developing appropriate dissemination products that go beyond the original intended scope of work. Because creative and enthusiastic teams may easily develop a long list of analysis ideas that exceed available time, labor, and project financial resources, the project leadership on the publications committee may need to prioritize and coordinate these product dissemination efforts.

A third general area to consider when developing analysis and dissemination plans concerns the needs and expectations of the intended audiences for the products. The general idea of tailoring evaluation research and dissemination of results to optimally meet the needs of audiences, stakeholders, or other end users is a well-established principle in social marketing, as well as in the literature describing techniques to maximize the utility and impact of qualitative research (e.g., Kotler and Roberto 1989, Patton 1997, Schensul et al. 1999a). When developing plans for a journal manuscript in team-based research, it is prudent for the group to consider a range of possible journals to ensure that the selected journal reaches the desired readership, it publishes papers on similar topics, and is receptive to the proposed research design, analysis methods, and planned method of presenting the results. Valuable information can be gained by examining the journal's past issues and editorial guides for authors. For example, when considering options for disseminating the findings from the New York Vietnamese study (Carey et al. 1997), the research team explicitly chose a journal that would reach a broad audience that potentially included both researchers and public health practitioners beyond tuberculosis treatment and control. Even though the study relied upon semistructured qualitative data, most of the findings were presented in numeric formats and tables because of the journal's editorial and readership preferences. It is very likely that without substantial revisions, the same manuscript would not have been accepted or published in a strictly qualitative health research journal that preferred findings presented in traditional ethnographic case study formats. Namey et al. in chapter 7, this volume, discuss an array of other options for using quantitative methods in the analysis of coded themes or text-based content attributes (e.g., also see Krippendorf 2004, Weber 1990).

Likewise, when considering outlets for oral presentations, materials should be tailored to audience needs and conference organizational specifications to as great an extent as possible. When presenting study findings to nonresearchers or community members in either oral or written forms, additional care should be taken to use formats that are understandable. For example, many community members may lack formal research or statistics training, and might be overwhelmed or not understand complex tables and charts that would be acceptable in a scientific journal. On the other hand, a lay audience might be very open to hearing a series of descriptive case studies presented in a way that resonates with their own experiences. Experienced health educators or community advisory boards not only may help a research team design better studies that are acceptable to a community, but also assist a team in communicating usable and understandable findings or recommendations back to the affected populations.

It is worth emphasizing that there is no single correct way to analyze qualitative data or to present findings in written reports or oral presentations. Likewise, there is no single correct statistical procedure that should always be used for the analysis of different types of quantitative data sets. As in all types of scientific research, the choice of appropriate analysis methods in qualitative team-based research should depend upon the project's substantive goals and objectives. Although a full review of qualitative data analysis options is beyond the scope of this chapter, numerous excellent resources exist that describe a very broad array of qualitative data analysis options (e.g., Beebe 2001, Bernard 2002, 2006, Boyatzis 1998, Crabtree and Miller 1999, Creswell 1998, Denzin and Lincoln 1998, Drisko 1997, Field and Morse 1985, Kolbe and Burnett 1991, Lambert et al. 1995, LeCompte and Schensul 1999a, Miles and Huberman 1994, Patton 2002, Ulin et al. 2005, Weber 1990).

The range of qualitative data analysis options expands or contracts depending upon prior choices made by the team regarding the overall project research design, sampling methods, final sample size, data collection techniques, data organizational formats, QDA software used, and data coding schemes. The most common and broadly applicable option entails presentation of findings in dissemination products in a manner consistent with traditional ethnographic descriptions. This approach can be used with nearly all types of qualitative studies, regardless of their design, sample characteristics, or data collection methods. Assuming that the data have been well organized and reliably coded, most contemporary QDA software programs have features to search the database for instances of coded themes, or phrases and words present in the text (see Namey et al.'s chapter 7, this volume, for a more detailed discussion on the uses of Boolean searches). Code searches might be very simple (e.g., a search designed to "find all the text segments where Code X occurs in the responses to Question 7") or much more complex (e.g., "find all the text segments where

Code X and Code Y occur together without the presence of Code Z in the responses to Question 7, but only among male sample respondents that are between the ages of twenty to thirty years"). Many contemporary QDA programs also allow the user to search for specific words or phrases that occur in the text. The results identified with these types of searches may be used to identify relevant illustrative quotes or to help develop case studies. These text passages can be copied, organized, and included in either the narrative of a written document or summarized in tables or other types of graphics (Miles and Huberman 1994 describe a wide array of options for organizing and presenting qualitative findings). Likewise, search results can be used in oral presentations or in other dissemination products. Use of illustrative text passages and case studies can help researchers describe the range of variation with regard to respondent behaviors, ideas, beliefs, or other perspectives that are relevant to the study's purposes. Further insight may be gained by dividing the sample into separate strata and comparing the similarities or differences between and within subgroups (e.g., males versus females, young versus old, residents of Community 1 versus Community 2, persons with different morbidity conditions).

Presenting illustrative text passages and case studies in written documents or oral presentations helps convey a sense of what respondent behaviors and beliefs exist in the sample (and presumably also are prevalent in the larger population from which the sample was drawn). Moreover, researchers can examine the types of variation within and between groups using this approach. Another advantage is that ethnographic descriptions often are quite vivid, and are easily understood by audiences unfamiliar with complex research methodologies or statistics. However, researchers may not only need to describe the breadth of variation of behaviors and beliefs, but also the proportionate distribution of those behaviors and beliefs. For example, Hutcheson et al. (2006) explored the reasons why forty HIV serostatus-naïve MSM residing in Seattle had anal sex without a condom with partners they knew for certain to be HIV-seropositive, based off a thematic analysis of semistructured qualitative interview data. During the coding process, reasons cited by the respondents were condensed into eighteen different categories: they believed their sexual behaviors with their seropositive partners were unlikely to lead to HIV infection; they thought they were immune to HIV infection; they did not care if they became infected with HIV; they preferred sex without a condom, and so on. In addition to describing the range of variation of cited reasons and providing illustrative quotes from the respondents, Hutcheson and her colleagues also computed simple percentages to identify the proportions of the sample that endorsed the various reasons for having unprotected sex. This provided a simple way to identify the most commonly held rationales for engaging in this behavior. If the sample had been larger, it might also have been useful to compute 95 percent confidence intervals for these percentages to help gauge their precision as estimates of the true population proportions, and perhaps examined differences between various strata of the MSM.

Beyond computation of frequencies or percentages, researchers may also want to examine the patterns and strength of association between different behaviors, beliefs, or other variables collected from respondents (e.g., sociodemographic characteristics, quantitative variables from medical charts). Namey et al. (chapter 7, this volume) discuss use of cluster analysis, multidimensional scaling, and other methods for examining co-occurrences of coded themes. Provided that a number of essential conditions are met (see below), it may be useful to treat the assignment of thematic codes as dichotomous nominal variables (i.e., the respondent either does or does not ascribe to a specific belief or behavior). Various contemporary QDA programs have the ability to export respondent-by-code matrices containing binary nominal variable data. Co-occurrences of themes or associations of themes with other variables (e.g., demographic indicators, health outcomes) could then be derived using common statistical procedures, such as contingency table analyses, available in SPSS, SAS, or other statistical software packages.

Before attempting the construction of contingency tables or any other type of quantitative analyses of coded qualitative data, we very strongly urge researchers to make certain that all appropriate assumptions are met for generating meaningful and valid statistical output. These assumptions and conditions may vary depending upon the procedures used; researchers are ultimately responsible to select and use appropriate statistical methods given the nature of the data they have collected. For example, suppose that a researcher wants to compute chi-square and odds ratio statistics for ascertaining if a dichotomously coded theme is correlated with a dichotomous health outcome variable by deriving these statistics from a simple 2 $\times$ 2 table. We suggest the following minimum list of caveats would need to be in place:

1. *Ensure that essential assumptions for using the statistic are met.* More detailed discussions can be found in common statistical textbooks; research teams would be well advised to make sure that they are not abusing the statistic (see, e.g., Moore and McCabe

1989:443–500 for a more extensive discussion of proper use and pitfalls in the application of common statistical significance tests).

2. *Have a statistically representative sample of the population* (i.e., this usually means some type of random sampling method was employed). For example, use of chi-square statistics in a qualitative study that utilized a nonprobability sample likely would not be appropriate; at best, chi-square results derived from a nonprobability sample would have questionable external generalizability beyond the sample. Except under very limited circumstances (usually when there is little or no variation between respondents), researchers who gather qualitative data from small nonrepresentative samples run the risk of having findings that are biased in unknown ways. And findings drawn from small, nonrepresentative samples may lead to incorrect conclusions about the larger general population from which the sample was drawn.

3. *Adequate cell sizes are available.* The typical rule of thumb for computing chi-square statistics in contingency tables is for having at least five or more persons counted in each cell of a simple 2 × 2 table, and five or more in at least 80 percent of cells in larger tables but have no cells with a zero count. Other statistics may have other similar special needs. Again, it is the responsibility of the researcher to understand these types of assumptions, or run the risk of generating meaningless statistical output.

4. *Observations are counted only once in a single cell within the table.* In studies such as those described in this chapter, an *observation* usually would be a person in the sample, and the total of all the cells would equal the sample size if there are no missing data. A person would only be tallied once and be counted in just one cell.

5. *Beware of searching for "statistical significance" that has no genuine meaning.* Many studies with long surveys will have a very large number of variables. Large and complex qualitative data sets may easily yield codebooks containing well over a hundred thematic codes. By chance alone, a researcher is likely to find some "statistically significant" associations if they were to compute chi-squares for every theme and their health outcome variable. Researchers should avoid such statistical "fishing expeditions."

6. *Do a power analysis during the research design phase to ensure having an adequate sample size needed to detect associations of a desired magnitude.* Not finding a statistically significant association between a theme and an outcome variable may simply mean that the sample size is

too small to detect a true association; *p* values typically are affected both by the strength of the underlying association, as well as the sample size. Insufficient sample size planning during the initial phases of a project can destroy or seriously damage the ability to analyze data after data collection has ended. When planning for sample sizes and conducting power calculations, it is essential to use realistic assumptions about refusal rates, dropout rates, or ways respondents may fall out of the final data set.

7. *Examine the magnitude and direction of the association.* Statistical significance tests only provide information about whether there is an association between variables. But by itself, statistical significance says nothing about the strength or direction of the association. If one has a very large sample, it may be possible to detect a very weak but statistically significant association that has little practical meaning in the "real world." It also is important to examine the row and column proportions in the contingency table to have an accurate understanding of the direction of the significant associations. Use of odds ratios, or other statistics that assess magnitude and direction of association, may help.

8. *Eliminate nonrandom classification bias.* Any source of systematic error in the research design, sampling, instrument wording, data collection, data entry, data coding, or data analysis for any of a study's variables may bias estimates of statistical significance or magnitudes of association in a nonrandom upward or downward direction. In the simple 2 × 2 table situation, systematic bias will mean that persons have an unjustified higher or lower chance of being incorrectly included in one column versus the other, one row versus the other, or a combination of both problems. If an odds ratio was computed, for example, it could either over- or underestimate the true population value of the magnitude of the association (Schlesselman 1992). It is essential that research teams do everything possible to identify and eliminate the sources for these problems at all project stages.

9. *Eliminate random classification bias.* In our view, this is one of the largest potential pitfalls in the collection, coding, and analysis of themes derived from qualitative data. Again in considering the simple 2 × 2 table situation, random classification bias will mean that persons have a high but nonsystematic chance of being incorrectly included in one column versus the other, one row versus the other, or a combination of both problems. Computed odds ratios will tend to be biased toward the null value when

random misclassification takes place (i.e., underestimate the true population odds ratio values, which means that researchers may not infer associations that are legitimately present in the general study population; Schlesselman 1992). In large qualitative studies, one major potential source of random error is insufficient standardization in the administration of open-ended questionnaires by different interviewers, or by the same interviewer at different times with different respondents. This problem can be reduced through very thorough interviewer training, rigorous pre–data collection practice exercise, and meticulous quality assurance supervision during data collection and writeup. The idea is to do everything possible to ensure that all respondents have a comparable opportunity to respond to the same set of open-ended questions, and also receive comparable levels of follow-up probes. This helps ensure that each respondent provides complete and accurate answers to all the questions, and similarities or differences between responses are not due to differences in how they were interviewed. If resources permit, an ideal method is to have different interviewers interview a subsample of respondents and compare results for potential differences in interviewer technique. As discussed earlier in this chapter, we have used this method with considerable success as an exercise during our interviewer trainings in our CDC projects. However, in spite of their best efforts, interviewer biases may still affect the quality of the data (see Namey et al., chapter 7, this volume). It may be useful to allocate interviewees at random to the different interviewers to ensure that random interviewer bias does not become a systematic bias. As with analysis of structured data sets, during analysis it is a good idea to look for possible differences in results when stratifying the sample by interviewer. Another major potential source of random error occurs in the coding of themes present in the data. As we discussed earlier in this chapter, there are a number of practical steps that can be taken to ensure inter- and intracoder reliability in coding (Hruschka et al. 2004). Having high coding reliability helps reduce this source of random classification error, and thereby helps reduce bias in the computation of statistics from contingency tables. Some other potential sources of misclassification bias may be related to the memories of different respondents, or respondent beliefs about disease–exposure associations (e.g., in a retrospective case–control study, the respondents with a disease differentially search their recollections for reasons why they became sick).

10. *Beware of overreliance upon simple bivariate associations.* Examination of possible statistically significant crude associations between themes and outcome variables is a useful first step. However, the magnitude and even the direction of associations may vary among different sample strata (e.g., when one compares results for men versus women, residents of one city versus a different city, injection drug users versus non–drug users). Potential correlates of the outcome variable may interact, and crude bivariate associations may be spurious due to confounding. Provided that they have a sufficiently large and representative sample, researchers may wish to employ a variety of sophisticated statistical methods for examining these situations (e.g., Schlesselman 1992). Also, as noted earlier, if the sample size permits, it can be useful to employ methods such as factor analysis, cluster analysis, multidimensional scaling, or other techniques to explore co-occurrences between themes among various sample strata (Namey et al., this volume).

Discussion

An underlying theme running throughout the examples and recommendations in our chapter is that the success of team-based qualitative studies depends on development and implementation of a well-crafted overall research protocol and project management plan. This should be the case in all scientific research regardless of the methods, size of the study, or subject matter. In small-scale studies that involve just one or a few researchers, mistakes in original research design and project management sometimes can be noticed and successfully fixed before they lead to permanent damage. However, in larger team-based investigations that may involve many persons from varied disciplines working in different locations, lack of adequate research planning or administrative oversight can quickly magnify, and result in a chaotic project that yields a poor-quality data set.

To underscore why careful research and management plans are so important in team-based qualitative studies, we will describe what happened to a very unfortunate project for which we have knowledge (*not* one of the case studies we have discussed earlier in this chapter). Almost none of the recommended best practices described in this chapter were carried out in this project. In this example, project personnel were supposed to implement a shared qualitative data collection protocol in five cross-sectional studies in different populations residing in various urban locales in the

United States. The original main goal was to compare and contrast variation in health-related beliefs and treatment-seeking behaviors within and between the five groups. There were separate interview teams working with each group. One of the earliest identified problems was that the sampling plan lacked the necessary features to include the most relevant persons as potential study respondents. Subsequently, the project coordinators did not provide satisfactory and consistent training to all the local interviewers, which meant that the local personnel did not understand or correctly implement their roles in achieving the project goals. Local interviewers were permitted to independently modify the interview instruments, which destroyed the possibility of comparing results among the five groups. There was almost no timely quality assurance implemented during data collection to ensure that all question topics were thoroughly addressed as intended. After the fact, it was discovered that some interviewers completely failed to sufficiently address critical parts of the questionnaire until it was too late, and so data were completely unusable. In addition, local interviewers were allowed to write up their qualitative interviews using different software and idiosyncratic data organization. These inconsistent data formats made it extremely time consuming to analyze and compare data collected by different interviewers, often including data writeups from interviewers working within the same study population in the same locale.

In spite of these mistakes, the project generated a huge volume of qualitative data that included hundreds of pages of text. However, even after an intensive post–data collection analysis effort was implemented to rescue something from this project, it became apparent that the data were thoroughly disorganized and of overwhelmingly poor overall quality. There also were expensive cost overruns and lengthy delays beyond the original completion date. In spite of considerable effort to save the project from total failure, in the end the decision was made to not write up the findings for any scientific journal or for any other applied public health purpose because of the project's methodological flaws. Ultimately the data set was destroyed.

To avoid catastrophic project failures such as this, it is essential to have a well-thought-out research design that matches project goals and objectives as well as available project time, funding, and staffing resources. These plans must be detailed, thorough, and well justified and investigators must make these plans before data collection starts. We occasionally have reviewed some qualitative research proposals and protocols in which investigators fail to provide these types of plans in sufficient depth, and erroneously claim they do not need to have this type of careful planning merely because they are doing qualitative research.

In contrast to having poorly developed research designs, we strongly advocate that qualitative research sampling plans should be realistic, and yield relevant respondents, regardless of whether a probability or nonprobability approach is used. We also advise that data collection instruments need to be well planned and thoroughly pretested before use. All staff—including but not limited to interviewers—must be trained and have an accurate shared understanding of project goals and procedures. Data management and rigorous data quality assurance plans must be developed and consistently carried out throughout the study. Systematic qualitative data coding plans should be created and carefully managed, including procedures to ensure strong statistical reliability of thematic coding. To assist other team-based qualitative researchers, the appendix at the end of this chapter provides a partial checklist of considerations that may help during the development of qualitative research plans and protocols.

If qualitative research teams implement these steps, we believe that the team is likely to have a defendable and usable set of qualitative data for subsequent analysis and results. For example, assuming that a qualitative data set has been well collected and rigorously coded, many QDA software programs will help researchers search their database for text passages they can use in creating ethnographic case studies. Ethnographic case studies have been used to present qualitative research findings for many decades, and they remain a valuable approach. In addition, and if the researchers believe it is appropriate for their data sets and substantive study goals, sometimes the presence or absence of a theme in a text passage can be viewed as a simple dichotomous variable. For example, respondents may either report a specifically defined belief or behavior, or they do not when they were asked the same open-ended question from a semistructured questionnaire. In that situation, and depending on how samples were generated and how the open-ended questions were administered, it may be useful to use statistical software to further understand frequencies and distribution patterns of reported beliefs or behaviors in a sample (e.g., Carey et al.1997 used this approach for reporting findings for a multidisciplinary public health audience unaccustomed to results presented in traditional ethnographic case study formats; also see Krippendorf 2004 and Weber 1990 for a broader discussion of using quantitative methods for presenting content analysis results from qualitative data). Numerous other options are available for presenting qualitative findings for varied audiences and purposes (LeCompte and Schensul 1999a; Miles and Huberman 1994).

Finally, if the research team is working in an applied field, it is helpful to tailor reports to the needs of the different stakeholders and intended audiences. Program planners and evaluators will have different reporting needs than scientific peers, and information should be presented in ways that are easy for nonresearcher audiences to understand. Our experience suggests that question-by-question or theme-by-theme reports and oral presentations can be a useful format for describing results to program planning and policy decision makers. In the end, if qualitative studies have been well designed and implemented, the results often can be extremely valuable for addressing both theoretical and practical applied needs.

References

Abdul-Quader, A. S., D. D. Hechathorn, C. McKnight, H. Bramson, C. Nemeth, K. Sabin, K. Gallagher, and D. C. Des Jarlais
2006   Effectiveness of respondent-driven sampling for recruiting drug users in New York City: Findings from a pilot study. *Journal of Urban Health* 83(3): 459–476.

Ackoff, R. L.
1953   *The Design of Social Research*. Chicago: The University of Chicago Press.

American Psychological Association
2001   *Publication Manual of the American Psychological Association* (5th ed.). Washington, D.C.: American Psychological Association.

Appleton, J. V.
1995   Analysing qualitative interview data: Addressing issues of validity and reliability. *Journal of Advanced Nursing* 22:993–997.

Beebe, J.
2001   *Rapid Assessment Process: An Introduction*. Walnut Creek, Calif.: AltaMira.

Bernard, H. R.
2002   *Social Research Methods: Qualitative and Quantitative Approaches*. Thousand Oaks, Calif.: Sage.
2006   *Research Methods in Anthropology: Qualitative and Quantitative Approaches* (4th ed.). Walnut Creek, Calif.: AltaMira.

Boyatzis, R. E.
1998   *Transforming Qualitative Information: Thematic Analysis and Code Development*. Thousand Oaks, Calif.: Sage.

Carey, J. W.
1994   Improving international HIV program planning: Systematic interview methods in the context of programmatic needs assessment. Masters of Public Health thesis, Emory University, Atlanta, Ga.

Carey, J. W., T. Bingham, K. Sey, D. Schwartz, and the CHIP Research Team
2005   Social context and individual risk factors associated with recent HIV seroconversion among men who have sex with men in Los Angeles, California. Presentation at the Annual Meeting of the Society for Applied
Anthropology, Santa Fe, N.M.

Carey, J. W., M. Morgan, and M. J. Oxtoby
1996   Intercoder agreement in analysis of responses to open-ended interview
questions: Examples from tuberculosis research. *Cultural Anthropology Methods Journal* 8(3):1–5.

Carey, J. W., M. J. Oxtoby, L. P. Nguyen, V. Huynh, M. Morgan, and M. Jeffery
1997   Tuberculosis beliefs among recent Vietnamese refugees in New York State:
Implications for improving patient education and therapeutic adherence.
Public Health Reports 112(1):66–72.

Carey, J. W., P. H. Wenzel, C. Reilly, J. Sheridan, and J. M. Steinberg
1998a CDC EZ-Text: Software for management and analysis of semistructured
qualitative data sets. *Cultural Anthropology Methods Journal* 10(1):14–20.

Carey, J. W., P. H. Wenzel, C. Reilly, J. Sheridan, J. Steinberg, and K. G. Harbison
1998b *CDC EZ-Text User's Guide, Version 3.06.* Software manual for "CDC EZ-
Text," Pp. 1–128. Software developed by Conwal Inc. for the Centers for
Disease Control and Prevention, Atlanta, Ga.

Centers for Disease Control and Prevention
2004   *AnSWR: Analysis Software for Word-based Records, Version 6.4.* Atlanta, Ga.:
Centers for Disease Control and Prevention.
2005   *CDC Authorship Policy.* July 2005 update. Available at: www.cdc.gov/od/
ads/authorship.htm.

Cochran, W. G.
1977   *Sampling Techniques.* New York: Wiley.

Coyne, I. T.
1997   Sampling in qualitative research. Purposeful and theoretical sampling;
merging or clear boundaries. *Journal of Advanced Nursing* 26(3):623–630.

Crabtree, B. F., and W. L. Miller
1992   *Doing Qualitative Research.* London: Sage.

Creswell, J. W.
1998   *Qualitative Inquiry and Research Design: Choosing among Five Traditions.* Thousand Oaks, Calif.: Sage.

Daly, J., A. Kellehear, and M. Gliksman
1997   *The Public Health Researcher: A Methodological Guide.* New York: Oxford
University Press.

Denzin, N. K., and Y. S. Lincoln (eds.)
1998   *Strategies of Qualitative Inquiry.* Thousand Oaks, Calif.: Sage.

Drisko, J.
1997   Strengthening qualitative studies and reports: Standards to promote academic integrity. *Journal of Social Work Education* 33:185–197.

Field, P. A., and J. Morse
1985   *Nursing Research: The Application of Qualitative Approaches.* London: Croom Helm

Fielding, N. G., and R. M. Lee
1998   *Computer Analysis and Qualitative Research.* London: Sage.

Galavotti, C., L. E. Salzman, S. L. Sauter, and E. Sumartojo
1997   Behavioral science activities at the Centers for Disease Control and Prevention: A selected overview of exemplary programs. *American Psychologist* 52(2):154–166.

General Accounting Office
1992   *Using Statistical Sampling. GAO/PEMD-10.1.6.* Washington, D.C.: U.S. General Accounting Office, Program Evaluation and Methodology Division.
1993   *Developing and Using Questionnaires. GAO/PEMD-10.1.7.* Washington, D.C.: U.S. General Accounting Office, Program Evaluation and Methodology Division.

Gorden, R. L.
1998   *Basic Interviewing Skills* (rev. ed.). Long Grove, Ill.: Waveland.

Guest, G.
2005   The range of qualitative research. *Journal of Family Planning and Reproductive Health Care* 31(2):165.

Guest, G., and E. McLellan
2003   Distinguishing the trees from the forest: Applying cluster analysis to thematic qualitative data. *Field Methods* 15(2):186–201.

Hahn, R. (ed.)
1999   *Anthropology in Public Health: Bridging Differences in Culture and Society.* New York: Oxford University Press.

Heckathorn, D.
1997   Respondent-driven sampling: A new approach to the study of hidden populations. *Social Problems* 44(2):174–199.

Higgins, D. L., K. O'Reilly, N. Tashima, C. Crain, C. Beeker, G. Goldbaum, C. S Elifson, C. Galavotti, C. Guenther-Grey, and The AIDS Community Demonstration Projects

1996   Using Formative Research to Lay the Foundation for Community-Level HIV Prevention Efforts: The AIDS Community Demonstration Project. *Public Health Reports* 111(Suppl 1):28–35.

Holtgrave, D. R., and J. W. Curran
2005   What works, and what remains to be done, in HIV prevention in the United States. *Annual Reviews in Public Health* 27(15):1–15.

Holtgrave, D. R., L. S. Doll, and J. Harrison
1997   Influence of behavioral and social science on public health policymaking. *American Psychologist* 52(2):167–173.

Hruschka, D., D. Schwartz, D. C. St. John, E. Picone-DeCaro, R. A. Jenkins, and J. W. Carey
2004   Reliability in coding open-ended data: Lessons learned from HIV behavioral research. *Field Methods* 16(3):307–331.

Hutcheson, R. E., R. A. Jenkins, J. W. Carey, R. Mejia, R. Stall, M. Golden, and H. Thiede
2006   Sexual behaviors with known HIV seropositive sex partners among men who have sex with men (MSM) testing for HIV in Seattle/King County, Washington. Unpublished manuscript.

International Committee of Medical Journal Editors
2006   Uniform requirements for manuscripts submitted to biomedical journals: Writing and editing for biomedical publication. February 2006 update available at: www.icmje.org.

Iverson, C., A. Flanagan, P. H. Fontanarosa, R. M. Glass, P. Glitman, J. C. Lantz, H. S. Meyer, J. M. Smith, M. A. Winker, and R. K. Young
1998   *American Medical Association Manual of Style* (9th ed.). Baltimore, Md.: Williams and Wilkins.

Jeffery, M., M. Oxtoby, J. Castiglione, P. Bogan, and J. Grabau
1996   Improving adherence among Vietnamese refugees using directly observed preventive therapy. Presentation at the International Conference of the American Thoracic Society, May 11–15, New Orleans, LA.

Johnson, J. C.
1998   Research design and research strategies. In H. R. Bernard, ed. *Handbook of Methods in Cultural Anthropology.* Pp. 131–171. Walnut Creek, Calif.: AltaMira.
1990   *Selecting Ethnographic Informants.* Newbury Park, Calif.: Sage.

Kolbe, R. H., and M. S. Burnett
1991   Content analysis research: An examination of applications with directions for improving research reliability and objectivity. *Journal of Consumer Research* 18:243–250.

Kotler, P., and E. L. Roberto
1989   *Social Marketing: Strategies for Changing Public Behavior.* New York: The Free Press.

Krippendorf, K
2004   *Content Analysis: An Introduction to Its Methodology.* Thousand Oaks, Calif.: Sage.

Kruger, R. A.
1994   *Focus Groups: A Practical Guide for Applied Research* (2nd ed.). Thousand Oaks, Calif.: Sage.

Lambert, E. Y., R. S. Ashery, and R. H. Needle (eds.)
1995   *Qualitative Methods in Drug Abuse and HIV Research.* National Institute on Drug Abuse Research Monograph 157. Rockville, Md.: U.S. Department of Health and Human Services, National Institutes of Health.

LeCompte, M. D., and J. J. Schensul
1999a *Analyzing and Interpreting Ethnographic Data.* Walnut Creek, Calif.: AltaMira.
1999b *Designing and Conducting Ethnographic Research.* Walnut Creek, Calif.: AltaMira.

Levy, P. S., and S. Lemeshow
1999   *Sampling of Populations: Methods and Applications* (3rd ed.). New York: Wiley.

Lyberg, L., P. Biemer, M. Collins, E. De Leeuw, C. Dippo, N. Schwartz, and D. Trewin (eds.)
1997   *Survey Measurement and Process Quality.* New York: Wiley.

Mack, N., C. Woodsong, K. MacQueen, G. Guest, and E. Namey
2005   *Qualitative Research Methods: A Data Collector's Field Guide.* Research Triangle Park, N.C.: Family Health International.

MacKellar, D., L. Valleroy, J. Karon, G. Lemp, and R. Janssen
1996   The Young Men's Survey: Methods for estimating HIV seroprevalence and risk factors among young men who have sex with men. *Public Health Reports* 111(Suppl 1):138–144.

MacQueen, K., E. McLellan, K. Kay, and B. Milstein
1998   Code book development for team based qualitative analysis. *Cultural Anthropology Methods Journal* 10(2):31–36.

MacQueen, K. M., and B. Milstein
1999   A systems approach to qualitative data management and analysis. *Field Methods* 11(1):27–39.

Mansergh, G., S. Naorat, R. Jommaroeng, R. A. Jenkins, S. Jeeyapant, K. Kang-garnrua, P. Phanuphak, J. W. Tappero, and F. van Griensven
2006   Adaptation of venue-day-time sampling in Southeast Asia to access men who have sex with men for HIV assessment in Bangkok. *Field Methods* 18(2):135–152.

Mantell, J. E., A. T. DiVittis, and M. I. Auerbach
1997   *Evaluating HIV Prevention Interventions.* New York: Plenum.

Marshall, C., and G. B. Rossman
1989   *Designing Qualitative Research.* Newbury Park, Calif.: Sage.

McLellan, E., K. M. MacQueen, and J. L. Neidig
2003   Beyond the qualitative interview: Data preparation and transcription. *Field Methods* 15(1):63–84.

McLellan, E., R. Strotman, J. MacGregor, and D. Dolan
2004   *AnSWR Users Guide.* Atlanta, Ga.: U.S. Centers for Disease Control and Prevention.

Miles, M. B., and A. M. Huberman
1994   *Qualitative Data Analysis: An Expanded Sourcebook.* Thousand Oaks, Calif.: Sage.

Mobley, S., V. Sierra, and J. W. Carey
1993   Nicaragua Ministry of Health National AIDS Control Program Technical Assessment. Prepared by AIDSCAP for the U.S. Agency for the International Development mission in Managua, Nicaragua, pp. 1–47.

Moore, D. S., and G. P. McCabe
1989   *Introduction to the Practice of Statistics.* New York: Freeman.

Morse, J. M.
1991   Strategies for sampling. In J. Morse, ed. *Qualitative Nursing Research: A Contemporary Dialogue* (rev. ed.). Pp. 117–131. Newbury Park, Calif.: Sage.

Muhib, F. B., L. S. Lin, A. Stueve, R. L. Miller, W. L. Ford, W. D. Johnson, and P. J. Smith
2001   A venue-based method for sampling hard-to-reach populations. *Public Health Reports* 116(Suppl.):216–222.

Mutchler, M. G., T. Bingham, M. Chion, R. A. Jenkins, L. E. Klosinski, and G. Secura.
2003   Comparing sexual behavioral patterns between two bathhouses: Implications for HIV prevention intervention policy. *Journal of Homosexuality* 44: 221–242.

Patton, M. Q.
1997   *Utilization-focused Evaluation.* Thousand Oaks, Calif: Sage.

2002   *Qualitative Research and Evaluation Methods* (3rd ed.). Thousand Oaks, Calif.: Sage.

Qual-Software
2006   Archives of QUAL-SOFTWARE@JISCMAIL.AC.UK. Internet discussion group. Available at www.jiscmail.ac.uk/lists/qual-software.html. Accessed September 8, 2006.

Rugg, D. L., R. Levinson, R. DiClemente, and M. Fishbein
1997   Centers for Disease Control and Prevention partnerships with external behavioral and social scientists. *American Psychologist* 52(2):147–153.

Ryan, G. W., and H. R. Bernard
2003   Techniques to identify themes. *Field Methods* 15:85–109.

Schensul, J. J., M. D. LeCompte, B. K. Nastasi, and S. P. Borgatti
1999a   *Enhanced Ethnographic Methods: Audiovisual Techniques, Focused Group Interviews, and Elicitation Techniques.* Walnut Creek, Calif.: AltaMira.

Schensul, J. J., M. D. LeCompte, G. A Hess, B. K. Nastasi, M. J. Berg, L. Williamson, J. Brecher, and R. Glasser
1999b   *Using Ethnographic Data.* Walnut Creek, Calif.: AltaMira.

Schlesselman, J. J.
1992   *Case-Control Studies: Design, Conduct, Analysis.* New York: Oxford University Press.

Scrimshaw, N. S., and G. R. Gleason (eds.)
1992   *Rapid Assessment Procedures: Qualitative Methodologies for Planning and Evaluations of Health Related Programmes.* Boston: International Nutrition Foundation for Developing Countries.

Snider, D. E., and D. Satcher
1997   Behavioral and social sciences at the Centers for Disease Control and Prevention: Critical disciplines for public health. *American Psychologist* 52(2): 140–142.

Spradley, J. P.
1979   *The Ethnographic Interview.* New York: Holt, Rinehart, and Winston.
1980   *Participant Observation.* Fort Worth: Harcourt Brace Jovanovich.

Stueve, A., L. N. O'Donnell, R. Duran, A. San Doval, and J. Blome
2001   Time-space sampling in minority communities: Results with young Latino men who have sex with men. *American Journal of Public Health* 91:922–926.

Sykes, W.
1991   Taking stock: Issues from the literature on validity and reliability in qualitative research. *Journal of the Market Research Society* 33:3–12.

272 JAMES W. CAREY AND DEBORAH GELAUDE

Tashima, N., C. Crain, K. O'Reilly, and C. S. Elifson
1996   The Community Identification (CID) Process: A discovery model. *Qualitative Health Research* 6(1):23–48.

Tesch, R.
1990   *Qualitative Research: Analysis Types and Software Tools.* New York: Falmer.

Ulin, P. R., E. T. Robinson, and E. E. Tolley
2005   *Qualitative Methods in Public Health: A Field Guide for Applied Research.* San Francisco: Jossey-Bass

Ulin, P. R., E. T. Robinson, E. E. Tolley, and E. T. McNeill
2002   *Qualitative Methods in Public Health: A Field Guide for Applied Research in Sexual and Reproductive Health.* Research Triangle Park, N.C.: Family Health International.

Weber, R. P.
1990   *Basic Content Analysis* (2nd ed.). Newbury Park, Calif.: Sage.

Weitzman, E. A., and M. B. Miles
1995   *Computer Programs for Qualitative Data Analysis.* Thousand Oaks, Calif.: Sage.

Appendix: Checklist for Planning a Systematic Team-based Qualitative Research Project

Research Design
___Are the goals and objectives clear, specific, and realistic?
___What is the broad intent of the study (evaluation, program planning, formative, intervention development or testing, etc.)?
___Are the research questions focused around the needs of the study?
___Does the research design match the needs of the study?
___Can the research design be carried out within the study timeframe?
___Will the needs of primary audiences or stakeholders be met by the research design?

Sampling Design
___What sample size is needed to answer research questions and meet the needs of study?
___Given the project needs, is it better to learn a lot from a small sample of a few respondents (depth), or is it better to learn patterns in a larger number of respondents (breadth)?

___Which specific probability or nonprobability sampling method should be used?

___Do the sampling plans match with planned analysis methods that will be used to generate results and reports?

___Are the sampling plans thoroughly documented?

Instrument Design

___Who will coordinate instrument development and gather input from key personnel?

___Do the data collection instruments cover all aspects needed to thoroughly address the goals and objectives?

___Have clear intents lists been developed for each instrument?

___Is there a good rationale for asking each item, and have redundant or less useful items been deleted from the instruments?

___Have the instruments been sufficiently pretested and refined?

Data Collection

___How will interviewers and other project personnel be trained to follow the project common protocol?

___What specific methods will be used to hire, train, and supervise interviewers and other data collection personnel?

___Have plans been made to provide follow-up training?

___Are quality assurance plans in place prior to data collection?

___Will you need verbatim transcripts or interviewer summaries?

Data Management

___What software systems will be used to support data collection? Do the features of the software program match all project needs, and are personnel sufficiently trained to use the software properly?

___Are there sufficient resources (staff, money, and time) available to cover all data management needs?

___Are there standardized procedures across sites for transcribing and entering the data?

___Are key personnel trained in data entry procedures, and are there appropriate quality assurance plans in place to ensure that data are entered in a correct and comparable manner across the entire team?

___Who specifically is responsible for data management and electronic/paper trail?

Data Analysis

___Which staff member will oversee codebook development, and how will they coordinate efforts of coders?

___Have data analysis/coding team personnel been identified, and have they received sufficient training in the coding protocols being used by the project?

___How will codebooks be structured?

___What standards and statistics will be used to measure inter- and/or intracoder reliability?

___How will new coders be trained if they join the staff at a later point in time?

___Is there sufficient time and staff for the coding and analysis process?

___What specific qualitative or statistical procedures will be used to analyze the final codes data set?

___How will the final coded data be used for meeting project goals and objectives?

___Will results be presented using traditional descriptive case studies, or statistical outputs? Will these presentations match needs of intended audiences?

Index

About the Contributors

Betty Akumatey obtained her MPhil in social anthropology from the University of Cambridge in the UK. Presently, she teaches sociology of the family and social anthropology at the Department of Sociology, University of Ghana, Legon, and has recently joined the Legon Regional Institute for Population Studies, where she will be pursuing her research interest in culture, gender, and HIV prevention and giving lectures in qualitative research methods. She recently worked as the principal investigator for two team-based qualitative research projects involving women at high risk for HIV in Ghana. Betty is also keenly involved in providing sexual and reproductive health education at the community level, and has facilitated many workshops in schools and faith organizations toward enhancing communication skills for HIV prevention, especially among youth, parents, and teachers. One of her recent endeavors in community education focuses on the "sociocultural aspects of gender-based violence and rape," and was presented during a series of nationwide training workshops, involving private medical and dental practitioners in Ghana. That's the academic Betty; the other (real) Betty is the one that sings about love and other nonquantifiable human qualities.

Kelly Bartholow, MPH, is the Deputy Branch Chief for the Program Evaluation Branch in the Division of HIV/AIDS Prevention at the Centers for Disease Control and Prevention. She received her graduate training at the Rollins School of Public Health at Emory University in behavioral science and health education. She has worked in HIV prevention since 1994 and joined CDC in 1996. She has worked on several multi-site qualitative evaluations of HIV prevention programs implemented by community-based organizations. Outside of the office, her family keeps her very busy, grounded, and grateful.

Arwen Bunce received her MA in medical anthropology from Case Western Reserve University. Her diverse interests have led to a variety of research positions, including managing a joint anthropology/epidemiology project investigating the meaning of self-rated health among the elderly in Philadelphia, and a more public health–focused position as Health Education Coordinator with Doctors Without Borders in Kashgar, P.R. China. While at Family Health International, Arwen worked in teams to develop, manage, and analyze several qualitative research projects based mainly in India and West Africa. Arwen is currently working at the Duke University Medical Center, Division of Community Health. Here she is responsible for evaluating the community impact of several local clinics and public health initiatives, as well as working with a team to develop a diabetes management initiative in partnership with predominantly African American churches in Durham, NC. Whenever possible, Arwen relaxes by rehabilitating and releasing birds of prey.

James Carey, PhD, MPH, received his graduate training in anthropology and epidemiology from, respectively, the University of Massachusetts at Amherst and Emory University in Atlanta. He presently is the Team Leader for the Operational Research Team within the Prevention Research Branch in the Division of HIV/AIDS Prevention, at the Centers for Disease Control and Prevention. Since joining the CDC in 1992, he has directed numerous multidisciplinary research projects aimed at understanding individual- and community-level factors influencing HIV risk behaviors, tuberculosis control, behavioral science research methods, and effective public health program design in the United States and in other countries. A selection of some of his most recent publications includes "Reliability in Coding Open-ended Data: Lessons Learned from HIV Behavioral Research" (with Hruschka et al., *Field Methods*, 2004), "Fixed Choice and Open-ended Response Formats: A Comparison from HIV Prevention Research in Zimbabwe" (with Hruschka et al., *Field Methods*, 2004), and "HIV/AIDS Research and Prevention: Anthropological Contributions and Future Directions" (a chapter in the *Encyclopedia of Medical Anthropology*, volume 1, Human Relations Area Files, 2004). In June 2005, three more of his articles on the use of behavioral and epidemiological data in HIV prevention program planning in health departments and community-based organizations were published in a special issue of *AIDS and Behavior*.

In his free time, Jim enjoys gardening, woodcarving, camping with his family, and traditional Celtic instrumental music.

Deborah Gelaude, MA, is a behavioral scientist in the Prevention Research Branch of the Division of HIV/AIDS Prevention at the Centers for Disease Control and Prevention. She received her graduate training at Georgia State University in Applied Medical Anthropology. Since joining the CDC in 2002, she has worked on large multisite team-based qualitative data collection projects. She currently helps lead a multisite mixed-methods research study exploring the contextual factors of recent HIV infection. A selection of recent publications includes "Reliability in Coding Open-ended Data: Lessons Learned from HIV Behavioral Research" (with Hruschka et al., *Field Methods*, 2004), "HIV/AIDS Research and Prevention: Anthropological Contributions and Future Directions" (with Carey et al., a chapter in the *Encyclopedia of Medical Anthropology*, volume 1, Human Relations Area Files, 2004), and "Between the Sheets and Between the Ears: Sexual practices and Risk Beliefs of HIV-positive Gay and Bisexual Men" (a chapter in *HIV+Sex: The Psychological and Interpersonal Dynamics of HIV-seropositive Gay and Bisexual Men's Relationships* (American Psychological Association, 2005). Deborah is an avid amateur photographer and photoblogger and spends many hours exploring Atlanta's neighborhoods, documenting a rapidly changing urban landscape with her camera lens.

Greg Guest, PhD, received an MA in anthropology from the University of Calgary and a PhD in anthropology from the University of Georgia. Over the past decade, Guest has implemented and managed multidisciplinary projects in various fields of applied research including human ecology, agricultural development, human–computer interaction, consumer experience, and international health. Greg is currently a behavioral scientist at Family Health International, where he manages multicountry research projects related to HIV prevention and reproductive health. His topical interests focus on the political and ecological dimensions of public health, HIV risk behavior, response bias in self-reported behavior, and mixed-methods research. Greg's publications include the edited volume *Globalization, Health and the Environment: An Integrated Perspective* (AltaMira, 2006), and articles in journals such as *AIDS Care, African Journal of AIDS Research, AIDS and Behavior, Journal of Family Planning and Reproductive Health Care, Human Ecology, Culture and Agriculture*, and *Field Methods* (various titles). He also coauthored the chapter "An Ethnographic Approach to Design" in *Human–Computer Interaction Handbook* (with J. Blomberg and M. Burrell,

Erlbaum, 2003) and his work is profiled in *Applying Anthropology: An Introductory Reader* (McGraw-Hill, 2002). Greg fancies himself as an amateur gardener and spends much of his spare time muddling about in his backyard. He also has a passion for exotic sports cars, although he's still figuring out how to afford one.

Laura Johnson, MA, is a Research Associate at Family Health International. She performs qualitative and quantitative data analysis on a variety of research topics including sexual experiences of adolescent girls, faithfulness messages for youth, and experiences of participants in clinical trials. Laura is currently working as an analyst and data manager for a formative research project connected to a multicountry clinical trial that tested the HIV-prevention properties of a daily pill. Her recent publications include "The Value of Contraception to Prevent Perinatal HIV Transmission" (with Reynolds et al., *Sexually Transmitted Diseases*, 2006), "How Many Interviews Are Enough? An Experiment with Data Saturation and Variability" (with Guest and Bunce, *Field Methods*, 2006), and "Respondent Perspectives on Self-Report Measures of Condom Use" (with Waszak Geary et al., *AIDS Education and Prevention*, 2003). Laura is also a devoted Star Wars fan and decorates her office with Star Wars posters and collectibles.

Natasha Mack, PhD, MA, earned a BA in comparative area studies at Duke University, and an MA and PhD in linguistic anthropology from the University of Arizona. Since joining Family Health International as a researcher in 2004, she has expanded her geographical experience from the francophone and Spanish-speaking Caribbean to west and southern Africa and Latin America. Her favorite research interest is how the intersection of political economy, emotional attachment, and gender norms affects HIV risk behavior among people with multiple partners, cross-culturally. She is also interested in HIV risk behavior in Latin America among men who are married but who also have sexual relationships with other men. Recently, in Malawi, she analyzed the role of alcohol consumption in the social ritual of transactional sex as a risk factor for HIV infection. True to her roots, she has also conducted a linguistic analysis illustrating how the media coverage of a controversial HIV prevention trial in West Africa contributed substantially to early closure of the trial. On the horizon is development of a tool to help researchers elicit culturally relevant explanations for concepts essential to obtaining truly informed consent in clinical trials. She is comfortable with contradiction, in both herself and others.

Kathleen M. MacQueen, PhD, MPH, is Coordinator of Interdisciplinary Research Ethics and Senior Scientist with the Behavioral and Social Sciences Division at Family Health International in Durham, NC. She is also adjunct faculty with the University of North Carolina at Chapel Hill in the Department of Social Medicine, School of Medicine, and in the Health Behavior and Health Education Program, School of Public Health. She has a PhD in anthropology from Binghamton University and an MPH from the Rollins School of Public Health at Emory University. She has been working in the area of applied research ethics and HIV prevention trials for more than fifteen years. Both domestically and internationally she has provided leadership on the social, behavioral, and ethical dimensions of trials of HIV vaccines, microbicides, and the prophylactic use of antiretrovirals to prevent acquistion of HIV. Before coming to FHI in 2001, she worked ten years at the Centers for Disease Control and Prevention as a research anthropologist and science director in the National Center for HIV, STD, and TB Prevention. Her scientific publications have appeared in journals as diverse as *Medical Anthropology Quarterly, American Journal of Public Health, American Journal of Preventive Medicine, AIDS Care Journal,* and *Field Methods.* Kate's haiku have appeared in *Frogpond, Acorn, Heron's Nest,* and *Modern Haiku* among other journals. She has, regrettably, been neglecting her sumi-e brushwork.

Eleanor McLellan-Lemal received her MA in applied anthropology from Northern Arizona University, where she focused on international development and public health. Since 1991, she has been involved in HIV research and is currently employed as a Behavioral Scientist in the Epidemiology Branch in the Division of HIV/AIDS Prevention at the Centers for Disease Control and Prevention in Atlanta, GA. Over this fifteen-year time period, she has worked on more than ten large-scale qualitative team-based research projects, domestically and internationally. She is experienced in qualitative research design and data collection and analysis, and has conducted both rapid and in-depth ethnographic HIV/AIDS research among vulnerable populations, including drug users, men who have sex with men, and commercial sex workers, women, and ethnic minorities in the United States. Internationally, her work focuses on community accessibility and HIV vaccine clinical trials. Her newest project involves a mixed-methods approach to assessing HIV risk factors for African American and Hispanic women in the southeastern United States. She is one of the codevelopers of AnSWR: Analysis Software for Word-based Records and the Global AIDS Program's International Rapid Assessment, Evaluation, and Response (I-RARE) curriculum, and provides training for both. Her qualitative methods publications include "Distinguishing the Trees from the Forest: Applying Cluster Analysis to Qualitative Data" (with Guest, *Field Methods*, 2003), "Beyond the Qualitative Interview: Data Preparation and Transcription" (with MacQueen and Neidig, *Field Methods*, 2003), and "Codebook Development for Team-based Qualitative Analysis" (with MacQueen et al., *Cultural Anthropology Methods*, 1998). When she is not working or spending long hours commuting to and from work, Eleanor devotes her time to pattern-recognition hobbies (e.g., knitting, crocheting, painting, jewelry making), cooking for family/friends, and reading. Although less inclined, she provides tech support to her husband and lends a hand in home restoration projects.

Bobby Milstein, PhD, MPH, has worked for more than fifteen years at the Centers for Disease Control and Prevention, where now he leads the Syndemics Prevention Network and coordinates planning/evaluation activities for emerging investigations and policy initiatives. Dr. Milstein has guided the development of CDC's framework for program evaluation; helped build a focus for the combined prevention of HIV, STD, and unplanned pregnancy within the Division of Reproductive Health; coordinated preparedness modeling activities throughout the agency; and supported numerous efforts to enhance health protection research, place-based health promotion, and initiatives to eliminate health inequities. With colleagues in the Syndemics Prevention Network he explores transformations in public health work that arise in situations where there are multiple interacting epidemics, or "syndemics." He often teaches and leads dialogues on innovations in planning/evaluation, analytic methods, and the role of dynamic democratic practices in protecting the public's health. Dr. Milstein is a codeveloper of CDC's AnSWR software system for integrating qualitative and quantitative data. Outside of work he plays tennis, swims, sails, SCUBA dives, water-skis, and cooks.

Emily Namey completed her MA in applied anthropology at Northern Arizona University, where she focused on medical anthropology and public health. During her three and a half years at Family Health International, she worked on several large qualitative research projects in conjunction with international multisite HIV-prevention clinical trials. There she managed field communications, tracked data, planned and executed analyses of multiple large qualitative data sets. Her research interests extend beyond

HIV prevention to women's health more broadly, in both international and domestic contexts. Emily currently coordinates qualitative research at Duke University Medical Center, in the Division of Obstetrics and Gynecology, where her work involves research into what constitutes a good childbirth experience for women. Outside of the office, Emily can often be found in the pool, where she competes as a masters swimmer.

Lucy Thairu, PhD, MSc, is a postdoctoral fellow in the Division of Infectious Diseases at the Stanford University Medical School. She received her MSc and PhD in Nutrition from Cornell University in Ithaca, New York. Her research focuses on the sociocultural context of mother-to-child transmission of HIV through breast milk, and the historical, social, and medical aspects of health crises in Africa. Her recent publications include "Acceptability, Feasibility and Affordability of Infant Feeding options for HIV-infected Women: A qualitative study in South-West Nigeria" (with Abiona et al., *Maternal and Child Nutrition Journal*, 2006), "Socio-cultural influences on Infant Feeding Decisions among HIV-Infected Women in South Africa" (with Pelto et al., *Maternal and Child Nutrition Journal*, 2005), "Improving Infant Feeding Practices: Current Patterns, Common Constraints and Designs of Interventions" (with Pelto & Levitt, *Food and Nutrition Bulletin*, 2003), and "Infant Feeding Options for Mothers with HIV—Using Women's Views to Guide Policies" (Nutrition Policy Paper, UN Sub-Committee on Nutrition, 2001). Lucy is a budding cook in her free time. Her recent experiments include "Madeleines de Commercy with a German crumb topping" and "mahamri" (Swahili doughnuts).

Cynthia Woodsong, PhD, has more than twenty years of field experience in the areas of international health research, population policy, health care delivery systems, and international development. She has designed and executed projects used in the development and evaluation of HIV/AIDS, reproductive health, and family planning programs for populations in sub-Saharan Africa, Latin America and the Caribbean, Asia, Eastern Europe, and the United States. Dr. Woodsong is a senior scientist at RTI's International Program in Global Health Technologies. For the past six years, Dr. Woodsong's work has centered primarily on aspects of development of topical vaginal microbicides for HIV prevention, including the ethics issues that such research raises. Other project experience and interests include HIV/AIDS prevention, dual protection for pregnancy and HIV/AIDS prevention, postabortion care, and the integration of traditional and modern approaches to health care. Woodsong's professional focus on prevention has led her to concentrate more finely on preventing stitching errors in the Zen approach to Japanese embroidery. She conducts training in qualitative research methods, research ethics, advocacy for HIV/AIDS and reproductive health policy, and evaluation methodologies, as well as integration of qualitative and quantitative research design. Two of Woodsong's more recent publications are "The Generation of Knowledge for Reproductive Health Technologies: Constraints on Social and Behavioral Research" (*Journal of Social Issues*, 2005) and "Women's Autonomy and Informed Consent in International Microbicide Clinical Trials" (*Journal of Empirical Research on Human Research Ethics*, 2006).